The School Media Center: A Book of Readings

compiled by
PEARL L. WARD
and
ROBERT BEACON

The Scarecrow Press, Inc.
Metuchen, N. J.   1973

Library of Congress Cataloging in Publication Data

Ward, Pearl L   comp.
    The school media center.

    Bibliography: p.
    1. Instructional materials centers--Addresses,
essays, lectures.   I.   Beacon, Robert, joint comp.
II. Title.
LB3044.W37   021'.2   73-4901
ISBN 0-8108-0618-5

PREFACE

The changes taking place today in the nation's schools are truly amazing and exciting. From the concept of the library as merely a repository of printed materials, there has developed the view of the library as a materials or media center. Within the last decade this idea has taken imposing shape in both our elementary and secondary schools. Although some educators have been reluctant to accept the library as the all-media center, forward-looking individuals long ago saw it as one of the most dynamic and central units of the modern school.

This book of readings is designed to show what the media center is and what it does. A general, overall picture of the center will be found here: the educational developments which have brought about the form of its existence and the direction it must take, various aspects of its administration, the collections it houses.

The readings have been selected with the student in mind--the student who is preparing to take his or her place in the media center of a modern elementary or secondary school. No attempt has been made in this book to include articles on reading or literature for children or young people, reference work, or various other areas generally covered in separate textbooks.

This selection of readings, therefore, is a beginning for the student; it should not be considered a complete text or the only book a student should read about media centers. He will, for example, want to read more than the introduction and first chapter of The School Library by Ellsworth and Wagener included here, because the entire volume is valuable, with its detailed diagrams of study carrels and architectural designs. The small section from the School Library Manpower Project report should be followed up by at least a cursory glance at the entire report and the Task Analysis Survey Instrument. The few sections of the 1970 Standards for the Development of School Media Programs in California are just an introduction to the publication which

iii

should be read as an example of state standards developed by media personnel.

What we have brought together here, in this convenient format, is a coherent group of representative articles about media centers selected from the abundance of available material. These cannot cover all aspects of media center operation, but we hope that they are of value for what they do cover. Several of them have not appeared previously in print. All these articles, we feel, will add to the student's knowledge and will make a substantial contribution to a growing and extremely valuable aspect of today's school: the modern media center.

This collection of readings is a beginning in another sense. Knowledge in this area cannot remain static; obsolete ideas, concepts and practices must give way to the new. More recent research into the financing, arrangement, development and use of Instructional Media Centers must be disseminated widely.

The authors hope that this collection is one medium through which the growth of IMC's may be encouraged. Readers' suggestions of items to be included in a revised collection are invited. They should be sent to the authors at the School of Library Science, University of Southern California, Los Angeles, California 90007.

CONTENTS

v

vi

vii

PART I

TRENDS AND DEVELOPMENTS IN
EDUCATION AND IN MEDIA CENTERS

1. Introduction to The School Library

by Ralph E. Ellsworth and Hobart D. Wagener

Reprinted with permission from: Educational
Facilities Laboratories, Inc., The School Library,
Facilities for Independent Study in the Secondary
School, by Ralph E. Ellsworth and Hobart D.
Wagener, 1963.

Change--rapid, radical, and often beyond our com-
prehension--is the keynote of our time.

Consider this: A commercial airline finds it no longer profitable to fly from New York to Paris. The trip by
jet is too short, just 6-1/2 hours. To make business
sense, it has had to extend the same flight to Rome, some
700 miles and 1-1/2 hours farther. According to one pilot,
"In a way the speed creates a problem. You get where
you're going so fast that you have to make more trips to
get in the required flying time."[1] Fifteen years ago, it
took 16-1/3 hours to cover the same distance by piston
plane.

It is said that in the recent 1960 census 50 statisticians did the job that required over 4,000 statisticians just
10 years earlier.

Even death has yielded to change. A decade or two
ago, it was considered a state in which the heart stopped
beating and respiration no longer took place. Today that is
regarded as "clinical" death and not necessarily final. As
the result of new knowledge, the resuscitation of certain
cases of sudden death has become a practical matter in
many hospitals.

That education is changing--that its goals, methods,
and even its schoolhouses are in transformation--is consistent with our times and a reflection of them.

Changing Pressures in the Schools:

During the nineteenth century education was largely a matter of firm subjects taught with firm discipline. The rigors of Latin declensions not only trained the mind; they trained the man as well. Strength of character was held to be the natural by-product of arduous mental labor. But the twentieth century differed. Its educators hailed the psychic security of the child as the key to development of the man. Teaching methods, along with the school curriculum, became involved with the "whole child"; that is, with his personality growth and social adjustment. And like plants forced to early flower in the benign environment of a greenhouse, learning ability, it was thought, would blossom in a classroom climate of psychological and social warmth.

But once again, since World War II and more particularly since Sputnik, the American public has shifted its view. It is asking the schools to restore the mastery of subject matter as their primary concern, and encouraging the assignment of specially trained workers to the personal and social problems of children. This, briefly, is the motive force behind the shifting emphasis in education today.

Along with the demand that education focus on intellectual achievement, there has been a parallel demand for change in the training of the personnel who manage our schools. For over 30 years society placed more and more responsibility on the schools for teaching an increasing range of subjects that arise out of the problems faced by parents and children in our modern culture--driver education, sex education, social adjustment, citizenship, etc. As a result, the role of the school administrator shifted. He was forced more and more to assume the role of an arbitrator between the school and community. By the same token he became less and less the educational leader of an academic institution of learning. To qualify for the job, therefore, his professional training consisted, largely, of direct analyses of the problems of the schools and courses in educational administration, philosophy, and methods, rather than in the content of learning itself. But that too has been challenged.

With the renewed demand for the primacy of subject matter, the idea of studying the form rather than the content as a basis for teacher preparation and school administration, is quickly diminishing. Schoolmen themselves these days acknowledge that they must cope with problems that require

deep insight into the nature of knowledge in the traditional
subject fields. As N. B. Burbank, president of the American Association of School Administrators, puts it:

> No longer is it enough to have had some courses
> in education and administration, and a subject
> major and minor. He (the school administrator)
> finds himself frequently in deep water if he
> doesn't have a fair degree of familiarity with such
> cognate fields as economics, sociology, anthro-
> pology, philosophy, and political science. In other
> words he needs a broad cultural preparation in
> liberal arts as well as thorough training in the
> field of educational administration.
> --Challenge to School Administration,
> Boulder Camera, May 14, 1962

Even in the elementary schools the demand for teachers who
know more about the subjects they are to teach (and students
are no longer thought of as "subjects") is becoming the rule.

Another area of education placed under sharp scrutiny
in the new pursuit of "academic excellence" is the traditional
approach to methods of instruction. The prevailing view
holds that these emphasize teaching too much at the expense
of learning, that they encourage an attitude of passive recep-
tivity on the part of the student. At all levels of education
there is currently a great interest in developing curricular
patterns and teaching methods that help students learn how
to formulate attacks on problems, as well as to acquire information for its own sake. Advances in technology--the
widespread use of instructional television, the design of
automatic systems for the retrieval of information, and the
development of individualized audio-visual equipment which
can be carried from place to place throughout the school--
all place at the disposal of teachers and students new ways
to learn and new places in which to do so.

The old idea of handling students as groups, as
though each member of the group were like all the rest,
now seems wasteful of the time and talent of the best teachers and students. Attempts are being made to break up the
lockstep aspects of secondary education and to place more
responsibility on the student for the manner in which he
studies and for the rate of progress he maintains.

The patterns of individual study and varied group

sizes and time schedules set forth in J. Lloyd Trump's
Images of the Future[2] have already had considerable impact
on the educational scene, to the point of changing the very
nature of the schoolhouse itself.[3] Some planners are even
thinking of schoolhouse designs based on the concept that all
formal instruction will be given solely by television reception to students based in their own study carrels. In this
system, the classroom as it is traditionally known is virtually eliminated.

Whatever the variations on the theme, the motif of
self-instruction and individual inquiry rings loud and clear.

But if students are to pursue knowledge on their own,
if they are to study independently, then they must be provided with the facilities to do so. A logical starting point
is the school library, the only academic area ordinarily
planned for individuals rather than groups. And that--the
creation of good working libraries--is the subject of this
report.

An accurate barometer of the intensity of interest in
knowledge qua knowledge is the kind of library service provided by a school. In most of today's secondary schools the
library will be found in a small room with a few hundred
books around the walls. Seats for a few readers are pre-
sided over by a librarian whose main task is to keep order
over a reluctant group of students who are there, not because they want to be, but because they have been sent
there to study their textbooks. The students are likely to
be more interested in attracting attention than in pursuing
the study of a problem. They are there not as individuals,
but as captive groups.

This thumbnail sketch is unfortunately true of all but
a small percentage of school libraries today. The most enlightened school librarians, teachers, and administrators
have not been happy with this situation. Many of the standard texts which molded the attitudes of today's administrators, however, either sanctioned or were content to
tolerate this kind of school library. Though most of the
more recent books on school administration advocate an enlightened concept of school libraries, due to inertia, or un-
willingness to make the necessary expenditures, or special
local factors, few school districts have an enlightened library
policy.

Barriers to Progress:

      Since the purpose of this study is to help schools plan
the kinds of library facilities that are currently needed and
will be needed in the future, it is important to explore some
of the existing problems. By isolating the deficiencies which
make today's school libraries ineffective, indeed, cause them
to operate as barriers to learning, progress can begin.

      What are some of the barriers?

      Here are two important ones, both part of a complex
of long-standing antagonisms and misunderstandings that must
be eliminated or minimized:

      School Administrator-Librarian Attitudes. School li-
brarians tend to think of school administrators as men who
have been trained in methods rather than educated in the
liberal arts. Librarians consider that administrators are
not bookmen and therefore are not interested in school libraries. The administrators, so librarians claim, impose
limiting conditions on the library that prevent the librarians
from making the contribution to the instructional program
they know they should be making. The resulting frustrations,
well known in the profession, represent a barrier that inter-
feres with the recruiting of enough good school librarians.

      School administrators, on the other hand, tend to
think of the librarian as a Victorian maiden lady whose major
interest is to see that all the library books are safely on
the shelves all the time and who likes to preside in the middle of a reading room with a sharp-edged ruler poised for
use on any student who makes noise or disturbs the tidiness
of the school library.

      We have found all kinds of school administrators and
librarians, and, as is undoubtedly true of many professional
groups, the unworthy practitioners often overshadow the
worthy ones. School librarians are most often blamed for
the unsatisfactory library service in schools. They in turn
blame administrators. What are the dynamics that operate
behind the scene?

      In the case of administrators, one has only to follow
in the footsteps of a school superintendent and watch him
wrestle with the problems and pressures that make up his
day's work. It becomes clear at once that only a superman
can have enough energy left at the end of a day to spend his

free (if any) evenings reading the kinds of books school librarians think he should read. To quote N. B. Burbank again, from the afore-mentioned piece addressed to school superintendents:

> An overriding problem, one which may well outstrip all others in urgency, is found in the tensions which have come in recent years to be an integral part of your daily life and mine. The larger our districts become, the more our enrollment grows, the more we find ourselves embroiled in tension-producing activities. More and more prized is the ability to go home and relax in the evening, and get a good night's sleep. Too few of us can still do this--most of us are lucky if we get away for two or three weeks in the summer. The complexities of our responsibilities today are indeed far reaching.

Juxtaposed against this are the young school librarians with stars in their novice eyes who find they are licked before they begin. They quickly learn that they are unable to change the conditions which created the situation in the first place. What are these conditions?

--A philosophy of education that provides little motivation or time for student use of the library.

--A study hall concept of the library which discourages affection for reading, and turns the library into a forbidding place rather than a living room. Most often the library is too formal, too institutionalized, devoid of pleasant furniture, and lacking in imaginative displays and service.

--A physical setting that is not only isolated from the main stream of student traffic, but is also inadequate in size.

--A collection of books, periodicals, newspapers, and audio-visual materials so small that it stifles potential interests and meets only the needs of the poorest and most limited students in the school.

--A separation of book and audio-visual services.

--A library that fails to take into account the fact that the technology of communication is changing rapidly.

--A lack of understanding by the administration that competent librarians should be delegated the responsibility and
authority to administer the library and work with the
teaching staff as materials consultants.

--A concept of staff size that limits the librarians' energies
and time to the routine tasks, giving them no opportunity
to play an intimate role in the instructional program.

Given these conditions, it becomes apparent that the
situation wouldn't be much better if all librarians were perfect.   Clearly the underlying causes are to be found in the
philosophy that shapes our schools, in teaching methods that
don't require better libraries, in inadequate learning resources, in poor physical settings, in the low expectations
of student effort, and a host of other factors that have nothing to do with the capabilities of school librarians.   The librarians are a product of the conditions that have made
school libraries what they are, not the cause.   An appropriate school library operating in the right kind of instructional
relationships would encourage good school librarians to do
the kind of work they know they should be doing, and that
others expect them to do.

To be sure, this report is not concerned with passing
judgment on the points of view characterized here, but it is
concerned with their relationship to the presence or absence
of good school libraries.   We pay our respects to the many
thoroughly enlightened school administrators we have worked
with.   But they are in the minority.   We also pay our respects to the enlightened school librarians we have worked
with.   But they too are in the minority.   We trust this report will make clear to both groups that their own attitudes,
beliefs, and points of view may be the reason for the level
of library service that exists in their schools.

Confusion Between the Content and Carriers of
Knowledge.   A second major area beclouded by misunder-
standing is the relationship of the content to the carriers of
knowledge.   There is a frequent assumption that content
must be associated with just one type of carrier.   The confusion that grows from this is expressed in the often-heard
question: "Should the library contain audio-visual materials
and services, or should these be contained in a separate
'instructional services center' with the library limited to
books?"

The answer to this turns on whether one takes a static or dynamic view of what a library is.

Ever since man learned how to communicate above the level reached by animals, he has developed language symbols and has tried to record them so he would not forget them, and so that he could share his knowledge with his fellow men. At various times he has kept the record in the form of clay tablets, pieces of wood, papyrus, scrolls, handwritten books, machine-printed books, phonograph records, transparent films (moving or static), tapes, wires, electronic impulses, and so on. Today, knowledge can be recorded and shared in many ways.

There has been a tendency for man to get excited each time a new carrier for knowledge is invented. Opinions range from thinking the old better than the new to thinking the new better than the old.

For example, one can imagine that when words on parchment began to replace clay tablets, scholars must have thought the scrolls to be less permanent, and librarians probably found them difficult to shelve and keep clean.

Soon after Gutenberg developed a mechanical method of producing identical copies, we know that there were people who thought the printed books less dignified or beautiful than handwritten manuscripts.

We know, for instance, that the Dukes of Urbino would not allow a printed book in their library until a century after the invention of printing. They considered printed books ugly. On July 7, 1553, the Sorbonne recommended to Francis I that "to save religion it is necessary to abolish for all time in France, by a severe edict, the art of printing."[4] Renaissance scholars like Erasmus welcomed printed books. Opposition tended to come from scribes facing possible technological unemployment, and book collectors, like the Dukes of Urbino.

This age-old confusion in the relationship between the carrier and content plagues us today over the issues of the so-called audio-visual aids and the use of teaching machines. Today one hears absurd claims that the motion picture is better than, or poorer than, the book; that "one picture is worth a thousand words"; that books are old-fashioned and films are not; that a book can't teach because it isn't "programed. "

Librarians are reputed to be against audio-visual aids and audio-visual experts are reputed to be against books. School administrators are said to be willing to spend thousands of dollars for audio-visual materials and unwilling to spend tens of dollars for literary material.

It is undoubtedly true that certain carriers may prove to have specialized usefulness not shared by other carriers, but there is enough evidence to suggest that, since all carriers can serve individual as well as group use, it would be wise for schools to consider them all as legitimate library materials.   Similarly, as the already formidable list of available carriers grows, the library staff may have to be a balanced team of specialists trained to make optimum use of all the school's informational resources.

Largely because of the hardware needed to recover information from them, tapes, motion pictures, filmstrips, and recordings, present problems of technology and selection, and often of program development, that are not posed by the printed word.   During the early stages of accumulation of audio-visual media and materials, the librarian is competent to manage them and to guide students and teachers in their proper use.   But as the program and collection grow, the librarian is not likely to have the time or training to handle the specialized chores that accompany extensive use, nor should she be expected to.   An audio-visual expert or "media specialist, " as they are called, will be needed to fill the vacuum.   If, for example, the library should have a system for the electronic transmission of information from a central source, it could not manage without the services of the media specialist whose job it would be to design the components of the system and supervise the production of materials to be used in it.

The point is that schools need to adopt a dynamic concept of the library as a place which includes all kinds of carriers of knowledge so that the critical question will not be "Is television or film better than the book?" but rather, "Which carrier of knowledge is best to accomplish the task at hand?"

The air of mystery and novelty that surrounds the idea of knowledge appearing in the form of a little black box or a metal can containing a tape, will do no harm unless it prevents educators from making a realistic evaluation of the specific value each carrier is capable of contributing to the learning process in comparison with other carriers.

On the other hand, those whose natural enthusiasm for the new tempts them to overlook the values of the old might recall that the printed book is both "visual and audible"; that it is relatively inexpensive and highly mobile; that its use does not depend on an electric power source; and, further, that it is capable, as a thing in itself, of winning man's affections. At the same time, the new cannot be neglected out of loyalty to the old. If the school library is to realize its potential function as a learning center, old prejudices and complacent rigidities had better yield to a spirit of academic enterprise.

It is the intent of this report to develop a concept of the school library and a method of planning that will, hopefully, eliminate the base of the confusions and poor practices that now exist throughout the country. We hope administrators, library personnel, and architects will use it to help them design libraries that will be free to act as a vigorous force in the educational program of their schools.

Notes

1. John Bainbridge, "Profile," The New Yorker, November 10, 1962, p. 61.

2. J. Lloyd Trump, Images of the Future (Washington, D. C.: National Association of Secondary School Principals, 1958.)

3. Educational Facilities Laboratories, Inc., Schools for Team Teaching and High Schools 1962 (New York: EFL, 1961, 1962.)

4. P. Dupont, Histoire de l'imprimerie (Paris, 1954,) I, 191.

2.   A New Concept for a School Library

by Ralph E. Ellsworth and Hobart D. Wagener

Reprinted with permission from: Educational Fa-
cilities Laboratories, Inc., The School Library,
Facilities for Independent Study in the Secondary
School, by Ralph E. Ellsworth and Hobart D.
Wagener, 1963.

In this report the school library will be called a library, not an instructional or learning center, an instructional media center, a resource center, or any of the other
labels currently popular among schoolmen to convey an expanded concept of the library's function.   The reason for
this simply is that the word "library" has time-honored
meaning, it is untarnished by faddism or the caprice of
style, and it is understood by the public as the traditional
place where the carriers of knowledge are kept and used.

For similar reasons, and for simplicity as well, the
user of the library will be called a reader.   Though the
purist might insist that he be called a viewer if he is looking at film, or a listener if he is using tape, he has gone
to the library for the traditional reason: to pursue information, regardless of how it may be stored.   Viewing or listening, he is merely expanding his ordinary activity in the
library.

A concept of a school library begins with an analysis
of the kinds of activities it is expected to house.   Obvious
as the question may seem, the first one that must be asked
is: What do students do in school libraries?

--Find answers to specific questions that arise either from
   the teaching process or from ordinary curiosity.

--Go alone or as a member of a committee sent to get information.

--Carry out study hall assignments; that is, spend a specif-

12

ic amount of time studying in the library.

--Find material for projects such as a written report, a book review, a debate brief, or a research paper.

--Learn how to use the keys of a library--card catalogs, bibliographies, reference books, periodical indexes, etc.

--Look at motion-picture films, filmstrips, or other audio-visual materials. Study with a teaching machine, listen to phonograph records or tapes, listen and record voice for language study.

--Locate quotations, excerpts, or data for speeches or projects.

--Read just for the fun of reading--one book or a hundred.

--Browse through current magazines and newspapers or look at the new book shelf.

--Talk with other students.

The second part of the same question is: What do teachers do in school libraries? Activities similar to those mentioned for students, but they also

--Confer with the library staff on relevant materials to use for class work: those appropriate for general presentation in the classroom, those most suitable for students working in small groups, and those appropriate for use on an individualized basis.

--Preview films and filmstrips; confer on the purchase or rental of audio-visual materials, and on local production of same.

--Consult with librarians on book purchases, on the handling of special materials (pamphlets, sample magazines, government documents, etc.), on classification and cataloging problems, and on reader's problems and difficulties that the students may be having.

The Organization

A library usually involves three elements: the ma-

terials, the staff, and the physical setting. In all but the
very small school, it should be thought of as a system or a
network rather than as a single, enclosed room as it is so
often regarded. There are different kinds of libraries to
match the needs of different situations. In the past the
American school has been highly standardized, but if pres-
ent-day trends continue, individual schools will be developing
more individual personalities such as are characteristic of
many of the colleges and private preparatory schools in this
country and England. It is axiomatic that in writing a program for a college or university library, one never finds
two institutions exactly alike. Each library differs in some
ways from all others, so may one expect to find many different kinds of school libraries in the future.

    The factors that make for individuality are the nature
of the building or buildings, the school program and tradi-
tions, the availability of other usable libraries, and the
point of view of the planners.

    Among the various kinds of school library systems,
the following are typical:

    The single, inclusive central library which serves all
grades and all kinds of needs.

    A dual system, one for elementary grades and one
for the secondary school. Where the junior high school is
in a separate building, a separate library is provided, otherwise it is a part of the high school library.

    A central library which gives book truck service to
all classrooms and laboratories, or from which may ema-
nate closed circuit television or other audio-visual programs
received in class or lecture rooms.

    A decentralized system based on some form of sub-
ject grouping such as sciences, social sciences, and humanities, with one of the three or sometimes a fourth also
serving as the headquarters library. Each division is fully
staffed with competent librarians.

    A fully decentralized system in which, in a sense,
the whole building is a library. Here all types of learning
or teaching activities are subordinated to teaching centers.

    The library concept advocated in this report is intended to support a particular type of school organization, one that grows out of the current dissatisfaction with the "cells and bells" arrangement in which each school day is rigidly broken up into a series of equal time slots, and equal-sized classrooms, with a fixed and constant teacher-student ratio. The dissatisfaction is centered on these elements:

The student develops a passive attitude toward learning. The teacher takes the initiative. The student's day is filled with attending classes. He has little time for independent study, and it is not expected of him. School activities consume any free time he may have. Learning is fragmented into many small, unrelated classroom subjects and much time is wasted in the mechanics of going from place to place, subject to subject, and in the warm-up required by this process. The student has too little time for the "laboratory" part of learning, including the use of books and other resources as a laboratory kind of experience. There is too much "teaching" and too little learning.

Further, in a period of shortage of qualified teachers who are well educated in both the subjects they teach and the skill with which to teach, there is a waste of the teacher's time on activities that could just as well be performed by people with lesser ability and training. The fixed size of classes, always with 25-30 students, further wastes the talents of those able teachers who are available.

To repair these weaknesses, a different system of school organization has been proposed. Called "team teaching," one of its main objectives is to concentrate the time and talent of master teachers exclusively on teaching, leaving other activities to assistants who are not as highly qualified but have other specialized abilities. The particular pattern may vary from school to school, depending upon size, program, and other variables, but in general, master teachers, librarians, instruction assistants, and clerks work together in a team. A lead teacher is responsible for coordination of the team's work. By pooling their individual strengths, each teacher is given the opportunity to concentrate on what he does best. He is relieved of those tasks which a colleague, by virtue of preference or ability, may be better equipped to perform. He is relieved too, of those subprofessional housekeeping and clerical chores which can be carried out by less highly qualified personnel. Thus a master teacher especially gifted at lecturing, for example,

may be solely assigned to the formal instructional work of a
team, lecturing to as many as 150 students gathered together
at one time.   Because he has fewer classroom contact hours,
perhaps 9 to 12 per week, he is left with adequate time for
study and teaching preparation.   Other master teachers,
adept in other skills, may lead seminars, head creative
workshops, or work in laboratories with individual students.
The librarians, who are members of the team so their services can be more closely interrelated with the teaching-
learning process, meet with teachers to evaluate instructional programs.   Assistants, not as highly trained as either
teachers or librarians, may supervise places where independent study is scheduled, correct factual details in tests
or student papers, or make certain that materials for reading assignments are available in the library.   Clerical tasks
are performed by clerks and general aides.   It is assumed
that in every community there will be men and women available to handle the work of the assistants at a lower cost than
that commanded by teachers.

      The counterpart of this is a revision of the manner
in which students spend their time.   To permit each youngster to move ahead consistent with his own ability and to
provide opportunity for independent study, his schedule
might be divided roughly this way: 40 per cent of his time
in a large group receiving formal instruction delivered in
person by a teacher-lecturer or via centrally produced television; 20 per cent as part of a small seminar group which
provides opportunity for discussion and the interchange of
ideas; the remaining 40 per cent, in studying on his own,
or teaching himself.

      Americans may not yet be ready to accept the idea
of making full use of either "automated-" or self-teaching,
but these ideas are old.   They are the basis of the Oxford
and Cambridge concept of higher education.   The professor
gives a series of lectures for any student who wants to attend.   The student works with his tutor whenever he needs
help.   The rest of his time he studies independently.   The
initiative rests with him.   What is new is the nature of the
tools that are now available to help the student teach himself.

The Library as a Teaching Laboratory:

      The technological breakthrough represented by the development of the transistor tube, which permits electronic equipment small enough and light enough to be taken from place to place and used wherever the learner wishes to work, opens the way to new learning techniques and new places in which to learn. No longer is it necessary to plan entirely in terms of fixed-function space and built-in equipment.

Portables for the use of television reception, filmstrips and slides, phonograph records or tapes, and language laboratories have been in existence for some time. But new kinds are constantly being developed. One is a cross-media unit which combines a filmstrip viewer and audio-tape or record player packaged in one container. It is set up so that the tape activates the filmstrip to move on its own. Another new model has a tape in a cartridge, eliminating the threading and handling problem. Still another is a new battery-powered audio device that weighs only seven pounds, but contains as many as 22 separate programs on one tape, including a voice recording and playback mechanism for the study of a foreign language. With the development of 8 mm. cartridge film, the motion picture, traditionally confined to service in the classroom only, can be liberated for use by the individual student in the library.

Television kinescopes, video tapes, and "programed exhibits" of different kinds swell the number and variety of carriers and materials. An excellent example of a programed exhibit can be found in the Desert Museum near Tucson, Arizona. Here one walks along a path bordered by a series of displays depicting problems of conservation, erosion, water use, etc. The visitor presses a button which starts a sound track and activates the program which has been designed to teach a specific idea or concept or action. Although the idea is still new, schools are beginning to prepare exhibits of this kind for the teaching of specific projects. (Actually a well-constructed motion picture or book is also a type of programed exhibit.)

Then, of course, there is the teaching machine, perhaps the brightest star in today's constellation of teaching aids. A variety of programed teaching tapes has been prepared for the machines, to serve as study guides in a number of disciplines. The biology, mathematics, and physics teachers of the country have been hard at work revising the teaching programs for those sciences, and new books and materials are currently being prepared and tested. (Ameri-

can Institute of Biological Sciences Curricular Study; the
Physical Sciences Study Committee.) Similar developments
are under way among the chemists and mathematicians.
Many of the programs can be used by individual students
as a substitute for the lecture the teacher might otherwise
deliver to large classes.

We wish to emphasize the fact that educational institutions appear to be at the edge of a revolution in learning
techniques. As Harvard's then Dean Bundy describes it:

> The slogan words are 'self-instruction,' or 'pro-
> gramed learning,' or 'teaching machines'; the re-
> ality is as hard to describe as it is extraordinarily
> promising. The essence of the matter is not mys-
> terious: information can be so ordered and pre-
> sented that a learner actually engages in the rapid
> step-by-step control of the material; this has al-
> ways happened when a deeply interested learner
> met a particularly well-written text. The new
> technique simply multiplies the effectiveness of
> the process. It is a technique, not a monster....
> And the student is not taught by the machine--he
> learns with it. Indeed, it is precisely the ines-
> capable need for--and reward of--his active parti-
> cipation in the operation that differentiates this
> kind of study from reading a book. [1]

--and we wish to add, from watching a motion picture, listening to a phonograph record, or using any form of information carrier that has not been devised to take full advantage
of the personal, step-by-step, mechanical operation required
by the student. Dean Bundy continues:

> One particular advantage of teaching in this manner
> is that it becomes no hard thing to create a library
> of programs which will respond to the complex in-
> terdependencies of learning.... In college physics
> today it is not easy to provide instruction that is
> equally serviceable and relevant for the would-be
> biologist, chemist, and physicist, all three. In
> mathematics there is perhaps a still more search-
> ing difficulty in teaching analysis as it relates to
> both advanced mathematics and applied physics.
> Ordinary courses cannot readily be divided into a
> large number of subtly differentiated elements--
> but programs of self-instruction can. There is

no reason, except the effort of the programing, why a self-instruction laboratory should not have many kinds of sub-courses providing the student with the particular things he needs. Libraries do this already, of course, but programs can do it better, and indeed this instrument is neither more nor less than a better kind of book, for many purposes. 1

Dr. B. F. Skinner, one of the originators of teaching machines, places emphasis on what may be the heart of the matter with this statement:

It is curious that such suggestions (paying high salaries to teachers, trusting students as individuals and grouping them according to ability, bringing textbooks and other materials up to date) rarely deal with the actual processes of teaching or learning. They make no attempt to analyze what is happening when a student listens to a lecture, reads a book, writes a paper, or solves a problem. They do not tell us how to make these activities more productive. In short, the methods of education are generally neglected. The use of films and television does not constitute a new method; it is merely a way to amplify and extend old methods, together with their shortcomings. 2

His point, namely, that the teaching machines permit a kind of teaching and learning activity that books and other audio-visual devices cannot do so well, seems hard to grasp until one has actually worked with the machines.

No one at this time can be certain of when and how these machines will fit into the school program. It is safe to predict though, that the library staff will manage the tapes for teaching machines just as it now does printed books, pamphlets, slides, and motion pictures, as legitimate library material. Then, there will need to be "keys" to the tapes so that students will be able to find out which tape is relevant to their needs. These keys may well, at first, consist of the advice given by the teacher and the librarian or audio-visual expert, but sooner or later they will take the form of bibliographies and catalogs to be found in the library's reference collection. Some tapes will be consumed as the student uses them and will be thrown away when they have served their purpose; other will be returned to the library and re-used.

It would also seem safe to guess that the machines
in which the tapes will be read will be needed all over the
school building, and that eventually each student might own
one to be kept at home.

The teaching machines now available vary in size and
complexity all the way from an 8" x 8" x 10" box using a
simple lens with ambient light and costing a few dollars, to
large electronic machines costing thousands of dollars.
Similarly, the purposes they serve will vary all the way
from rote learning of words to exercises in the development
of the student's ability to reason.

The physical requirements for teaching machines are,
naturally, not well understood today.   Most of them require
electrical outlets.   Some require a slightly darkened room,
and some make enough noise to require especially sound-ab-
sorbent surroundings.   Some generate enough heat to require
artifically cooled rooms.   There are those that are portable,
others quite heavy and immovable.   The kind of cubicle or
carrel used in foreign language laboratories would seem to
be appropriate for teaching machine use.

It is easy enough to discuss a reorganization of teaching methods, using new media to place the student on an independent study basis.   All of these ideas could be put into
operation today if the people involved--the administrators,
teachers, librarians, students, and parents--would accept
them.   To be sure, we have good teaching machines but
materials for them are still primitive.   We have good television receivers but too few good teaching programs.   We
have good motion-picture projectors but not enough good
films.   These problems, however, will solve themselves in
time.

The problems that will be difficult to solve will re-
volve around our lack of understanding of how to prepare
the mass of students at the elementary and high school level
for independent study.   No doubt this is a process that must
start in the very first grades and expand in scope and intensity up through the grades.   This is exactly what the best
teachers have always tried to do for their best students.
The difference now is that the teacher has new tools to
work with.   We propose to use these tools for all students--
good and bad, and average.   The intent here is to show how

the new ideas, machines, and learning materials might be used in a new kind of library setting. Some schools will be able or willing to adopt only a few of the suggestions offered. Others may try to go all the way.

The Individual Study Carrel:

Unless independent study is made possible by giving youngsters the time and the place to work on their own, it becomes a matter of mere lip service. Today the student's typical day consists of six hourly periods. For each of these he goes to different classrooms and laboratories, to the gymnasium, and to the library for a study period. To accomplish practically the revised patterns of time and study proposed here, we would start by providing each student with a study carrel base. From this he would go to the other activities of his school day, some of which might be large group lectures, committee work, special projects, laboratory work, and sports. The youngster would spend part of his day at his study carrel where he would work with all types of carriers--books, teaching machines, records, tapes, radio, and individual television, movie, or slide projectors. When he needed guidance he would go to the teachers and teaching assistants who would be in charge, as they now are, of his learning progress. That progress would be judged on the basis of evidence submitted in regular examinations, oral and written reports, personal conferences, and teaching machine scores. When he needed study materials or bibliographic guidance he would go directly to the materials or to the library staff, which has the same relation to the materials of instruction as the teachers do to the content of instruction. Each is master of his part of the learning situation.

In the beginning stages of such a program, both machines and materials might be checked out at the library's circulation desk, just as books and printed materials are checked out. The student would carry the equipment to his carrel, use it there, and return it to the desk when finished.

Should the media program and collection grow extensively to the point where it might involve thousands of tapes, records, kinescopes, films, and the like--and should the size of the student body warrant it--the school might consider some means for transmitting information electronically from a central storage bank. There is a variety of such systems, some simple and others highly sophisticated, but their common denominator is that the student or teacher can recover information without handling the hardware in which it is stored. Rather, he signals an electronic control room where materials are kept, and the program of his choice is transmitted to him. In that case the carrel is fitted with a television screen for the reception of visual materials, headphones for sound, and a telephone mechanism or dial system for communication with the control room. These are fixed components of the carrel. (Via such systems, connected with the school's public address system, the teacher could also receive information in the classroom.)

The growth pattern in some schools might evolve as a combination, with both the check-out of portable equipment as well as a central electronic system for transmitting information. If the school foresees such a pattern of growth, it should plan for the use of both types of carrels.

In either case the carrels can be movable, an important consideration in the flexible arrangement and use of total library space. Their dividers would be of several types, some supporting a book shelf, some containing cabinets or lockers where the student might store his materials between work periods without having to go through the tedious task of assembling them each time.

Because the cost of providing each student with his own study carrel is likely to be well beyond the means of many schools, some carrel dividers could be designed to contain two storage cabinets to permit double use of the space. Additional cabinets for triple use of each space could be hung on the uprights of adjacent book stacks. If the student were to spend 40 per cent of his time in independent study, the school would need to make only double assignments of each carrel.

Since the study carrels are intended to be grouped in or near blocks of books, they would already be part of the library. Auditoria, music rooms, laboratories, and special classrooms would not be in the library section of the school building, but would have their own specialized quarters. It is possible, though in our judgment undesirable, to group study carrels in special rooms outside the library. The weakness of such an arrangement is that it separates the student from the library collections. Moreover, with regard to student traffic and behavior, if the carrels are an integral part of the library, students would be influenced by the decorous atmosphere of the library itself. This in turn would help to establish desirable behavior.

The physical library setting needed for this concept of school organization could be very much like some of the new modular libraries found on many college and university campuses today such as Baldwin-Wallace, Louisiana State, Barnard College, the University of Michigan Undergraduate Library, or Oklahoma State.

Notes

1. McGeorge Bundy, "Science as a Way of Life," Harvard Today, Autumn, 1961, pp. 23-4.

2. B. F. Skinner, "Teaching Machines," Scientific American, November, 1961, p. 91.

3. Monuments or Footprints?
   The School Library in the Decade
   of the Seventies

   by Pearl Ward

Reprinted with permission from <u>California Librarian</u>, January 1970.

William Faulkner, in his book, <u>The Town</u>, has one of his characters, Mr. Snopes, make the following observation about his accomplishment: "Except that it was not a monument: it was a footprint. A monument only says 'At least I got this far' while a footprint says 'This is where I was when I moved again. '"[1] As school librarians stand on the threshold of the 1970's, looking both backward and forward, they have the opportunity of assessing where they have been in the recent past and anticipating the possibilities which lie ahead in the new decade. Realistically, we can say with Faulkner that the past has not been a monument, but we have left footprints which are pointing into the future as we move on. For school libraries and school librarians have been making noticeable footprints in recent years.

Before considering what the 1970's hold for us as we move on, it is profitable and appropriate to review and assess what the developments, trends, and influences of the late 1960's have been. A backward view, like looking in a rear view mirror, shows us the following: (1) the trend toward materials or media centers, (2) publication of new national standards for the media centers, (3) a revolution in education, especially in the teaching and learning processes, and (4) the effect and the influence of federal aid and private funding for school libraries and other segments of the school system.

Let us look briefly at each of these items before turning to the future:

(1) <u>Materials or Media Centers</u>. Chief among recent developments in school libraries has been the library

24

as a materials or media center in which the collection encompasses much more than the printed word. The conventional school library in a growing number of schools across the country has changed and expanded to include all types of media from print to very sophisticated electronic devices. With the additional materials go the equipment, the facilities, and the services to augment them. Needless to say, all libraries have not moved in this direction. Many stages in media services exist today. The trend, however, is and will continue to be toward the unified approach of all learning materials.

(2) New National Standards. As the 1960's came to an end, new national standards were published, prepared jointly by the American Association of School Librarians and the Division of Audio-Visual Instruction of the National Education Association. The Standards For School Media Programs[2] reflect the thinking of the last few years and provide the guidelines for the all-media library at the building level of the 1970's. The California State standards are currently being revised to reflect the recent philosophy of school libraries. These standards will be published very soon.

(3) Revolution in Education. Many changes have taken place recently in the concepts of learning, in teaching, and in patterns of school organization. These changes affect the school library, particularly as to the place of the library in the educational structure of the school. The greater emphasis on the individual learner has placed the library as a media center in a very strategic position, at the center of the learning process. Changes in instructional materials and services are being made to individualize instruction. In the schools which apply the new educational concepts, the library must provide all types of materials for students and teachers as well as the machines and the facilities for effective usage. In many cases, students take home machines as well as materials. Flexibility in service is the developing pattern. The wisdom of Robert Frost is being realized today: "The good teacher knows how to get more out of a student by surrounding him with an atmosphere of expectation than by putting the screws on him."[3]

(4) Federal Aid and Private Funding. Numerous federal programs have provided funds, both directly to school libraries and indirectly to other segments of education within recent years. The Elementary and Secondary

Education Act, since its passage in 1965, has greatly aided
school libraries and school districts and has been the impe-
tus for many innovations. Other programs such as the
National Defense Education Act, the Vocational Education
Act, and more recently the Education Professions Development Act have contributed to the improvement of school libraries and material centers. Private funding, particularly
through the Knapp Foundation and its School Library Development Project, made possible the development of fine school
library programs. These demonstration libraries, set up or
improved with Knapp funds, and many of the libraries established or augmented through Special Purpose Grants under
ESEA, Title II, have become examples of what can be done
with more adequate funds and a dynamic philosophy of school
libraries. The more recently funded School Library Manpower Project of the Knapp Foundation will make a substantial contribution in the needed area of personnel.

II

        Turning now from the past and the present to the fu-
ture, what can be said, realistically, of the decade ahead?
What does the decade of the Seventies hold for school libraries?

        (1) First of all, the new national standards for the
all-media library will be the guidelines and measuring stick
for the immediate future. These standards, together with
the revised California State standards, are important documents which, if accepted by school administrators and librarians and applied seriously, will make the library an active participant in the educational process rather than a mere
storehouse.

        (2) The all-media library will continue to be the ac-
cepted pattern, the availability and proliferation of materials
and equipment increasing: printed materials, records, tapes,
prints, slides, films, television, microforms, etc.

        (3) Information retrieval systems, open and closed
circuit television, computer-assisted instruction, and other
sophisticated methods and devices will become more widely
used if not standard equipment for the average library.

        (4) Materials and equipment will not be confined to
one location in the school but will be found in various areas

such as in resource centers, classrooms, and laboratories.

(5) Newly constructed libraries will reflect the newer educational concepts. Space for individual and small group study in the form of carrels and conference rooms will become standard. The library complex will include, in addition to the traditional space, a classroom or rooms, a materials production laboratory, a lecture hall or area for large group viewing, and possibly a television studio.

(6) Librarians and other educators will apply in the seventies many valuable ideas and lessons learned from participating in federal programs regardless of whether federal funds are restored to any degree to the average library. Important among the things learned were the need and value of the library in the elementary school, the importance of individualized learning, and the recognition of many and varied ways of learning by today's students.

(7) Librarians will function most effectively as teachers and will be important members of the school team. The all-media library will not be administered by a single individual but will have specialists on the staff in various areas of responsibility.

(8) Librarians as materials experts will have increasing responsibility in the evaluation of all types of materials. Emphasis will be on evaluation and use rather than merely organization and storage.

III

These, then, are a few of the developments or the directions which school libraries may take in the next few years. The decade will have been successful if these developments and general trends are realized. The great hope of the seventies will not, however, be the sophisticated technological developments found in a few libraries, but the expansion, revitalization, and conversion of the multitude of traditional, print-oriented libraries into dynamic, relevant, all-media, curriculum centered libraries. If the majority of libraries can truly move ahead in this direction, the next ten years will be memorable ones and the footprints left will be large ones.

One last word, as we pause on the threshold and con-

template the new decade.   It is of the utmost importance
for each and every one of us to ask how best we can contribute to the growth and development of the young people
who come within our sphere of influence.   We must not become lost or enmeshed in the morass of materials, gadgets,
and techniques to the exclusion of the individual child or
young person who needs us instead of the device, be it a
film, a dial access system, an electronic instructional system, or a book.   We as the human element must live up to
the developments in technology and materials.   We must
make our libraries humanistic institutions.   The individual
student, as a person, must remain our chief reason for
being.   And we, as the intermediaries between the individuals seeking knowledge and the knowledge itself, must never
stand in the way of anyone's development.   We ourselves
must be the best kind of individual we can possibly be in
order to make the school library all it can be for students
and teachers in the 1970's.

Notes

1.   William Faulkner.   The Town (New York: Random
      House, 1957), p. 29.

2.   American Library Association and National Education
      Association.   Standards for School Media Programs,
      1969.

3.   Sidney Cox.   A Swinger of Birches, a Portrait of Rob-
      ert Frost (New York: New York University Press,
      1957), p. 67.

4. Learning to Learn in School Libraries

by Frances Henne

Reprinted, by permission of the American Library Association and the author, from School Libraries, May 1966.

Not surprisingly, discussions of changes being effected in school library programs by curricular and instructional developments, educational technology and facilities, automation, federal and state legislation, networks of library resources and services, computerized information services, and innovations too numerous to mention lead frequently to a consideration of teaching the use of the library and its resources. This venerable subject of library instruction is currently getting new nomenclature (methods of inquiry, for example), attracting critical examination and reappraisal, and generating some controversy.

Learning, with its many elements and variables of what is to be learned and how it is to be learned, what is to be taught and how it is to be taught, constitutes a complex discipline--the core of the educative process. Teaching study and research skills represents but a small segment, and teaching the use of the library and its resources falls within that segment.

Determining the objectives, content, and methodology of library instruction in contemporary elementary and secondary education is not the simple matter that it may appear to be, and our traditional approaches, shaped by long service and practice, may be affording librarians a specious form of security. The current emphases in the schools on self-directed learning, inquiry, and independent study all too often contribute to an automatic solidifying of these established methods, with little or no critical evaluation of their current appropriateness.

With the widespread interest in and exploration of techniques for teaching learning, the art and methods of in-

29

struction, and the psychology of learning, it can reasonably
be assumed that some agreements concerning the program
of teaching study skills and methods of inquiry might eventually be reached in much the same way that decisions have
been made in the last decade in planning programs in numerous substantive fields of the curriculum.   (Analysis of
these curricular programs for implications and suggestions
for study, learning, and research skills holds great value.)
It is true that designs for library instruction have been constructed on local and system levels, involving librarians,
teachers, and curriculum specialists, but it seems timely
that a systematic study on a national basis be implemented,
utilizing techniques of discussion (symposia), study, and experimentation that the various commissions or other deliber-
ative groups in the substantive fields have employed.

    For the specifics of content (types of knowledge and
skills) to be acquired by individual students and the decisions
regarding the appropriate time, place, and methods for acquiring them can best and only be determined by the pooled
judgments of experts in the academic subject fields, in curriculum construction, in instructional methods, in the psychology of learning, and in school librarianship.   (This suggestion is a variation, and a significant variation, of one of
the proposals made at the Conference within a Conference.)
The expectations of college specialists would also be relevant.   This recommendation in no sense rules out the importance of the school librarian's participation in the planning and implementing of programs thus evolved; but instruction relating to study skills and methods of inquiry, including the use of the library and its resources, is always a
means to an end, and this end and the ways to reach it
must involve the philosophy and experiences of curriculum
specialists and specialists in the theory of learning.

    Until we have the benefits of deliberations of the
kinds suggested above, the nature of teaching library instruction will be shaped primarily on a local level.   (It
should be emphasized that the proposals noted here do not
rule out the desirability of or the need for making adjust-
ments necessary for the individual school.   The integration
with the school's curriculum would always be local in a
very real sense.)   Some current theories and developments
that are occupying the attention of many school librarians
in the area of library instruction are presented in the re-
mainder of this paper.   Many represent topics that have
been with us a long, long time, but now seem to be pres-

sing forward for action and decision on a wide scale.

The Nature of Library Service

Recommendations about the nature of library instruction will affect, and also be affected by, philosophy concerning the scope of library services. Current thought about the distinctions to be made between independent use of the library by students and desirable library services provides an example. In the viewpoint of many school librarians the mere process of locating and finding materials in the library holds little intellectual benefit for students, and time thus spent is generally wasted time. The many processes involved in what students do with materials--evaluation, synthesis, reflection, thinking, appreciation, or whatever--are the important factors, not the searching, locating, and assembling of materials.

At points like these, it is essential for new thinking and new decisions in order to determine how much students should know about the use of the library and its resources, how consistently and persistently they must apply their skills and knowledge independently and without assistance from librarians, when this independent pursuit of materials results in a waste of time, and what variations should be recommended for different groups of students. Deploring the spoon-feeding of students, as librarians so frequently do, may actually mean deploring a more intelligent use of a student's time and efforts; and self-directed study or learning is not necessarily synonymous with self-directed finding of materials.

Thus expanded location, information, and bibliographic services are being recommended, and in some cases in actual operation, on school building and system levels for both teachers and students. The centralized bibliographic and abstracting services developed by Leonard Freiser in Toronto are well known. The potential of system and regional centers, with their bibliographic apparatus, retrieval machinery, and specialized services is briefly described in the national standards for school libraries. All of these developments, ongoing and projected, can make materials and the content of materials more accessible and facilitate and expand information and other library services. The philosophy of expanded library service for teachers and

students pertains to the library program in the
school, and is not restricted to centralized system operations.

How Much, For Whom, When, and Where?

        In the program of library instruction, the recognition
of individual abilities (individualization) is stressed. Various
designs in curriculum construction (ungraded schools, track
curricula, advanced placement and accelerated programs,
provisions for exceptional children, among others) are geared
to the individual and varying abilities existing among students,
and so must the library program of instruction. These adaptations will vary from school to school and within schools.
For the most able students, regardless of whether they are
economically able to go to college, the school's program of
research skills is required in full. For others, the amount
of instruction may range from practically nothing to other
levels, depending upon the abilities and characteristics of
the students. For some students, and in certain schools
this may be many students, the only library skill that they
should have to acquire is an awareness, imprinted indelibly
and happily upon them, that the library is a friendly place
where the librarians are eager to help. To these students,
the esoteric delights of periodical indexes and other library
tools must ever remain closed. When the program of library instruction is truly integrated with classroom instruction, the needs of the retarded, the slow, the underachiev-
ing, the average, and the academically talented are taken
care of in a realistic and natural way.

        When decisions about what students need to know are
reached by the school, their implementation requires careful
planning by the school's administrators, teachers, and librarians that is comparable to, but obviously not identical with,
the planning required for the substantive areas of the curriculum. The principal assumes responsibility for this area
as seriously as he does for other parts of the instructional
program. The head school librarian can serve, and frequently does, as the chairman of the school's committee (or
equivalent) that plans and implements the school's program
of teaching study skills and methods of inquiry. This committee includes teachers representing the various subject
areas and grade levels in the school. All faculty members,
of course, are ultimately involved in the program.

Local circumstances may necessitate or commend variations on the principles enumerated above, but basic objectives and desired outcomes remain essentially the same. For example, a system curriculum coordinator may work with the school committee. In some school systems the school library supervisor or coordinator develops the study and research skills program with the cooperation of the system subject and area specialists or with librarians and teachers representing each of the schools. Whether plans are developed at building, system, or state levels, the program must be geared to meet the needs of the objectives and instructional methods of the individual schools, and the administration, librarians, and faculty of the school must become actively involved in these procedures.

Analysis of Assignments

Whether in conjunction with developing a research skills program or in some other context, analysis and evaluation of assignments are high priority pursuits in many schools. Since the program of library instruction is integrated with the curriculum and objectives and content of the component parts of the curriculum determine the kinds of library resources to be used and any skills needed for their use, an analysis of all assignments made in the school proves useful. Theoretically, analyses of curricular content should reveal the kinds of study and research skills to be taught, but this cannot be assumed to apply to every school. In any event, knowledge of the assignments provides information needed to indicate an appropriate integration of the program with curriculum content.

This analysis also enables the librarians to evaluate the adequacy of the library's resources to meet student needs. For the program of teaching study skills and the methods of inquiry involves not just teaching the types of knowledge and skills entailed, but also opportunities to put them into operation through the use of a wide variety of school library resources. Independent research and inquiry are important in themselves, whether the student locates the necessary materials or has them located for him, and the library's resources must therefore be comprehensive and adequate for his purpose. Analysis of assignments can be and frequently is delegated to the head school librarian when the major objective relates to determining the adequacy of the school library resources. This form of evaluation is kept up-to-date by the teacher's reporting assignments to the school librarian on a continuing basis, and by having the librarians serve on the school's curriculum committees. A long history in the school of such reporting and representation will obviate the need for innovating a systematic analysis of assignments in terms of available library resources.

Scrutiny of assignments is important, as experience has frequently shown, for reasons other than those already noted, including locating busywork, pointless duplication, antiquated exercises, and sheer foolishness--and then making the improvements in order.

Teaching Study Skills

No matter how the school may allocate the responsibilities for teaching the various study skills, whether to teachers alone, or librarians alone, or a combination of both--the librarians' responsibilities and opportunities for observing and helping students in the use of materials (and, in the process, evaluating their competencies) are clearly indicated. This principle applies to all schools. In those schools where independent study and self-directed learning are carefully planned for the students, these activities of the librarians represent key factors in a successful program. The librarian is the one who has the opportunity to observe, among other matters, the student's ability to use materials, to take notes, to outline, and to evaluate and synthesize materials. The school librarian's role in the program of study skills and methods of inquiry is that of a teacher and guidance specialist. The librarian's follow-up services in seeing how effectively students are using the library materials they have selected for their immediate needs are strategic and valuable ones.

All of which means that school librarians must have a knowledge of recent developments and approved techniques concerning the skills and psychology of learning and related topics. More is implied here than the content covered in the educational or teaching requirements commonly required for the certification of school librarians. From part of the school librarian's double-pronged certification requirements, comes some understanding, enriched later through experience, of teaching methods and developments; but the content prescribed in the principle stated above goes beyond this rudimentary preparation. (Being taught how to construct lesson plans is not the point intended!)

The Learning Center

The library forms a natural environment for the kind of guidance that has just been described, and the designation of the school library as a study or learning laboratory does not need to have the chill connotation that some attach to it. A library is a learning center, and learning embraces reading a book for fun or aesthetic enjoyment as much as it does examining materials to abstract information or ideas for a term paper. It is not unnatural that in many schools the library is called the Learning Center. The Learning Center evolves directly and purely from the recent emphasis in the educational programs of the schools on the processes of learning: learning skills and competencies to be acquired by students; the materials and apparatus to be used by them (including traditional library resources as well as newer media); and the careful planning of time for study in the students' schedules--now done in some schools by computers. Inquiry, independent or individual study, and self-directed learning occupy a strong position in the philosophy of modern education, and in this development the school library's resources and its program of teaching study and research skills form a key and integral part at all levels of elementary and secondary education.

Along with the new focus on the library as a learning center, we can note changes in the attitude toward the library as the place for study. The image of the old-fashioned library study-hall rightly evokes chilling horror in the hearts of school librarians, and the comments that follow do not apply to this concept. Today, students should and must have the opportunity to study, to learn, in a library and not in the bleak and barren environment of a study-hall. Now, with the developments in school library facilities--library areas, resource centers, and all the multi-dimensional forms they take--the goals have changed. The idea portrayed in the oft reiterated cliché that curricular and instructional changes have made modern high school libraries comparable to those in many liberal arts colleges of yesteryear and to junior college libraries of today is true, and it must be put into operation in all respects, not just in raising the maturity level of the resources collections. Making it possible for all students to study and work in a library environment requires certain conditions, since no one is

asking for a return to the old-fashioned library study-hall
with its frequently attendant policing and disciplinary problems. The minimal conditions include: sufficient quarters
and facilities for the library, sufficient staff, sufficient resources, and, if students have scheduled study periods, in-
telligently and carefully planned programs for study. Let it
be stressed that current national standards for school libraries relating to facilities and to staff do not sufficiently
provide for an automatic conversion of library areas into
study halls or vice versa.

The I. M. C. and the Skills of Learning

With more and more school libraries becoming instructional materials centers with fully equipped facilities
and with functional programs of service, the librarian's
role has expanded. Students, in the pursuit of their studies,
use a cross-media or multi-media or single medium approach, and receive appropriate guidance from the school
librarians in the selection of these materials and in their
effective use. This principle means more than showing a
student how to use a filmstrip viewer, or machinery for
teaching tapes, or an 8mm sound film projector, or the
micro-reader, or the apparatus for listening to recordings,
or the dial equipment for banks of resources now making
their appearance, or the apparatus for making transparencies, or machines and devices for programed instruction.
The program of teaching the use of library resources includes guidance in teaching students viewing and listening
skills. Opportunities to help students to acquire film literacy are rapidly increasing for school librarians.

Learning how to view and how to listen and acquiring
the skills of perception that evaluation and appreciation of
the media require represent abilities that young persons
have to acquire through time, effort, and guided experiences,
in much the same manner they master the mechanical skills
and developmental aspects of reading. Such instruction includes guidance in helping students to turn naturally to media
other than print as the best and possibly the only appropriate
or artistic forms of communication, to realize when audio-
visual media complement printed materials, and to know
when they have no relevance or are inferior for the purposes
at hand. School librarians also have exciting opportunities to
present to students the realm of the cinema as an art form.

The Vanishing Student Assistant?

    In view of the amount of time that students have and
need for study and for other learning experiences of a rich
variety, it would seem that the student assistant program,
as we have known it, should become a happily forgotten
relic of the past. Many librarians share this belief.
Among the reasons that are advanced are the following:
misuse of student time and effort; the substitution of student volunteer work for the salaried clerical and technical
assistance that is needed; the demands of educational programs and instructional methods that make it more desirable, and generally imperative, for the student to spend his
time in using the library's resources rather than squander-
ing it by helping with the library's housekeeping, janitorial,
and clerical tasks; and the avenues recently opened in various economic opportunity laws to employ salaried personnel
(including students).

Academic Credit

    Unfortunately, the importance attached to the skills of
learning and methods of research sometimes results in the
revival of outmoded techniques or the implementation of undesirable practices. No academic credit at any grade level
should be given for instruction in the use of the library and
its resources. Logically, this principle is a superfluous
one, since the well-planned program, fully integrated with
the curriculum, would not make such an eventuality possible.
Library skills are means to other educational ends, and not
ends in themselves. Library skills do not represent a separate substantive discipline and hence should not be designated
as course content carrying academic credit. Nonetheless,
there seems to be a growing and alarming tendency to for-
malize this instruction. Even when no academic credit is
given, no justification exists for having either courses in
this area or a detached string of lessons. Ironically enough,
the use of programed aids and of audiovisual materials in
conjunction with library instruction often contributes to the
perpetuation of arbitrary, non-integrated instruction.

Accessibility

    The materials of learning are made easily accessible
to students, and the schools provide the necessary materials,

time, facilities, and staff that give students optimum benefits
in the pursuit of their studies and for non-academic purposes as well.

This principle covers many vital parts of the school
library's program. For library facilities, the following developments can be noted: the expansion of library quarters
(main library areas, resource centers, learning areas, and
other space provisions) and new organizational patterns for library areas on a subject or grade level basis. Equipment
has been expanded to include wet and dry carrels, language
laboratories, teaching machines, micro-readers, audiovisual
equipment of all types, machinery for the production and reproduction of materials, and other items. Experiments with
electronic machines for dialing materials, or comparable devices, are under way.

In order to meet the needs of students, the resources
of school libraries are constantly being improved and expanded. Particular emphasis is being given to developing
reference resources (including those in the elementary
schools, since the requests of teachers and children constantly require consultation and use by the librarians of resources that are far from being elementary), the periodical
collections, the collections of audiovisual materials, and the
professional materials for teachers. In secondary schools a
major drive has been made to provide the resources needed
for accelerated, advanced placement, honors, and enriched
courses. In order to satisfy quantitative demands for particular materials school libraries are providing materials in
sufficient duplication. The acquisition and use of paperbacks
in school libraries have rightly assumed sizable proportions.

Making materials easily accessible can also be seen
in the current circulation policies of school libraries that
are elastic and flexible, making it possible for students to
withdraw all kinds of materials easily, and some kinds of
equipment. Further evidence can be noted in the extension
of the hours and days that many school libraries are open
for student use. Even recent movements toward printed book
catalogs and new classification arrangements have a direct
bearing on making materials accessible.

The need to meet, at the very least, existing national
standards for size of library staff becomes critically imperative, since so much individual work with students in the
school library and group work with them in the library areas

and elsewhere form a basic part of the research and study skills program--and this but one part of the school library's services.

Quite probably, the notoriously substandard conditions relating to size of school library staff that have persistently plagued school libraries--and not the lack of a carefully delineated philosophy of library instruction--have led to an over-emphasis on teaching and requiring students to work independently in libraries, rather than providing them with library services that would do much of this location and collection of materials.

Students and Other Libraries

Amidst what must be millions of words written and spoken about students crowding into public libraries, the essential points are sometimes lost in the welter of verbiage. As far as elementary and secondary school students are concerned, the most immediate fact to recognize and concentrate upon is that school libraries must be developed and they must meet the standards for resources and programs. The important goal to reach and to be concentrated upon is that of bringing school libraries up to these standards as quickly as possible. Providing substitutes for these measures, no matter how noble the intents, simply means supporting the perpetuation of inferior conditions in the schools. When the schools fully meet their responsibilities in providing the resources of teaching and learning, in having library programs and services that meet recognized standards, and in making the school library resources and services truly accessible, lamented pressures on the public library might even fade away; and colleges would no longer have to give elementary and secondary school level courses in library instruction.

If endeavors to improve school library conditions fail or improvements come too slowly, and if the public libraries continue to assume responsibilities for providing services and resources to meet curricular needs of students, then what implications can be drawn? One would be that the principles outlined for teaching students about study skills and methods of inquiry must be recognized and followed by the public library in its own program of service. This is relatively simple in those numerous instances where students attend schools that have programs of library instruction but still flock to the public library because of inadequacies in

the collections of the school libraries, the inaccessibility of
the school libraries, or for other reasons.   Otherwise it is
not simple, and even quite unmanageable, because library
instruction must be related to curricular content and assignments, must stress the multi-media approach in the process
of learning, and must provide group and individual guidance
of many kinds--clearly functions of the schools and the educational process.   (It is not as simple a matter as just
knowing in advance what the assignments are.)

    In the current scene, a paradox emerges.   On the
one hand, we have the numerous references to the problems
created by student use in libraries other than those in
schools (most often public, but sometimes college, university,
and special libraries), and, on the other we have a proliferation of community, regional, and state plans setting forth
various proposals for reference and research resource centers to serve all groups (including students) and also proposals for other types of cooperative library services.   As
we hear more and more about the latter (not infrequently,
with the pleasant jingle of federal and state funds in the
background), we hear less and less about the evils emanat-
ing from students swarming into libraries outside their
schools.

    There is no question that the future holds changes,
even marked changes, in the forms of library services, the
audiences served, the organizational and administrative patterns, and the kinds of cooperative planning.   The philosophy
behind some of these possible trends was introduced decades
ago.   A plea is made that proposals for cooperative resources and services be based on sound evidence and sound
theories.   The viewpoint is submitted that we have not yet
assembled all the essential facts and that we will never have
a true picture of conditions until school libraries reach
recommended standards for resources, facilities, and services.   Only then will we be in a position to collect the data
needed for planning.   We do not even know enough now about
the nature of the materials that students use for their academic purposes in the school library or elsewhere, or about
the number and characteristics of students using or not using
library resources.   As part of their responsibilities in
planning the program of study skills and methods of inquiry,
school librarians might well find out about the specific materials used by students, the purposes for which they use
them, where they get them, and the reasons for using resources other than the school library.

We tend to assume that students need materials for their curricular purposes that are too rare or too scholarly or too expensive or too infrequently used to justify their inclusion in school library collections, and this assumption is probably fallacious. (We also tend to assume that all public library collections are superior to all school library collections, and this is definitely fallacious). We tend to ignore existing and proposed school system and multi-school system plans for materials centers, for centralized processing, and for other cooperative library services among schools. Too often the creators of state and regional library plans have little real understanding of what a good school library program is or of the reasons why modern schools must have the resources of teaching and learning. Under any circumstance, state regional, and local planning for libraries should actively involve school administrators and other educators, and too often this has not been the case.

Plans and practices that perpetuate sub-standard conditions in school libraries or that recommend organizational patterns which violate the educational objectives and services that are uniquely characteristics of school libraries, do a disservice to students and teachers. There are innumerable reasons why this is true, but the one to conclude with here is that learning to learn in libraries forms a natural part of the education of youth, best achieved where a richness of materials is easily accessible and under the guidance of teachers and librarians expert in their knowledge of the students, the curriculum, the ways of teaching, and the ways of learning.

5. The Library--An Environmental Learning Center

by Mary Joan Egan

Reprinted, by permission of the Association for Educational Communications and Technology, from Audiovisual Instruction, September 1969.

The Burnt Hills-Ballston Lake School District is a quiet, residential community on the edge of bustling, industrial Schenectady. It is within easy driving distance of the noted academic institutions and lively cultural programs in the humanities and sciences that are available in New York State's capital district region.

The community's school system is comprised of six modern, well-equipped schools: four elementary, one junior high and one senior high, with a total of approximately 5300 students. Each school contains a library meeting current standards. In 1965 the library system of the Burnt Hills-Ballston Lake School District received the Britannica Award as one of 10 elementary library systems in the nation evidencing notable achievement.

Under ESEA grants one of these libraries--the junior high--was selected to become a pioneer in a progressive plan extending an excellent library program. The project encompasses print and nonprint media, a computer terminal, and video-audio dial access to information. This innovation was christened an Environmental Learning Center.

Over a three-year period, federal grants amounting to $200,000 from Titles II and III, together with local funds, produced a transformation in facilities, equipment, materials, and personnel. Ten study carrels, each specially equipped with its own video screen, dial access system, and earphones were installed. These permit the individual student using the carrel access to slides, video- and audio-tapes, ETV programs, films, and filmstrips by dialing code numbers for his preference in the bank of instructive materials.

Students using other carrel stations in the Environmental Learning Center are surrounded by ample provision for their needs. Filmstrips, 8mm single concept films, microfilm, records, tapes, books, periodicals, pamphlets, pictures, and math games are at hand for immediate use. In this learning environment students individually reap the benefits accruing from independent research and study or gain significant support from the repetitive teaching possible from the media.

Multimedia carts, supplying books, nonbook materials, plus audiovisual equipment, can be wheeled to classrooms for individual use, group, or classroom instruction. Teachers, students, and librarians plan together for the use of materials for specific lessons or units.

All materials in the Center receive complete processing: classification, labeling, and indexing were extended to each piece of print and nonprint material that came to the Center. Newer media materials were treated to the same procedures as books to provide one integrated system of indexing and locating materials. All materials--books, pamphlets, pictures, 8mm loops, 16mm films, transparencies, audiotapes, videotapes, and slides are cataloged and processed. All materials are technically indexed in the card catalog to facilitate rapid location of appropriate learning materials.

To provide immediate accessibility of materials, a new and original system of shelving was instituted. For the filmstrips, shelves with special compartments were designed. Single concept 8mm films were labeled distinctively on one side of their plastic containers and shelved as books are shelved. Audiotapes, microfilmed magazines and newspapers, 16mm films, multimedia kits, and records receive similar treatment. Slides and transparencies, when possible, are shelved in the same manner. Borrowers scan shelves of media as familiarly as they scan a shelf of books to discover the precise material they seek. Both student and teacher have expressed enthusiasm for the efficacy of these arrangements of learning tools.

Materials located in the Environmental Learning Center are available through interlibrary loan to all schools in the district. These materials supplement the resources in the various school libraries.

The junior high library was selected to be a demonstration center by state and federal agencies because of the quality educational program and many other factors. As a demonstration project the center has welcomed over 1700 visitors from outside the district. Questionnaires, letters, and other methods of communication have revealed that educators are impressed with the unique character and organization of the project as well as the quality and enthusiasm of the faculty. The interest, acceptance, and good use of materials in the Environmental Learning Center by students have caused many visitors to apply numerous aspects of the project to their own schools or, in some cases, to another type of institution.

Typical Comments

Students: "You find things you wouldn't find in any library ordinarily. It informs you on just about any topic. "

"You can get more information than you could from just the encyclopedias and books. "

Teachers: "I make extensive use of our available facilities to plan and prepare unit guides for my students, and they in turn must consult all forms of media from books to videotapes. Materials programed on audio-video dial access and materials available for loan play vital roles in the learning process. "

"In the program of independent study in grade 9 well over 300 students have made significantly greater use of library type resources than they would have previously. "

Visitors: "This project has shown that the electronic approach to information-seeking is time-saving and that a bright future is ahead. "

"My first view of this innovative project was a complete surprise. I did not realize that such techniques, equipment, and innovative approaches existed. "

"I have always considered the library as the only logical place to handle not only books but other forms of media since it is the general information center. "

"My concepts have been broadened through the new

information acquired on the use of modern media techniques. The on-site visit was most educational for my professional associates."

To maintain and operate this modern-as-tomorrow Environmental Learning Center to full and efficient capacity, a competent, well-trained staff is essential. The staff is composed of three librarians (media specialists according to AASL and DAVI), and three aides who are available to work with students and teachers using the Environmental Learning Center. There is also a media production specialist, recently added to the staff.

Cooperating agencies involved in the planning and implementation of the project are the New York State Education Department (Bureau of School Libraries, Frank Stevens, chief; Division of Innovation in Education, Norman Kurland, director; Division of Education Communications, Lee Campion, director) and the State University of New York at Albany (School of Library Science, Susan Smith, school library consultant; NDEA Institute, Murray Philips, director).

Other agencies contacted included the Capital District Regional Supplementary Educational Center, public library systems, CASDA, manufacturers of equipment, and vendors of materials. Visitors are welcomed at the Center by appointment.

6. The I. M. C.

by Margaret E. Nicholsen

Reprinted, by permission of the American Library Association and the author, from School Libraries, March 1964.

What is an Instructional Materials Center? It might be defined as a collection of print and nonprint materials and equipment so selected, arranged, located and staffed as to serve the needs of teachers and students and to further the purposes of the school. To be a true center it must include print and nonprint and the necessary equipment for their use. Sometimes a collection of motion pictures, filmstrips and tapes and their hardware is called an "instructional materials center." This collection may need some kind of a name, but surely it is not an Instructional Materials Center.

Test tubes are used in chemistry, baseballs in Physical Education, skeletons in anatomy, foods in Home Economics. Do these items belong in an IMC? What are "supplies" and what "materials"? What are the practical limits to the materials to be located in a center? It seems to me that it is impossible to make any hard and fast rule that would apply to every school in the country. Under certain circumstances it might be perfectly appropriate for basketballs to be distributed by the IMC or for musical instruments to be housed there for loan to students. If the IMC has the space and staff, there is no reason why it could not handle any type of material or even supplies which would help students and teachers, as well as administrators.

What materials should certainly be found in every IMC: books, filmstrips, maps, motion pictures, pamphlets, periodicals, phonograph records, slides, and tapes, as well as the necessary equipment to use them. If a collection lacks any of those nine items it is not a true IMC, in my estimation. I think most would agree that transparencies and realia should be included, as well as overhead and opaque projectors and teaching machines. There are a

46

number of "gadgets" which are not materials and which do
not use materials, but which for the sake of convenience
and accessibility might be housed in the IMC. These might
include book copiers (which are found in most Centers today),
laminating machines, tachistoscopes, portable public address
systems, cameras, radios, television sets, typewriters,
duplicators, language laboratories, and adding machines.
All of these would be found useful by some teachers or students at some time or other. The final decision will depend, of course, upon the space available and upon the administrative organization of the school. However, the nine
items must be in the IMC before one should call it that. To
repeat, those are: books, filmstrips, maps, motion pictures,
pamphlets, periodicals, phonograph records, slides, and
tapes, as well as the equipment necessary to use them.

Why An IMC?

Why have an Instructional Materials Center? What
are the advantages of that over an old-fashioned library and
an unrelated audio-visual room?

First, from the teacher's point of view: He has to
go to only one place in the building, the IMC, to locate all
kinds of materials and equipment. He does not have to remember that for this I go to the library, for that I go to
the audio-visual room, and for these others I ask the Principal. When he goes to the IMC, he finds all the materials
available with staff members who know them. He can ask
advice, examine varied types of materials on the subject,
and then select the kinds of materials which best serve the
purpose for that particular class at that time. He may
want to use only books and magazines for this particular
lesson. He may want a filmstrip and phonograph record
for the next; and he can arrange for both in the one place
with no fuss or bother and without feeling that if he goes to
the audio-visual room he is neglecting the "library," or if
he goes to the library that he is neglecting all the new technological devices and is "old-fashioned."

Another advantage for the teacher in using the Center
is that it is open every minute of the school day as well as
before and after school. In some areas it is also open on
Saturdays and in the evenings. Separate audio-visual rooms
in many schools are often closed at certain times of the day
and are not open before and after school, thus presenting

the necessity for the teacher to remember the audio-visual
room schedule and adapt to it.   Another advantage to the
teacher in having materials in one location is that bibliographies he requests will include not only books, but also per-
tinent filmstrips, phonograph records and other nonprint materials on the subject.   Under the separate system he would
have to ask the library and the audio-visual staffs to each
make a list of the materials available on the subject.

Even more important than the increased service to
teachers, which results from having all types of materials
brought together in one place, is the increased service to
students.   They feel free to come to the Center for reading, for using the card catalog, for using reference books,
for looking at filmstrips or for listening to phonograph records.   They feel that the Center belongs to them and that
the materials are there to increase their knowledge.   Teaching machines for individual study, single concept films in
the 8mm projectors, filmstrip viewers, tape recorders with
the tapes of the lessons missed when they were ill, all
these are available to them in different areas of the Center.
The students are learning that when they want information
and inspiration they should go to the Center and look for
background knowledge and for cultural experiences in whatever media serves best the specific need.

Probably the centralization of materials is not going
to result in much financial saving to the school as the arrangement will increase the demand for materials and the
efficiency with which these can be provided and will marked-
ly increase the use made by both students and teachers.
Thus, the same amount of money may be spent, but the
service and the quality and effectiveness of the teaching will
be improved.   Likewise, a staff of approximately the same
size may be needed, but it will be better utilized combined
in a Center.   Instead of having two staffs in charge of two
separated areas, the Center would double the staff working
in one area.   The result--better service to both students
and teachers.

Personnel Needed

Who is needed to operate an Instructional Materials
Center?

The professional staff should have training in both

print and nonprint materials, their selection, organization and use. In a large staff there will be areas of specialization, but all should know literature for children or young adults as well as films, filmstrips, phonograph records, and slides suitable for use in the school. This is a large order; there is no doubt about it. However, the materials specialist is probably the only person in the school who has a picture of all types of materials suitable in all areas. Naturally, he will rely upon the subject specialists in the school for aid and assistance in selection of materials to be added to the collection. Perhaps as important as the training in both nonprint and print is the choice of professional staff members who are actively interested in all types of materials and who believe and can demonstrate that in some cases books are the perfect answer and in others filmstrips will do the job best, while in others a magazine article followed by listening to a phonograph record is the most suitable. Of the greatest importance is the philosophy that all types of materials should be so arranged and located that the professional staff member can assist the teacher or student in locating that type or types best suited to his purposes. The professional staff members must know the content of the materials; they must read books, view filmstrips, listen to phonograph records, look at motion pictures, and read magazines. There should be specialization in large staffs, but every member should be aware of and conversant with the total resources of the Center.

In addition to professional staff there should be an adequate number of clerks. These clerks must be able to type, to be accurate, and to deal with students, and, when necessary, with a demanding or unreasonable teacher. Much of the work of checking in motion pictures, of giving out projectors, of seeing that equipment and materials are returned can be done by clerks. A professional staff member will have to work out the system of scheduling, delivering, circulating, etc., but once it is well organized, a capable clerk can handle it. A professional staff member should not need to be concerned about telling Miss Jones that she has kept a phonograph too long and must return it as soon as possible. The clerks also do all the typing needed in processing new books and in typing the catalog cards, not only for books, but also for filmstrips and phonograph records.

During the school day most IMC's will find a number of students who will volunteer to work. Their assistance is

invaluable and they usually get a feeling of rendering service
to the school as well as a feeling of importance.   They can
check out books, check in books, operate projectors, etc.
However, it is sometimes a temptation to exploit these students and to give them deadly dull tasks which they must do
daily.   Some jobs, such as shelving books and magazines
and delivering equipment, can be done before or after school.
For these jobs, students should be paid and expected to come
on schedule every day, working as on a regular job.

Another type of staff member who will be needed in
a large IMC is a technician.   He is not a professional nor
on the regular faculty, nor is he on the clerical staff.   He
has charge of repairing the equipment and of preventive
maintenance.   Small Centers will find it less expensive to
contract with a local commercial company to repair their
equipment than to hire a technician--just as the Business
Education department expects to have typewriters repaired
by a local company rather than by a teacher or maintenance
staff member.

The staff of an IMC, then, should consist of a director or head, professional staff, technicians, clerks, paid
student help, and volunteer student aides.

Location

Where should the IMC be located?

It should be located as near the center of the school
as possible so that it is accessible to all students and teachers.   It should be open every minute of the school day, as
well as before and after school, and in some schools it
should be open on Saturdays and evenings.   There should
be separate rooms for reading, for listening, for viewing
and for the production of materials.   The reading area
should be able to accommodate 10% of the students, according to the standards of the American Library Association,
and should have spaces for individual study.   The listening
area can be a small room adjacent to the reading area and
equipped with booths or headphones.   Some schools have
placed phonographs with headphones right in the reading
areas, but this makes some disturbance due to "needle
talk."   The viewing area should be adjacent to the reading
area, and the space needed can be reduced by using a pre-
view machine or a rear projection screen.

There should also be a room for the production of materials. These rooms and areas should all be in one place for the convenience of teachers and students and to increase the effectiveness of their selection of materials. The equipment should be available in the Center, so that a teacher who comes for a phonograph record does not have to go elsewhere to obtain the necessary phonograph. What good is a filmstrip projector without filmstrips? It is entirely possible to work out a system of locating large equipment, such as motion picture projectors and overhead and opaque projectors elsewhere in the school.

Those items have to be delivered to classrooms for use, but the IMC must keep previewing or auditioning equipment for each type of material to make teacher or student examination possible before deciding what to use.

All materials for reading, i. e. books, magazines, pamphlets; materials for listening, i. e. phonorecords and tapes; materials for viewing, i. e. filmstrips, motion pictures and slides, should be located in one place, the IMC, accessible to all students and teachers. Permanent classroom collections and permanent collections of books shelved in various departmental offices should be avoided.

When To Start

When should an Instructional Materials Center be started? Immediately, of course. This can be done by either revolution or evolution.

The former would mean that tomorrow all materials and equipment would be brought together in one place and under one head. However, no superintendent should expect his present overworked librarians to assume responsibility tomorrow for all audio-visual and nonprint materials and equipment without additional staff and/or training. Personnel could be added who have had training in both types of materials, and present library staff could be urged (i. e. required) to take training in nonprint materials this summer. Likewise, no superintendent should ask his overworked audio-visual specialist to assume responsibility for the print materials unless he is given additional staff trained in both print and nonprint, and the former audio-visual staff required to take courses this summer in the organization, administration and content of print materials. The principal

advantage of the quick change from two separate areas to
the centralized materials is that teachers learn quickly that
they are to go to just one place henceforth for all types of
materials.

Changing to an IMC by evolution has the disadvantage
that for some time certain materials are still in one location
and others in another. Assuming that all print is in one
place and all nonprint in another, it would be possible and
practicable to move just the filmstrips and the filmstrip projectors and viewers to the library. Then with additional
staff next Fall, the phonograph records and phonographs
could be added. An additional clerk, or one transferred
from the present audio-visual room, could assume responsibility for the motion picture schedule, as well as the
scheduling of the overheads and opaques. Thus in a year
or two all nonprint materials and equipment would have
joined the print in one location and administered by one
staff.

Whichever method is used, the most important job of
the IMC professional staff is to gain as rapidly as possible
a thorough knowledge of the content of the materials of all
types.   .

Throughout this presentation I have obediently used
the term "Instructional Materials Center," for that is sup-
posed to be the topic of this meeting. However, the term
LIBRARY is familiar to all teachers and students and means
to them a place where they will find materials of communication well-selected, well-arranged, and well-cataloged, and
staffed with experts who can help them find answers to their
questions or find the material needed. The public library
has added phonograph records and motion pictures to its collections but still is called a library. Why not enlarge our
view of school library service and use the well-known term,
library rather than the long and cumbersome "Instructional
Materials Center" or "Learning Resource Center"? They
mean the same thing, for a library should contain all types
of materials which transmit the ideas, images, and sounds
of yesterday, today, and tomorrow.

PART II

ADMINISTRATIVE ASPECTS OF MEDIA CENTERS

7. Good Materials Centers--
    Through Principles or Principals?

    An interview with C. William Riley
    Principal, Lomond School, Shaker Heights City
    School District, Shaker Heights, Ohio

    Reprinted, by permission of the American Library
    Association, from School Activities and the Li-
    brary, 1968.

Certainly Materials Centers need firm, rational principles on which to grow. But they also need strong support
from the principals who develop and nurture them.

A most outstanding elementary center is the Lomond
School Learning Center at Shaker Heights, Ohio. Originally
funded by the Ford Foundation as an action-research project,
it is now operating for its third year totally supported by
the Shaker Heights school district.

Ideologically and operationally, the Center is supported by the Lomond principal, C. William Riley. It is he who
assumes the responsibility for establishing and expanding its
services. Because the results are so positive, Mr. Riley
was asked to answer some questions about its operation:

Recent studies strongly establish the principal as
the deciding factor in the quality of instruction.
Do you feel he is equally important to the materials center?

Mr. Riley: Definitely yes. A principal has the same
concern for the materials center as for the school's instructional program. Some principals argue that a materials center is largely supplementary, but they are thinking of an
adult-based program which affords little opportunity for responsibility or determination on the part of the children.

I view my Learning Center as the focal point of the
school and plan my classroom observations, conversations
with teachers, and analyses of the needs of children with

this in mind. When my librarian comes to me with recommendations, I consider them not only in terms of the Center but of the total school program.

On a theoretical basis that sounds good, but can you name specific ways in which you support your librarian?

Mr. Riley: I hope so, for strong lines of communication between librarian and principal are in many ways more necessary than accomplishing this same goal with any one teacher.

A prime responsibility of any principal is the selection of the librarian. Many considerations must be kept in mind, such as personality, communications skills, adeptness in selecting and promoting new materials, and familiarity with the total school program. A willingness to revise plans of presenting materials and flexibility in altering the Center's organization are also important.

I say very earnestly that I have a deep professional respect for a good librarian. The person in this position is so vital to the improvement of instruction that I would be foolhardy not to supply maximum support.

I accept the librarian's budget recommendations when ordering new materials. My librarian selects not only books and encyclopedias, but also filmstrips, tapes, transparencies, and other audio-visual materials.

I seek the librarian's opinion on how to reach teachers more effectively and how to involve them in the use of the Center. I come to the librarian for leads about children who have difficulties or who seem to be working below their maximum level.

I expose the librarian to the parents of the community and let them know how important her job is. I support the librarian by observing lessons and supplying any ideas I have for upgrading them.

One other kind of support, sometimes overlooked, is sincerely complimenting the librarian when her ideas have met with success, when an innovation opens up new areas, or even for day-by-day successful operation of the Center. I am afraid that sometimes principals tend to be parsimonious with praise.

The materials center is supposedly organized to
render multi-services for its participants. As a
principal, what do you want to see?

Mr. Riley: The Lomond School supplies children--
kindergarten through grade six--with a wide selection of fiction and nonfiction books plus other new and exciting learning materials. Through the use of tapes, the children can
hear a narrative, such as "The Life of Benjamin Franklin, "
to stimulate reading, or they can listen to a record such as
"A Child's Introduction to Jazz. "

Materials in the Learning Center serve to give our
curriculum a wider base. When our fourth, fifth, and sixth
graders check a variety of encyclopedias for certain information and find varying reports, they are having experiences in
discriminating research. When they see films or filmstrips,
they are, in effect, gathering raw evidence on which they
can make assumptions or draw conclusions.

The Center borrows from the Cleveland Museum of
Art, and our children become acquainted with original works
and good reproductions. The librarian frequently sends collections of materials, including models and realia, to classrooms and goes to classrooms herself for discussions.

The Learning Center performs many small services
for students. Recently it taped a special assembly--includ-
ing the school orchestra and chorus numbers plus speeches
by leaders from the student council--so that the participants
and other interested students can relive the performance.
Significant tapes become part of the permanent tape library.

Our librarian supplies teachers with professional
books and magazines and calls their attention to new supplementary materials for classroom instruction. A special
teachers' bulletin carries information on new acquisitions,
helpful reference hints, and general information to make
the teacher's job easier and more effective.

How do the mechanics of your Center operate?

Mr. Riley: The Learning Center is open a half hour
before school and forty-five minutes after school. Practically everything in the Center can be taken home, including
filmstrips and viewers that have their own carrying cases.
Children have free access to all materials, including the

vertical files, throughout the entire day.

Kindergarten through third-grade classes have one assigned library period each week. This period may be used as a story hour for informal library instruction and, of course, book exchange.

We are fortunate to have a large room across from our Learning Center. From September to January, there is combined group instruction for grades four through six once a week. Sixteen basic library-work study skills are introduced. The goal is to give children fundamental tools of research for independent study, and the librarian and teachers incorporate use of these skills into assignments and projects to be undertaken in the Learning Center.

Individuals and small groups come to the Learning Center any time to work. We have two listening centers, study carrels with earphones, a console with three tape decks, one record turntable with earphones, and viewers for 8mm-film loops. Children work independently, regardless of what group is in the library for a story hour or other scheduled activity.

Both teachers and children react favorably to this kind of informal scheduling, and there are practically no problems of disorder either in the Center or in going or coming.

Originally, how did you go about selling the Learning Center concept to teachers and librarians?

Mr. Riley: We must acknowledge some advantage from having a grant from the Ford Foundation. It required united action by the faculty. We had to get behind what we were doing and give it a serious try. But it did not take teachers long to see that the materials center provided exposure to more sources of information than our previous program did. Grouping materials in the Center rather than in separate classrooms meant that many materials were available to any child. Even halfway through the first year we could also see that audio-visual materials, such as filmstrips, records, tapes, and transparencies, combined with books provided opportunities to explore additional areas of interest.

Administration support was a big factor, and here, I

think, the principal had to supersede the principle. It is not easy for a teacher to change traditional modes of instruction. My teachers had to know that I would be behind every attempt they made. I could not expect change overnight, and I had to expect some failures along the way. My teachers knew that I was on hand to help, either by conferences or by working with them in the classroom. In fact, if I do not have this type of communication with a teacher, I know something is wrong.

When the first group with a year's experience in the Learning Center went on to junior high, teachers and students alike noted these children's ability to carry on independent study. Our former students increasingly report that the Learning Center facilities and materials are invaluable as they are exposed to more advanced academic work.

How do you orient parents and children?

Mr. Riley: I am glad you said "orient" rather than "sell." It is rarely necessary to do much selling to parents about independent study, but we do need to help them understand what it means.

Under the Ford Foundation grant, we administered standardized tests to show growth in library skills. Questionnaires filled out by children, teachers, and parents sought reactions on what would be improved. We still seek these reactions, and many parents say they notice a change in their child's attitude toward independent study.

Our monthly PTA newsletter has a Learning Center column. In addition, I frequently talk to parent groups about the goals of the Learning Center. Here is a comment from one of my parents: "I cannot overemphasize the benefit of the Learning Center. I have seen growth and independence in my son's works that were not demonstrated in my older child who lacked this opportunity."

If you were to name the single most significant benefit from your Learning Center, what would it be?

Mr. Riley: Let me name two. The first is that it establishes a favorable environment for the entire school. This is very important, because children's attitudes and work patterns are influenced strongly by the school climate.

The second benefit is the great increase in the work children do independently. I do not think any school can accomplish individualization all of a sudden. Teachers and children have to work up to it. Our Learning Center is making this possible.

In your thinking, is a materials center equally effective with children who are culturally deprived or underachievers?

Mr. Riley: Often people assume all Shaker Heights children are from higher socio-economic groups. This is not the case, and children who are less advantaged culturally and educationally are enrolled in our school. At first, they are amazed at having freedom to move from one area of the building to another without a teacher. It may pose a little control problem, but they become acclimated fairly quickly.

These children are also invariably surprised by the wide variety of materials. Some materials are chosen particularly with their needs in mind. Our librarian wants these children to experience early success on which they can build as they attack more sophisticated problems and use more involved materials.

With underachievers, it is important to arouse enthusiasm about materials--to help them find out how interesting a book can be. Once these youngsters become excited about being able to go ahead on their own, learning suddenly becomes rewarding. As a generalization, I would say that learning centers are even more important for the less-advantaged children or underachievers in building personal confidence and broadening their skill and knowledge base.

As a concluding question, what are your dreams for the future of your Learning Center?

Mr. Riley: I have all kinds of dreams. First I want more staff, and I would like one librarian who could devote most of her attention to emphasizing literature. We could also use more paraprofessionals to good advantage.

Lomond School is moving toward a humanistic emphasis in the curriculum. We are relating more and more elements of our learning patterns to the experiences and aspirations of the children, and this means expanding the facilities

for cultural expression.   If I wanted really to dream, I
could see a small theater adjoining the Learning Center,
with facilities for puppet shows or other dramatic perform-
ances and an adjoining art gallery large enough for three-
dimensional art as well as flat pictures.

I would welcome a plan whereby children had access
to the files of our local and national newspapers and could
share the materials from other learning centers.   I could
see small groups of children of different ages and grade
levels going unsupervised from the actual school building
during school hours to have interdisciplinary experiences in
the social, natural, and physical sciences.

I could see learning becoming even more individualized,
so that there would be individual prescriptions for each child
in his library-skill program.   Computers in the Learning Center would keep records, make analyses, and predict possible
gains for each child.

Actually there is no limit to what one can dream, but
in the meantime, we are glad that our Lomond Learning Center is functioning realistically and serving the total program
of our school to an ever increasing degree.

8. Standards--California

> The following statements on rationale, philosophy, and program were prepared by a Joint Committee of the California Association of School Librarians and the Audio-Visual Education Association of California. The complete state standards can be found in the publication Standards for the Development of School Media Programs in California, 1970.

Rationale

The purpose of standards is to provide guidelines for present and potential media programs that will aid schools in achieving educational goals. Schools which have not yet fully achieved their objectives can use the standards as a guide for charting goals to be reached in progressive steps over a period of time. Schools with innovative curricula and instructional techniques will need to go beyond the quantitative standards.

A media program is never static, because the education program on which it is based continues to change. A media program must meet new demands inherent in this transition. The standards should serve as one of the instruments for continuous evaluation of the media program's ability to meet evolving objectives of the education program.

The Committee believes that the standards can be realistically applied in schools where there is:

A firm commitment to a plan of education which incorporates a quality media program.

Successful application of recognized theories of learning.

Average economic support.

Strong community support.

61

Philosophy

Education programs that encompass a wide range of media permit learning situations with the potential to meet the demands and challenges of an expanding, changing environment. Utilization of a wide range of media is based on the premises that:

Learning occurs through all of the senses. These modalities are utilized with varying degrees of effectiveness by individuals who learn in different ways, at different rates, and for different purposes.

Learning can occur in large groups, in small groups, or in individual study.

The potential of each medium, when used either singly or in combination with other media, varies with the content, the subject area, and its presentation.

The use of educational media should enhance individual choice, creativity, and self-directed inquiry.

Specific minimum levels of media and media services should be available to all students regardless of school size and geographical location.

The media program must support the education program reflected in the philosophy of the school.

The new terms media specialist and media program denote more than a change in title. They denote more than the sum total of library and audio-visual. They are evidence of a fundamental change in media services and utilization developed in response to new patterns of learning, curriculum, and administration. New and unique roles for media and media specialists are implied. The interrelationship between learning and media is strengthened. The media program must have the recognition, promotion, and support of all segments of the education system. It is dependent upon the community and the governing board for active endorsement and financial support. The staff and administrators are responsible for the planning, development, and implementation of the program. The media program is an integral part of the education program only when teachers and students understand and use the media and services of the media center.

Program

As an integral and vital part of the total education process, the media program provides services to students, faculty, and administrators.

It merges school library services, audio-visual services, and other education technology services to bring about the improvement of learning.

It functions under the direction of media specialists who are involved with all aspects of curriculum development and implementation.

It provides opportunities for individual growth, enrichment, and enjoyment.

It serves as a catalyst for new ideas.

It provides for reading, listening, viewing, responding, and the production of materials.

It provides for activities in school and at home.

It supports innovations in both curriculum and school organization.

A media center is basic to this education approach. Specific needs necessarily vary with the type of education institution of which it is a part, but in all cases the media center is an essential component of the education system.

9. Budgeting for School Media Centers

Robert Wedgeworth

Reprinted, by permission of the American Library Association and the author, from School Libraries, Spring 1971.

Although in 1953 Alice Lefevre stated that "a search through professional literature brings to light a wealth of material on the administration of school libraries," there seems to be a conspicuous lack of information as to how school libraries seek, handle, and account for money (1, * p. 286). Ziskind noted in 1958 that school library budgets are prepared "almost universally by administrators"--meaning school principals, business managers, and superintendents (2, p. 424). This statement is partially supported by the results of a 1967 study by Ahlers and Morrison which revealed that in twenty-one of seventy-eight school districts studied there was no separate budget line for central materials centers (3, p. 457). These statements may suggest that the budgetary process has not played a major role in the management of school libraries. They may also suggest that school libraries and/or media centers have not achieved distinction as significant areas of interest to be separately considered in the budgetary process. Therefore, the primary purpose of this paper is to explore some of the major dimensions of the problem of budgeting for school libraries and/or media centers. Secondly, it will explore the nature of the budgetary process including a modern approach to budgeting. Finally, it will attempt to develop a framework within which budgeting can function as a powerful management and analysis tool for school media centers.

Given the sparseness of library literature on the subject of budgeting, this paper will raise more questions than it will answer. It will attempt to focus attention on the

---

*Numbers in parentheses refer to the numbered items in the references.

function of budgeting and the nature of the budgetary process rather than specifically how to develop or interpret a budget. As such it will be exploratory and even at times speculative. The intent is not to indict the adequacy of library literature or the administrative skills of school librarians but to present some ideas regarding the budgetary process and to suggest relationships to the effective management of school media centers.

Dimension of the Problem

During the past decade there have emerged four major levels of fund sources for school libraries and/or media centers: (1) local and school district funds; (2) state funds; (3) federal funds administered by the states (NDEA Title III and ESEA Title II); and (4) federal funds administered centrally (HUD Model Cities Program). The various levels of fund sources not only complicated the accounting procedures of school administrations, but also created the necessity for more comprehensive long-range planning at the state and local level. Initially, NDEA (1958) and ESEA (1965) provided fresh money which served to stimulate the development of school libraries and/or media centers (4, p. 544). However, such funds are not unlimited and are quite vulnerable to cuts in the federal budget, as evidenced by the original recommendation for ESEA Title II by the Nixon administration for the fiscal year 1971. Although the President subsequently reversed his position on school media resources, there is still the possibility of school media centers having to compete with other interests for a share of funds not earmarked for specific purposes (5, p. 1-2). This possibility not only places a premium value on budget justification but makes imperative the need to directly relate budget requests to the program of services to be provided with the funds sought. One can infer from the Coleman Report a decided inability of school media centers as well as other school services to differentiate themselves in terms of costs/benefits (6).

Organizational complexity is another dimension of the problem of budgeting for school media centers. In a one-school district the allocation and accounting for budget funds may occur at the building level. However, more frequently these activities occur at the district level for member schools. If there is a district supervisor for school media centers, the mechanism for coordinating building level media

interests will be present. But there is still the problem of
budgeting for special cooperative agencies such as book processing centers and film libraries. These agencies, in
some cases, receive funds directly from state, federal and
private sources for which they have fiscal and legal responsibility. Moreover, it is conceivable that school districts
will form systems in order to provide combinations of services such as computer assistance, closed-circuit television,
and technical processing. Both the supradistrict, single-
purpose agencies and their logical extensions as comprehensive system service centers are significant in that they represent additional levels of organizational complexity with attendant budgeting difficulties.

    Still another dimension to the problem of budgeting
for school media centers emerged with the historic achievement of the American Association of School Librarians
(AASL) and the Department of Audiovisual Instruction (DAVI)
of the National Education Association in developing the 1969
Standards for School Media Programs. For many school
librarians the adoption of the new standards will involve
them in an expanded program of services utilizing expensive
equipment and a wider range of professional skills. Not infrequently, sophisticated instructional systems will be developed based upon these skills and equipment. The task of
coordinating these service elements becomes quite complicated. Thus, it is appropriate, as Morris indicates, to emphasize the introductory statement in the new standards
which refers to the need for interpreting the standards in
terms of local conditions (7, p. 50). The objectives of the
instructional program and the funds available to implement
it should determine the specific configuration of service
elements which define the program of the school media center. For as Morris says, "It must be understood that the
standards are designed to implement a program. They are
not designed to stand by themselves and exist for their own
merit. ... " (7, p. 51).

    It may be appropriate at this point to ask about the
nature of the budgetary process; how does it operate so as
to accommodate fluctuations in fund levels, varying complexi-
ties of organization, and varying local conditions in its function as a management tool?

The Budgetary Process

"In the most literal sense a budget is a document containing words and figures, which propose expenditures for certain items and purposes. " (8, p. 1). This basic definition refers to what is traditionally called a "line-item" budget. That is, the budget is divided into a number of purposive categories, e. g. , personnel and equipment. Each category contains one or more lines of budget items and their associated costs. Wildavsky presumes that those who make budgets see a direct connection between what they include and future events. "Hence we might conceive of a budget as intended behavior, as a prediction. " (8, p. 1). "Another way of expressing this is that budgeting is a device whereby the same phenomena and the same ideas are progressively translated into different levels of meaning. " (9, p. 229). It is perhaps the different levels of meaning on which it operates which make budgeting difficult to study as a whole. If one were to ask a cataloger to describe what she was doing, she might reply, "I am indexing and describing these materials" or, "I am building a card catalog. " It is not likely that she would reply, "I am expending these catalog cards and depreciating this typewriter. " Yet all of these responses would be appropriate depending on the level at which the activity were being viewed.

Mosher identifies two broad categories of purpose for the budgetary process. In the policy category, the budget allows for regular, periodic review of the purposes and objectives of the organization. It facilitates cost/benefit analyses. It also provides a link between the administrative personnel who set the budget requirements of certain activities and the operating personnel who must carry out those activities within the budgetary limits prescribed (9, p. 230). In the administrative category, the budget provides the legal basis for fund expenditures. This applies primarily to governmental agencies. Administratively, the budget also provides the basis for accountability. That is, successive levels of employees in the organizational hierarchy are responsible for the expenditure of that portion of the budget which they, by virtue of their position, supervise. Accountability facilitates the delegation of authority as well as the systematic reexamination of operations (9, p. 230).

In principle, budgeting for school media programs should involve a planning mechanism, a management mechanism, and a control mechanism. As a planning device, it should communicate the purposes and objectives of management. As a management device, it should detail the responsibility for specific operations. As a control device, it should establish the basis for measuring progress toward stated objectives in dollars and cents.

In this regard, it is perhaps useful to look at some budgets of school libraries and media centers in order to see if these latter considerations are embodied in their function. An arbitrary selection of field seminar reports written by students in the Rutgers Graduate School of Library Service between 1961 and 1968 were reviewed. While these reports are not representative of school libraries generally, they do give some indication of how budgets communicate purposes and control operations. A major limitation of the reports is that they were intended to give an overall view of the respective school and as such do not focus much attention on the budget. However, this limitation lends some support to the contention that budgeting is an underutilized management tool in school libraries.

In a survey of a junior high school in 1961, it was found that the budget for the school library was submitted to the district library supervisor through the principal. The budget itself was divided into three categories: books and periodicals, supplies, and furniture and equipment. Budget increases were justified by citing the standards and/or increased enrollment. No audiovisual materials were budgeted at the school level, and in 1956-60, the expenditure for materials was $1.81 per pupil. A study in 1962 reported that the school board had no policy for elementary school libraries. A flat appropriation of $2.92 per pupil was made to each school principal for library purposes and was to be spent at their discretion. No formal budget procedures involving the librarians were indicated. A senior high school was evaluated in 1963. A close working relationship between the principal and the librarian was reported. The 1963-64 budget of $5.81 per pupil and faculty met the requirements of the 1960 ALA Standards. The budget consisted of three categories: books and periodicals, supplies, and audiovisual materials. The audiovisual budget was tabulated separately, however. The elementary school libraries of a school district were surveyed in 1964. It was reported that there was strong central control over the budget by the business manager. Although the total per pupil expenditure for all materials was $4.61 in 1962-65, the librarians had little budget influence. Unspent funds were diverted for other purposes without notifying the school principals or library personnel. Per pupil expenditure dropped to $2.50 in 1963-64, but was increased to $3.00 for 1964-65. A school library was surveyed in 1964. Here again a close working relationship between the principal and the librarian was reported. Per pupil expenditures were at the mean of the 1960 Standards for 1963-64 ($5.00 and $4.00 for books and audio-visual materials, respectively). No formal budget procedures were reported. A high school library was surveyed in 1968. No budget procedures were specified but the 1967-68 budget exceeded the 1960 Standards and was expected to exceed the 1969 Standards as well. A line-item budget was shown for 1967-68 divided into materials and equipment with subcategories under each.

While no valid generalizations can be made about this arbitrarily selected group of school libraries, there are some interesting features about their budget procedures which should be pointed out. First, the budgets simply list maximum expenditures allowed for certain categories of items. There is no indication of a stated coordination of the formal budget with programs of service. In those instances where the school library has strong support, the principal appears as a key figure in the budgetary process. The total exclusion of personnel and the frequent exclusion of supplies from the school library budget tend to obscure the nature of the library program. In no instance was there any indication that the librarian exercised significant influence in the budgetary process by means of a clearly articulated budget proposal based on clearly articulated program objectives. On the contrary, there were several instances in which the librarian had little input and virtually no control over the school library budget.

Several conclusions which appear in the professional literature may be advanced to explain the situations described by the reports reviewed. School budgets, for the most part, are highly centralized. Traditionally, those responsible for preparing school library budgets have relied upon standards to simplify their tasks (2, p. 425). Standards published by state boards of education generally are expressed in terms of minimum dollars per school or per pupil while those published by professional associations have gone into considerably more detail in designating minimum personnel and collection requirements as well as minimum dollar amounts (2, p. 425). Local criteria for school library budgets are determined "most frequently by the num-

ber of pupils enrolled or the daily average attendance in
each school" (10, p. 3, 552).

While quantitative formulas ease the computational
aspects of budget preparation they are valid only to the extent to which they are based upon empirical evidence regarding the cost of the services they project. The latest comprehensive cost accounting of school library services published in the literature appeared in 1941 (11). Also, budget
allocations based upon local criteria are generally made at
a level consistent with the internal political influence of the
fund-seeking department. Since the Public Library Inquiry,
repeated studies indicate that librarians as an occupational
group are apolitical. Given this characteristic plus the lack
of effective measures of the impact of school media service,
school librarians are in a poor position to justify increased
budget requests except where key administrative officials,
such as school principals, are sympathetic toward their
claims. Within this context a modern concept of budgeting
holds possibilities for assisting school librarians in planning,
managing, and controlling their operations.

Program, Planning and Budgeting

Since the mid-sixties a budgetary system called Program, Planning and Budgeting (PPBS) has been advanced as
a revolutionary concept (12, p. 271). Originally, PPBS was
developed for use by the Department of Defense in order to
enable it to plan, coordinate, and control its activities. It
has since been adopted by all of the federal agencies (13,
p. xv). The primary feature of PPBS is the central concept of accountability supported by eight operating or structural terms (12, p. 271). Accountability in the PPBS sense
does not refer to the responsibility for the control and expenditure of funds, but to the purposes and objectives of the
organization. For example, a school media center under
PPBS would be held accountable for supporting the general
educational program, as well as for facilitating the individual learning processes of its pupils. The eight operating
terms all function as factors in planning, implementing,
measuring, and evaluating the organization in terms of its
specific accountability. They are (1) objectives; (2) programs; (3) program alternatives; (4) output; (5) progress
measurement; (6) input; (7) alternative ways of doing a
given job; (8) systems analysis (12, p. 272).

It is not difficult to see that PPBS is geared for an organization with a clear purpose and with goods or services which readily lend themselves to unit measures. The Department of Agriculture may have as an objective the increased production of a certain vegetable. This vegetable may tend to be attacked by a certain beetle. A program could be established within the Department to eradicate this beetle. A program alternative could be to increase the acreage under cultivation of the vegetable. The output of the program could be a certain quota of beetles exterminated or, under the program alternative, a net increase in healthy units of the vegetable. Progress measurement could be in terms of healthy units of the vegetable or fewer beetles, as compared to some previous point in time. Input could refer to the men, equipment, time and/or acreage required for the program. Since there are many ways of exterminating beetles, there would be many choices in ways of implementing the program. Finally, systems analysis could reveal the cost/benefit relationships involved as well as the effectiveness of the whole program.

That PPBS is not so readily applied to organizations with vague or ambiguous goals or organizations whose goods or services are not easily measured, has not escaped the critics of the system. Mosher cites some intrinsic difficulties in applying PPBS to state and local organizations (12). He admonishes the advocates of PPBS for overselling their system by means of an oversimplified view of the world. He pointedly refers to objectives which cannot be specifically defined, services which defy present quantitative measures, and small programs for which complex budgetary procedures cannot be justified (12, p. 266). Criticisms such as this should act as a restraining force on those who may be eager to embrace PPBS as the budgetary panacea for school systems and social service agencies. On the other hand, PPBS introduces explicit qualitative factors into the budgetary process which point the way for substantial improvements in the budgetary procedures of the aforementioned agencies. Since there are some indications that state and local governments are increasingly adopting PPBS, it behooves librarians to identify the weak points and suggest modifications to the system before it is forced upon them. Perhaps by developing interim budgetary procedures which embrace some of the principles of PPBS, school media centers can improve their position in the budgetary process and, at the same time, prepare for more modern budget systems. A model for these procedures might be helpful in articulating these advantages.

Program Budgeting for Media Services

There are many aspects to be taken into consideration when shaping programs for school media centers--educational, demographic, organizational, and legal. A model for such plans should contain a combination of each of the following aspects:

1. The scope and depth of the responsibility for providing school media service within the local context must be established. What must be determined is the most effective combination of programs and services to support the general educational program as well as to provide for individual learning experiences at the appropriate level.

2. Trends in school population (size, age, family composition, and characteristics) and other change-producing influences should be reflected in the development of programs. This is especially helpful for inner city and rural poor school districts. These data are usually available from local or state sources.

3. Forecasts of the availability and level of fund sources need to be made in order to set the outside parameters of programs which can conceivably be offered.

4. Program forecasts are necessary to establish alternate program combinations depending on the availability of funds, personnel, equipment, etc. Long-range programs should be designed to be incremented in flexible increments which could be shifted as necessary.

5. Controls on programs and services should provide the means for evaluating the costs/benefits at regular intervals. These controls may be subjective and perhaps involve persons outside the media center itself.

6. Clientele should be developed at the building level and at the district level in order to give more weight to budget communications. Teachers and principals are obvious candidates. Cultivation of these two groups by providing them with special services can enable the media centers to use their influence to gain support for other programs. District administrators should not be overlooked in developing a clientele.

This model obviously assumes considerable responsibility for school media budgets at the supervisory level under a PPBS system.   For those media centers not operating under PPBS and for school librarians having little responsibility for the school media budget a simpler approach may be more appropriate.

First, a budget statement submitted with the normal budget calculations can be an effective device for communicating program information.   It should state briefly the objectives of the media center for the budget period under consideration and the programs to be offered to meet those objectives.   The programs in turn should be directly related to the specific budget request.   A New Jersey school district used a similar procedure in requesting a supplementary appropriation over a substantial time span which would bring all of the school media centers up to the level of the leading media center in the district.   Second, a clientele should be developed which will give substantial political support to the aspirations of the media center.   The provision of special services and frequent communication with potential supporters are possible means for accomplishing this objective. Third, a brief annual statement should be produced relating the proposed programs to actual programs and making an attempt to evaluate their effectiveness.   The emphasis here is on communication for the purpose of improving the political influence of the media center as it competes with other departments for funds.   Certainly, the evaluations will be quite subjective.   However, the intent is to use whatever criteria are meaningful in the process of budget justification and communication.

Research Implications

"Although these decisions [budget] demand good business sense, they are first and foremost a product of the ability to identify needs and the ability to plan to meet those needs at an optimum tempo" (4, p. 545).

This statement aptly captures the essence of what PPBS suggests for school media programs.   However, in doing so, it reminds us of all of the information we lack about these programs.   The pressures for increased numbers of research projects in the area of library budgeting are irresistible.   Some possibilities for topics are:

1.   What is the relationship between media center

objectives and the programs developed to meet them?
(normative survey)

    2.   How can the effectiveness of media programs
be measured both qualitatively and quantitatively?

    3.   What are the gaps in our knowledge about media
program operations? Research into these areas should go
hand in hand with Gaver's call for "...careful study by state
and school-district library supervisors of total school budgeting practices, of their own use of professional standards,
and of the effect of both factors on library expenditures in
the future" (14, p. 81).

    This paper focuses on changes in the budgetary pro-
cess to meet the current needs for media services in our
rapidly changing society. The concept of the media center
simultaneously supports a change in emphasis regarding how
children learn. Saettler calls it the dichotomy between theo-
retical-deductive and empirical-inductive modes of thought
(15, p. 356). The former refers to accepting theories and
deducing logical consequences from them. The latter refers
to accepting theories and deducing logical consequences from
them. The latter refers to observing phenomena and making
generalizations about what is observed. Librarians in
schools and colleges have long wished for the ascendancy of
thought patterns which encourage independent study. Now
that there are indications that we are moving in that direction the question arises as to whether we can develop programs to meet these needs. Certainly budgets cannot contribute much to this process. However, if effective budgeting can provide the means for accepting new challenges, it
is obviously a key component of administration.

Notes

1.   Alice L. Lefevre, "Administrative Control," Library
      Trends 1, no. 3: 286-97 (1953).

2.   Sylvia Ziskind, "School Library Budgets," Wilson Li-
      brary Bulletin 32:420-25 (February 1958).

3.   Eleanor E. Ahlers and Perry D. Morrison, "The Ma-
      terials Center at the School District Level," Library
      Trends 16, no. 4: 446-60 (1968).

4. Carlton W. H. Erickson, Administering Instructional Media Programs (New York: Macmillan, 1968).

5. ALA Washington Newsletter 22, no. 6 (1970).

6. James S. Coleman, and others, Equality of Educational Opportunity (Washington: 1966).

7. Barry Morris, "The Dollars and Sense of the Standards," School Library Journal p. 50-51 (April 1970).

8. Aaron Wildavsky, The Politics of the Budgetary Process (Boston: Little, Brown & Co., 1964).

9. Frederick C. Mosher, "The Study of Budgeting," in Paul Wasserman and Mary Lee Bundy, Reader in Library Administration (Washington: NCR Microcard Editions, 1968), p. 228-38.

10. E. C. Alexander, "Preparing the Library Budget," Library Journal 83:3551-53 (December 15, 1958).

11. Mary Evalyn Crookston, "Unit Costs in a Selected Group of High School Libraries," U. S. Office of Education, Bulletin, no. 11 (1941).

12. Frederick C. Mosher, "Limitations and Problems of PPBS in the States," Public Administration Review 29, no. 2 (1969).

13. David Novick, Program Budgeting; Program Analysis and the Federal Budget (Cambridge: Harvard University Press, 1967).

14. Mary V. Gaver, Patterns of Development in Elementary School Libraries Today: A Five Year Report on Emerging Media Centers (3d ed; Chicago: Encyclopaedia Britannica, 1969).

15. Paul Saettler, A History of Instructional Technology (New York: McGraw-Hill, 1968).

10. Budgeting to Meet the New Standards

by Barry Morris

Reprinted, by permission of the American Library Association and the author from School Activities and the Library, 1970.

How do you budget to meet the new joint Standards? You don't. Standards are guides to be used in planning, and a budget is simply a description of how resources are to be allocated in order to carry out the plan.

If we start out by budgeting to meet the new Standards, we will surely fail. On the other hand, if we do not use the new Standards to develop comprehensive, long-range plans for the school media program, we shall surely fail. Only when we have such plans is it possible to make good decisions about how resources must be allocated. Once this is done, presto, we have a budget. More importantly, we have a budget which is meaningful and convincing to administrators, school boards, and voting citizens who will decide the question of the amount.

Program Budgeting

Traditionally budgets have been made up in terms of what was known as functions and objects. Nearly all school systems in this country use a standard arrangement of six or eight functions including administration, instruction, coordinate activities, transportation, plant operation, maintenance, and fixed charges. Within each of these functions there are several objects of expenditure, such as salaries, supplies, books, travel, equipment, etc. These are often referred to as line items. The media services budget is included under the function of instruction and draws its support from the various object accounts in this part of the budget.

This system of budgeting is undergoing a dramatic

76

change. Most school systems in the United States are
either engaged in or planning for a more program-oriented
budget system. These plans are known by various terms,
the most popular being PPBS, Planning Programming Budgeting System. A number of states are developing plans to be
used by all local school districts; some school districts
have already instituted program budgeting systems; the Office of Education is sponsoring the development of model
programs and is revising its basic accounting handbook for
state and local school systems to facilitate program budgeting in the country. Administrators and budget officers are
now tuned to this new approach, and school boards regard it
as a means of evaluating school budgets in terms of potential output and productivity.

What is program budgeting and what does it mean to
the librarian and other media specialists at the individual
school level? A program budget system is a means by
which a school may impose upon itself a clear statement of
its objectives and a rigorous adherence to these objectives
in planning, budgeting, and evaluating its many programs.
It is further characterized by specific provisions for:

Long-range planning
Alternate solutions and innovation
Measurement of accomplishments or output.

Program budgeting requires that each program be
planned and budgeted by a program manager. In the case
of the media services program, the program manager is
the media specialist, the librarian. This does not mean
that planning budgeting is done in isolation. The media
specialist will, of course, work with many others in developing the media service program, but his is the prime
responsibility for the success of the program and his must
be the prime responsibility of design, planning, and resource allocation within the program. This means a great
deal more than simply requesting an increase in dollars per
pupil for library books, coupled with some requests for
more staff, more equipment, etc. It means the development of an integrated, long-range plan for the entire media
services program in the school.

In program budgeting a program is a group of activities designed to achieve certain goals and objectives. The
first thing to be done is to state these purposes, first in
terms of the ideal, ever to be sought after, and secondly,

in terms of specific objectives or accomplishments, to be
achieved within a definite time period and to be measured
at the end of that time period.

Let us look at the school as a whole. The function
of a school is to develop competence in such areas as communication, citizenship, and earning ability. These are
functional areas. They are given labels such as language
arts, social studies, and vocational education. The whole
educational enterprise is organized around these functional
areas or disciplines. They have become the basis for professional specialization, teacher certification, textbook writing, and curriculum organization.

Each of these areas constitutes a "program" and will
be the basis for program planning and budgeting.

The media services program is a little different. It
has a two-fold purpose: one, to provide support for each of
the instructional programs and two, to develop in each student the ability and the inclination to further his own education through independent inquiry. If your school has adopted
a program budgeting system, naturally that system should be
followed in preparing the program plan and budget submission.
If not, the following guide may be useful in preparation of a
stronger budget presentation incorporating the principles of
program budgeting.

The School Media Budget

The school media budget should begin with a statement of continuing goals or purposes indicating its two-fold
function of supporting service to the program of each instructional department and of developing independent inquiry by
students. This should be followed by a program description
clearly stating how the media service program is organized
and how it operates to achieve its purposes. This must be
abbreviated, no more than two or three pages, but it must
cover the subject so that any reader, be he layman or professional, will understand what the media program is and
how it works. It should follow the style of good journalistic
reporting, stating in simple direct language the who, what,
when, how and why of the program. It should be a description of what is, not of what should be.

The next step is to write a factual narrative evaluation of the program as it is, naming its strengths and weaknesses and including as much specific data as possible about how well it serves the teachers and students who called upon it for service. Do not make excuses or be defensive. Involve the teachers and students and perhaps even an outside consultant in the evaluation. It must really show up the weaknesses in the program for it will serve as the basis for your budget request.

The next step in your program budget preparation is the development of long-range plans for the total media service program. To do this, look carefully at your purposes and goals and at your evaluation. Then project some specific plans designed to achieve an ideal program at some point in the future, usually four or five years from now.

This is where the Standards come in. Your long-range plans should not be written in terms of media standards but should be written in terms of achieving certain objectives. These objectives differ from the continuing goals and purposes of the program in that they are more specific and measurable. They are stated in terms of level of performance to be achieved by a certain time; for example, to increase circulation to a level of x books per student, to reduce the average time between request and shelving of a new book from x days to y days, to extend open hours of the library from x to y, to meet 90 percent of first time-choice requests for audiovisual equipment, to provide free access by individual students to the full range of audiovisual materials recommended in the new social studies program.

The new joint Standards will be an invaluable guide in developing these long-range plans. The Standards represent the best thinking of a broadly representative group of specialists and generalists in the educational media field. They have been adopted or endorsed by much larger groups through their national organizations. They represent the best guide we have to the levels of support required to achieve fully the purposes of a full-service media program. However, the worst possible thing to do in making your long-range plans is simply to plan for a phasing in of everything expressed in the joint Standards.

Be selective. Include only those things which are necessary to accomplish the particular objectives you and your colleagues have established for your school. In some aspects of your program less may be required than is in-

dicated in the joint Standards. In other areas a greater
level of support may be called for.

The Next Year

Now you are ready to make your budget for next
year. It represents the first step in a multiyear program
to achieve the objectives established in your long-range
plans. For the first year, instead of reducing the average
time required for processing new material to thirty days,
you may settle for getting it down to an average of sixty
days. What is your plan of action for doing this? How
much clerical help will be required? What other provisions
need to be made?

Based on your evaluation and your long-range plans,
identify specific objectives to be achieved in the first year;
develop a detailed plan of action (but express it in summary
form in your budget presentation); and then list the specific
resource allocations necessary to carry out that plan of action. Be sure to make clear to any reader the relationship
of each of these resources to the plan of action itself.
Show why each is necessary and how it will contribute.
For example, if your plan to get materials on the shelves
sooner requires cutting down the processing time from an
average of two weeks in the workroom to an average of two
days in the workroom, show how much clerical time and
how much increase in supervision, if any, would be required.

Decide which aspects of your program need action
first and proceed accordingly. Two suggestions occur immediately. In most schools audiovisual equipment is inopera-
ble a good portion of the time and teachers may expect a
piece of equipment to have one or more common defects
when checked out for use: The lenses are not clean or the
take-up reel is missing or the slide carrier has been misplaced or something else is not up to specifications. Also
in most schools the librarian, for lack of clerical help or
some other reason, spends far much more time in processing, circulating, counting, reporting, or otherwise handling
materials than he does in seeing that Johnny and Mary are
able to get at the material they want and are able to use it
under satisfactory conditions.

Both of these problems lend themselves easily to the
program budgeting process and both will receive a sympa-

thetic hearing when presented in program budget fashion to administrators and to businessmen school board members. A good proposal on these problems will help to allay the often heard criticism, whether true or false, that we continue to ask for more equipment when our schools are full of projectors gathering dust and that we ask for more and more books when our library shelves contain volume after volume which has not been checked out in more than two years.

Your problems may be entirely different, but whatever they are, your chances of overcoming them will be much enhanced by the program budget process. Develop long-range plans to achieve clearly identified goals and base your plans on a hard evaluation of present strengths and weaknesses. Then program your resources and activities for the next year to reach specific interim objectives toward those long-range plans.

One final step is necessary. Decide which of your objectives for the next year is most pressing and assign priorities to all your proposals for improvement, giving alternatives wherever possible.

11. The Challenge of PPBS

by Garford G. Gordon

Reprinted by permission of the California Teachers Association and the author, from CTA Journal, January 1970.

Planning, Programming, Budgeting Systems (PPBS) represent an attempt to bring into governmental and other service operations some of the methods and procedures used in industry to determine the relative cost and effectiveness of various parts of their operation. The difference between this approach and cost-effectiveness and efficiency studies in business stems mainly from the fact that the product of governmental agencies is not generally measurable in terms of number of items produced or sales made. Also, government generally has to take what already exists as raw material for its operations, while industry may shop around for the type and quality that best fits its operations.

The foregoing is particularly applicable to public schools. They take the children as they come, the parents as they are, and operate in the community as it is. They produce something which is not measurable in all cases and which may manifest itself, even when measurable, only long after the individuals being educated have left the school program. Nevertheless, it is argued that schools, and each part of them, do have immediate objectives which can often be measured or at least judged by competent observers. Whether achieving these immediate objectives will lead to long-range success may be open to further study; but operating a program without a plan for achieving intermediate objectives can obviously not be justified. Hence, objections to the implementation of PPBS in schools amount to arguments against accountability for their operations.

The movement is here to stay, though not necessarily in its present embryonic form. It is necessary that all educators learn what it is all about to the end that its development will be along lines that help education rather than down paths that will hamper or actively harm it.

Planning, Programming, Budgeting Systems are just what the name says, systems. They are tools for better determining the resources needed to carry out plans and for improving the design of the programs used to reach the objectives chosen. PPBS does not choose the objectives nor does it decide upon the criteria for determining whether or not objectives have been achieved. Furthermore, while it is intended to provide information as to the resources going into a program, it does not say whether they are too much or too little or just right. If the objectives of the program are greatly exceeded, it <u>might</u> indicate that fewer resources should go to it; if they are grossly underachieved, it might mean that more resources should be allocated to the program. Or it might mean that the program should be changed; or that more realistic objectives should be chosen.

It is true that some have advocated PPBS with the thought that it will save tax dollars. An unsophisticated PPB System, used without adequate determination of what the various programs of a school or school system are, and especially if used without adequate determination of objectives and the criteria for deciding whether they have been met or not, will almost certainly lead to "meat-ax" changes in the curriculum and in school organization. Furthermore, failure to treat the "Budgeting" part of the system as something more than a pure dollar allocation to a program, particularly if coupled with inadequate evaluative techniques for determining whether objectives have been attained, will create tremendous personnel problems. Teachers could find their pay affected by the test scores of their students, or find themselves moved out of programs because they are "too expensive" for the results achieved. Obviously the better trained and more experienced teachers would be most seriously harmed. Nonteaching personnel such as counselors and principals would probably be even more adversely affected.

But PPBS need not save money. A sophisticated system with adequate objectives stated for each part of the educational enterprise, with clear definitions of the programs involved, and with relevant success criteria, can perhaps do what educators have long hoped for. It can show how thin school resources are spread. It can make crystal clear that placing additional responsibilities on schools must be accompanied by provision for additional resources --that is, by additional dollars.

Also, by stating objectives for each program level, it will be possible to make the operation of the school more flexible. There is no reason why objectives cannot be stated for each type of pupil, for each neighborhood, and for each community. With a little help from computers, budgets can be set up with due consideration for the differing needs of ethnic groups, socio-economic levels, types of handicaps, age groups, and many other individual differences.

To sum up, PPBS is a tool which probably could not be operated except at a trivial level without the use of computers. But, with the growth of computer usage and availability, it now has the potential to be a powerful force to help or to hurt education. It is like a stick of dynamite, which can be used to blast a rock out of the way of traffic or to blow up a bridge needed for that traffic. The important mission of California educators is to see that PPBS does the former and not the latter for the educational traffic of the State.

12. Interpreting the Standards:
     People Problems

     by John Rowell

          Reprinted, by permission of the American Library
          Association and the author, from School Activities
          and the Library, 1970.

     The widely promoted Standards for School Media Pro-
grams, issued by the American Association of School Librarians and the Department of Audiovisual Instruction of
the National Education Association, has new things to say
to the educational community. The instructional materials
programs, services, administration, and organization have
changed as the materials, developing technology, patterns
and emphasis of instruction, and instructional techniques
have changed. These changes are reflected in the Standards.

     However, the degree and quality of change are indi-
vidual to each school, and what is new in the Standards
should be interpreted personally by each school administrator. It is as inaccurate to assume that sweeping and instant
progress can be (or even should be) effected within a school
or school district to conform with every aspect of the new
Standards, as it is to react to them with hopelessness because they may seem too far beyond the realities of accomplishment. Consideration of the parts of the Standards
in terms of the variables peculiar to each school is essential if the total validity of a modern media program is to be
effected. The Standards provide for this interpretation.

     It was not intended by the two associations which
authored this document, nor by the twenty-eight professional
and allied organizations which support it, that it be interpreted as a universal and unqualified blanket blueprint for
action and application. Among the variables which preclude
any such intention are the differences between school districts
(and even between schools within a district) in the approaches
to the instructional program. For example, a school which
emphasizes individualized instruction requires educational

media programs of a different sort from those of the school
operating along more traditional instructional patterns.   But
the basic premise does not change--the media program exists
to serve the student and the teacher; it is use- and user-
oriented.   Within the flexible framework of guidelines to excellence,   the Standards should be interpreted in terms
of intent of use and the special requirements of the individual user.   The intent and the requirements are the
variables.   Therefore, whether in their qualitative or
in their quantitative aspects, the Standards should not
be interpreted as uncompromisingly prescriptive.

There are specific areas of use of the media center's
facilities and services which can be identified as potential
problems of interpretation, regardless of the administrative
pattern or the level or direction of the center's development
within the school.   Chief among these is the assignment and
utilization of the media center's staff.

To carry out effectively the unified program of the
traditional library and audiovisual services which the Standards advocate, the media center personnel must represent
a diverse range of professional, clerical, and technical competencies.   At this point (if ever) it is unlikely that a school
administrator is going to locate very many individuals who
have equal training and experience in the complex of all the
task analyses detailed in the Standards as essential to a topflight media program.   While school library science education today does include preparation in the nonprint communications fields, it is necessarily limited.   The same is true
regarding the education of audiovisual specialists in their
orientation to librarianship.   Although both the librarian and
the audiovisual specialist (or, if you will, the media specialist) have--or should have--educational and experiential background in instructional methodology and curriculum development, neither one may have these competencies in the depth
expected of the full-time practitioner.   Yet in terms of
operating a maximum-service media center which fully supports the instructional program and the educational demands
of the users, all these competencies, and more, are required.

Certainly, individuals will be found who have combinations of these skills: the librarian who may also be a
curriculum specialist or a subject area specialist; the audio-
visual specialist who may be a master teacher or an administrator.   Nor is the problem simply one of the general-

ist versus the specialist. The problems of interpretation
for the administrator staffing his media center are in assessing his expectations in terms of the goals of the total instructional program, and then to staff that center with people who have the complementary competencies to make it
work. There can be no "rule." Personnel form follows
educational function. So while the Standards offer explicit
guidelines to both form and function, the interpretation of
each is highly individualized.

It might be noted here that there are at least five
practical ways in which the administrator can extend the
professional effectiveness of his media center staff:

1. Provide adequate and appropriate clerical and
   technical back-up personnel to relieve the professionals from nonprofessional tasks

2. Refrain from assigning responsibilities and ex-
   pecting performance in areas for which a staff
   member has no training or experience merely
   because the Standards suggest he should have

3. Encourage continuing formal education, through
   financial assistance or released time, for the
   media staff so that they can update and/or acquire new skills

4. Offer in-service clinics for the staff wherein
   those with particular strengths may teach those
   with corresponding deficiencies

5. Create a climate and opportunity for staff experimentation and innovation.

Another staff problem needing administrative interpretation shifts from the administrator-Standards-media center to the administrator-media center-classroom teacher.
It is axiomatic that the worth of the media center, whatever
its standards, can be evaluated on the use made of it.
Teacher involvement in the media program determines this
worth, either directly through use, misuse, or no use, or
indirectly through positive, negative, or indifferent attitudes
passed on to the students. A great many instances of negative or indifferent teacher use and attitude can be attributed
to fear and/or lack of understanding (perhaps they are the
same) of what the media program is, what it can do to sup-

port (not supplant) classroom instruction, how its resources
can be directed to student use, and, principally, what those
services and resources are. The media center staff, however energetic and persistent, do reach a point of no return
(sometimes literally) in the promotion and interpretation of
their programs. It is clearly an administrative responsibility
in policy and by demonstration to support the program, to expect teacher participation, and to provide whatever interpretation and leadership is necessary to ensure comfortable and
easy communication between the classroom and the media
center.

Familiar barriers to this interplay and two-way communication are within the administrator's purview:

Rigid and restrictive scheduling of media center access
Inefficient media center use, e. g. , assignment of the
center as a general study hall
Inappropriate expectations of the media center professional staff, e. g. , alloting them time-consuming
para-professional technical and clerical responsibilities which do not allow adequate time to perform professional services for teachers and students
Unsuitable selection of media center materials and
equipment because of unexpressed teacher needs
Lack of time for professional consultation between
media center and teaching staffs, or, if the time
is provided, no interpretation to the teaching staff
of why and how the time can be used
No provision for center use extended before or after
the regular school day
No in-service workshops for teachers for their instruction in the value and techniques of examination,
evaluation, and selection of print and nonprint instructional materials
No locally based-demonstration clinics for the in-
service teacher-training instruction in the use of
print and nonprint instructional materials in the
educational process.

The removal of these barriers would substantially
thrust the media program into the orbit of the Standards,
however those standards are interpreted in an individual
situation. But because these barriers are sometimes
physical, sometimes psychological (both are real), and

always human, the highest order of administrative leadership and commitment is called into play. Budgetary needs,
facilities, equipment, and materials collections needs can
be statistically determined, evaluated, and plotted for improvement. While they do require a degree of professional
competence to ascertain, interpret, and implement, they
really are of secondary priority to the human factor. Paper,
print, and plastic may be programmed, and they are manipulative. But programs are people, and they must be interpreted.

The administrator is the electric link between the effectiveness or failure of the instructional media program.
It is his interpretation of the program to himself, his staff,
his board, and his community that will both initially and ultimately light up the land--or blow the fuse.

To be informed, to keep informed, to question, to
accept or reject on a rational and judicious basis are all
to the good. The fact of life that the Standards have been
formulated on the evidence of existing and generally ad-
mired programs should be the administrator's talisman, if
not his sandbur. There is no mystery, no harangue involved or implied. There is hard-core fact; proffered,
honest, defensible direction; and the unsupplied but implicit
requisite for administrative interpretation...

And decision...

And action.

13.   Who Should Do What in the Media Center

by Robert N. Case

The librarian faced the principal.   It was personnel
evaluation and review time.   The subject was job performance.   Never has a conference had such an honest beginning.

"I don't know what you do down there," the principal
began, "But it must be right.   Whenever I walk by, the library is full of students and teachers!"

The conference continued with a review of the progress
made in developing the school library media center into a
model program for the area: outstanding facilities, a substantially growing budget, an effective staff of three professionals each having clerical and technical support.   The program, which took years to develop, was making a strong impact upon the total school.   Did all of this happen because
of the librarian or in spite of him?   It's difficult to say.
The evaluation and review session concluded with the principal having these last words: "I know what I want.   I want
the best damned school library in the State!"   Quite an order
from a principal who thirty minutes earlier admitted, "I don't
know what you do down there!"

Judging from the articles appearing during the past
two years in the educational press, the above illustration is
not an isolated situation.   Further, if trends in education
continue, statements such as "I don't know" will no longer
be acceptable to the students, taxpayers, and the total community.   For too many years, education has not had to answer for its failures.   If a student didn't achieve, it was not
the fault of the system.   How could we fail?   We have the
best facilities, the finest instructional resources, and a superior staff all working toward the highest goals.   But to a
parent whose child can't read, advance, or even adjust, the

system has failed and is now under criticism.   A librarian
whose principal doesn't know what he does down there is as
much responsible as the principal for his failure in making
the system work to better effect student achievement and
outcomes.

In the next ten years, education is going to be on the
firing line to be held accountable for what it achieves.
School library media personnel, too, will have to stand up
and be counted with those who can relate their ability to
meet the job performance requirements directly to the successful development of the final product--the student.

Between four and five o'clock every school day afternoon across the country, thousands of school librarians col-
lapse of exhaustion from a full day of activity in doing what
they "do down there. " In truth, for many there was a lot
of wheel spinning and no traction.   Busy?   Never a moment's rest.   Accountable?   How can we say?

The 1969 Standards for School Media Programs has
given education a new definition for effective media service.
The broad scope of the Standards has brought about demanding job requirements for all levels of school library media
personnel.   Success in implementing these standards is one
thing, but our ability to measure up to performance is still
another.   Effective school library media service in the future may well have to be measured in terms of how well a
student learns.   The community which over the years has
invested heavily in the educational system now believes--
and rightly so--that it has every reason to expect educated
children as a result.   School library media personnel will
have to be deeply involved in meeting the new commitment
that every child shall learn.   In facing this challenge, ac-
tivating change, and accepting the responsibility to improve
the present status quo, school library media personnel will
be held accountable.

Our job requirements have changed and we have
changed with them.   Hopefully, there breathes no librarian
today whose job performance is comparable to the roles expected of him ten years ago.   In fact, if the job descrip-
tions under which a school library media specialist is performing have not been reviewed and revised within the past
three years, there is strong evidence of a weak link in the
process for establishing professional accountability.   The advances in education, technology, new teaching methodology,

and the impact of social concerns within the past year alone
have had a decided effect upon the total scope and responsibility which a school library media specialist has in the
educational process.

For two years, the School Library Manpower Project,
a five-year study of task analysis, education, and utilization
of school librarians, funded by the Knapp Foundation of
North Carolina, Inc., and administered by the American
Association of School Librarians, has focused its attention
on the development of new definitions for school library
media personnel. The Phase I activity has now concluded
with the publication of Occupational Definitions for School
Library Media Personnel. (School Library Manpower Project, 1971, 24p., pa., $2 from: ALA, 50 E. Huron St.,
Chicago, Ill. 60611). The Project was planned and implemented several years before accountability became "this
year's term" in education, but the results of Phase I are
becoming increasingly relevant to the questions asked of education today. In part, accountability begins with a clear
definition of responsibility, and to this effect the Occupational Definitions for School Library Media Personnel may well
serve as a first step for school systems to identify locally
the responsibility of school library personnel.

Initially, the process of developing new definitions for
school library media personnel within the framework of the
School Library Manpower Project was the completion of a
task analysis survey which identified the tasks performed in
694 outstanding school library media programs in the country. The results and findings of this study, made under the
direction of the Research Division of the National Education
Association, were reported in the publication School Library
Personnel: Task Analysis Survey, published by the American Library Association in 1969. Approximately 300 tasks
within twelve major categories were grouped according to
the school library position responsible for each task.

After the study was published, a special Task Analysis Committee was appointed by the Advisory Committee to
the Project to conduct an in-depth analysis of the findings
in the School Library Personnel: Task Analysis Survey.
The special study committee was composed of ten members
who represented a wide variety of position levels and disciplines in the fields of school librarianship, library education, library and educational administration, technology, and
public personnel. After an objective study of the survey

final report (which revealed the tasks presently performed
by school library personnel) the Task Analysis Committee
proceeded to determine the tasks which should be performed
and by whom in a school library media center with a full
complex of staff positions. As a result of this analytic process, many of the tasks and responsibilities were deleted,
added, and reassigned either upward or downward to the appropriate school library media staff position. This procedure brought a more meaningful approach to the development of the occupational definitions.

The work of the Task Analysis Committee, after reactions from the field, resulted in the development of occupational definitions for the school library media specialist,
the head of the school library media center, the district
school library media director, and the school library media
technician. The first three occupational definitions will be
used as examples from which the Phase II experimental programs of the Project will develop new curriculum approaches
and innovations for the education of professional school library media personnel.

As stated earlier, the changes taking place in education, and the continuing impact of technology support the
need for educators to pay increased attention and study to
position organization and design. The occupational definitions for school library media personnel are basic tools for
educational management to use to attain effective objectives
of the program.

Stated simplistically, an occupational definition is a
statement of the duties relating to a particular job and the
responsibilities for which a particular staff member in that
position is held accountable. The occupational definition is,
however, more than a listing of tasks, for it clearly describes the functions to be performed and reflects the skills
necessary to perform the activities within the function. What
tasks should be performed? Who should perform them?
Who retains responsibility for these tasks? What are the
necessary knowledges and abilities required to perform these
tasks?--These are four basic questions which need to be answered by a well developed occupational definition. It is important that the occupation definition fix the responsibility for
action as low in the organizational pattern as possible.

School library media personnel advancing to new positions must appreciate that an occupational definition is writ-

ten around the job and not the person doing the work. Additional education and training may be necessary to meet new job requirements. Such educational requirements may also need to be met as the present position definition is updated through the process of position evaluation and review. Once a management team has digested and organized the input data provided to assist them in preparing a detailed definition, the incumbent should have an opportunity to review the statement in terms of the total objectives of the school and library media center program. As new skills and responsibilities will probably be incorporated within a final occupational definition, the incumbent will need to face his professional responsibility to broaden his knowledge to best meet the requirements of the new definition statement.

The occupational definitions developed by the School Library Manpower Project identify the variety of persons needed to cover the span of responsibility, activities, and specific duties within a school library media program. As the four occupational definitions were developed as models, they represent typical specifications within each position category. It is not assumed that any one position included all responsibilities or activities listed within the definition. The four definitions and specifications will aid school administrators at the building and district level to differentiate among the duties and responsibilities of the various kinds of staff positions at the several school locations and levels. Such assessment will aid administrators to plan for the development of more complete and effective staffing patterns as the school library media programs expand to meet the educational goals of the school.

The occupational definition for the school library media specialist, as developed by the School Library Manpower Project, is identified as the first professional level position, since it relates to those basic duties, responsibilities, knowledges, and abilities fundamental to all other professional positions within a fully staffed school library media center. It is quite possible that a program may require two school library media specialists whose joint talents will meet the prescribed definition. This position definition also recognizes areas of specialization which may need to be incorporated in a particular occupational statement.

The only administrative position within the school library media center at the building level is represented by the occupational definition for the head of the school library

media center. As such, the position clearly identifies the
responsibility and primary leadership role the incumbent
must play in planning, developing, and implementing a successful school library media program. It is quite possible
that the head of the school library media center may be the
sole professional on the school library media center staff.
In this case, the position's administrative responsibilities
are in addition to those assigned to the school library media
specialist. When this situation occurs, as it certainly will
in many school library media programs nationally, it must
be recognized by education management that the head of the
school library media center will have limited opportunities
to perform as effectively as when the position is supported
by other professional and clerical personnel.

     The responsibilities for planning, coordinating, and
directing the district-wide school library media program are
incorporated within the occupational definition for the district
school library media director. The occupational definition
for this position requires a wider range of knowledges and
abilities to enable the district school library media director
to effectively meet the responsibilities of this key administrative role. In addition to administering a district school
media center, the director is also responsible for coordinating the school library media programs at a variety of levels.
A broad understanding of other disciplines, and an ability to
relate and communicate the total media field to others within
and without the educational system are essential elements in
this position's definition. The leadership and administrative
qualities of the district school library media director are reflected in the policy- and decision-making responsibilities
identified in the definition.

     The occupational definition developed by the Project
for the school library media technician represents the position as responsible for performing the technical function
unique to the successful operation of the school library
media center. The size of the school and the organization
of the school library media program and its staff at the
district level will often affect the numbers and kinds of
school library media technicians required at the building
level. Depending upon the size and scope of the program,
the school library media technician position may range from
trainee to supervisor of all technical operations under the
general supervision of a designated administrative authority.

     All the occupational definitions for positions identified

above are developed in greater detail in the Occupational
Definitions for School Library Media Personnel. Each complete definition model includes a series of statements which
directly relate to the nature and scope of the position and
details the major duties of that position. Each position
statement identifies a variety of areas of specialization
leading from that position and incorporates the knowledges
and abilities which directly relate to the successful performance of the position.

For school library media specialists who have not
yet had to face performance objectives and matters relating
to accountability--be assured that you are not being singled
out, punished, or blamed for failure. Just as business and
industry have for years exercised quality control of their
products, so now is education assessing the tools and processes to use for the qualitative improvement of education.
Establishing the criteria and compiling the data for more
meaningful definitions of the role of school library media
personnel are only a part of the total process which may include observation, interview, questionnaire, record logs,
task analysis, consensus and/or content analysis. We hear
a great deal about networks, system analysis, needs assessment, educational auditing, and behavioral objectives, to
name but a few. These, too, are some of the tools which
will be utilized in the future by education to reach its objective to produce students capable of meeting their individual and societal needs.

In the very near future, the principal we met earlier
will also have to face up to his accountability. It will no
longer be acceptable for him to say, "I don't know what you
do down there." But in the interim one can't help but wonder, "Do you?"

14. Occupational Definitions:
    School Library Media Specialist

    by Robert N. Case and Anna Mary Lowrey

    Reprinted by permission of the American Library
    Association from School Library Manpower Project,
    Phase I--Final Report, 1970, pp. 18-21. Robert
    N. Case, director.

Position Title: School Library Media Specialist

Reports to: Head of the School Library Media Center

Supervises: Clerk
(may include)   Technician
                  Student Assistant
                  School Library Media Aide

Nature and Scope of Position:

The school library media specialist represents the
first level of professional responsibility on the school library
media center staff.   This role includes expertise in the
broad range of both print and nonprint materials and related equipment.   It incorporates the evaluation, selection,
classification, scheduling and utilization of print and nonprint materials; the evaluation, selection, scheduling and
utilization of related equipment to provide the basis for
long-range program change and development.

The incumbent participates as a specialist in instructional media applying the knowledge of media categories to
the development and implementation of curriculum.   In addition the school library media specialist fills an active teaching role in the instructional program of the school through
instruction in the effective use of media and equipment.

Major Duties:

The school library media specialist applies expertise

in selection of all materials, both print and nonprint. This
includes the evaluation, selection, and acquisition of materials in terms of the criteria established to meet the needs
of the instructional program and the variation of pupil, faculty and community characteristics and interests. The incumbent relates the utilization of materials and equipment
to learning situations to serve effectively various instructional and organizational patterns encompassing subject area
and grade level instructional needs. The incumbent provides
supplementary resources through local production of materials and use of community resources.

The school library media specialist participates in
the development and implementation of policies and procedures for the organization of the physical facilities, materials and equipment to assure optimum accessibility. This
includes the organization of circulation procedures and
schedules. The incumbent may be responsible for the organization of materials when this service is not performed
at the district level.

The school library media specialist serves as a full
participating member of curriculum committees and study
groups at grade, subject or department levels. As such,
he applies knowledge of both educational principles and
media technology to enrich the instructional program. One
of the primary responsibilities of the school library media
specialist is to know and support the educational goals of
the school and community. The incumbent is aware of
teacher goals and classroom activities necessary to expedite services in the school library media center. Since
this liaison function provides the incumbent with information
for long-range planning and program proposals to meet the
needs of the school, the school library media specialist
analyzes and evaluates the present program and makes
recommendations to substantiate projected programs.

The school library media specialist provides reading,
listening and viewing guidance for students and teachers and
instills an appreciation for the knowledge acquired through
the utilization of a variety of media. He instructs and encourages students and teachers, both individually and in
groups, to use materials, equipment, and production techniques effectively, and contributes to the in-service education programs for teachers. The incumbent answers in-
quiries and assists students and teachers to locate resources
valuable to their educational needs and to the growth of their

personal interests and abilities.

The school library media specialist supervises supporting staff as assigned. The incumbent designates duties and
trains subordinate staff members, following the established
criteria for instructional, technical and clerical positions.
This supervision includes the diagnosis of the strengths and
weaknesses of the staff and the assignment of tasks according to the strengths, while providing opportunities to improve
the weaknesses.

Again, following the knowledge of instructional goals
requirements, the incumbent participates in the development
of procedures and the recommendation of policies. These
procedures and policies must provide an acceptable program
for evaluation, correction and improvement which permits
the flexibility necessary to meet the objectives and instructional methods of the schools.

The school library media specialist informs the faculty and administration of materials, equipment, innovations,
research and current developments in the field of instructional technology. The incumbent participates in implementing
an appropriate public relations program designed to communicate the philosophy and goals of the school library media center to the students, faculty, administration and community.

The school library media specialist has the expertise
as stated above. Through the attainment of additional knowledge and/or experience, he may elect to pursue a particular
field of specialization, such as:

Subject Area and/or Grade Level: an expertise in a
particular subject discipline or grade level and a
depth of knowledge in materials appropriate to the
educational objectives of the subject discipline and/or
grade level.

Organization of Materials: an additional expertise in
the organization of media including the classification
of print and nonprint materials.

Media Production and Design: additional expertise in
such areas as message design, production, photography,
graphic arts.

Media Technology: additional expertise in such areas

as reading and language laboratories, programmed instruction, dial access, computer technology, random access, electronics, radio and educational television, and communication systems.

Knowledges:

The school library media specialist must have knowledge of:

1. content of a broad range of print and nonprint materials.

2. evaluation selection criteria for print and nonprint materials.

3. organization of school library media collections.

4. print and nonprint materials related to literature for children and adolescents.

5. reference materials.

6. reading, listening, and viewing skills to assure proper guidance for the utilization of print and nonprint materials.

7. evaluation, selection and utilization of equipment.

8. administration of school library media programs.

9. theory and function of school library media programs.

10. instructional methods and techniques.

11. curriculum development.

12. learning theory.

13. student growth and development.

14. human behavior.

15. communication techniques.

16. production techniques.

Abilities:

The school library media specialist must have the ability to:

1. interpret content of print and nonprint materials.

2. determine and apply suitable criteria for the evaluation and selection of materials and equipment.

3. involve faculty and students in the evaluation of materials.

4. organize materials and equipment.

5. communicate knowledge of materials and equipment and their appropriate use.

6. apply administrative principles within a structural framework.

7. implement established policy.

8. apply the results of institutional experience to the future development of educational goals.

9. contribute effectively to curriculum development.

10. analyze, evaluate, and apply basic research data.

11. establish rapport with students and faculty.

12. plan cooperatively programs involving many variables.

13. work cooperatively and effectively with the head of the school library media center, other school library media center staff and teachers.

14. teach students how to use materials and equipment critically and independently.

15. assume a leadership role.

15. The Librarian: Consultant in Curriculum

by Anna M. Beachner

Reprinted by permission of the American Library Association and the author, from School Activities and the Library, 1964.

The new curriculum guide is ready for distribution, and the staff looks at it with satisfaction. It is attractive and readable. The removable plastic binder is strong evidence that it can be evaluated and revised. The foreword speaks a clear philosophy from which it was evolved, as well as notes that the priority for the study was given by a Central Curriculum Coordinating Council. The listing of committee members shows a good cross section of all grade levels and schools so that articulation and communication have been assured. As we measure this guide against the criteria for developing a curriculum publication, our satisfaction changes to pride.

But what assurance is there that the changes in content and method outlined here will reach the classroom? How can we be sure that children will have some new and better learning experiences because this guide was written? How can we guarantee an honest chance for these ideas, yet an equally honest appraisal of them so that the curriculum can remain dynamic?

No one can describe with complete reliability the "how's" required for such assurances or guarantees. It is possible, however, to lower the margin of risk if we make responsible use of key staff members--the school librarians. Let us trace the development of this particular curriculum guide to see where a librarian has helped us cut the risks.

Long before this matter of curriculum change went to the Curriculum Coordinating Council, the librarian was in the picture, building a climate of change. Because he worked with teachers in selecting materials for a good professional library, and because he read these books and magazines himself, he was able to recommend reading for teachers. It was the librarian who called to the attention of the staff that a School Mathematics Study Group had extended its work to elementary arithmetic, and that the National Council for Geographic Education had released a recommended scope and sequence of geographic concepts for all grades. What is more, he consults with the principal and staff to determine which of these research reports to purchase.

Also, early in the fall, when teachers are fresh from summer study, the librarian frees himself at intervals from back-to-school routines in order to hear their suggestions for changes or additions to the book collections or audio-visual aids. While the librarian is planning, during the year, with teachers of a certain grade level which book and nonbook materials are appropriate to a unit, he notes their concern about outdated content and materials. So a grass-roots realization of the need for curriculum change is planted and grows. When the Curriculum Coordinating Council asks for priorities to be set, these teachers have some clear ideas of what needs to be done. Because their librarian has furnished background reading for them, they come to the Council with a clearly conceived and expressed request which wins its place in the action of the district for the year.

It goes without saying that the Curriculum Council has a librarian as a member. As a result, all librarians will receive regular reports of the discussion and action of the Council. Not only will this help them to see more clearly their responsibility in providing timely professional reading, but also when librarians are appointed to curriculum com-mittees, they have a head start as informed participants.

On the Council, the librarian voices the point of view of the generalist. This can be a stabilizer in a group made up of teachers who bring to a discussion the concerns of their particular grade level or subject matter area.

Not all priorities for curriculum change require a guide, but some form of communication needs to be de-veloped if the change becomes vital. Let us assume for the sake of this argument, that this priority requires a curriculum guide.

What part does a librarian plan in the development of such a publication? As was mentioned before, he brings to the committee personal reading on the subject and the knowl-

edge of the problem gained by close working relationships
with teachers.   Even more valuable, however, will be his
expert advice on sources of information for other committee
members.   If a district does not have a central professional
library, more than one librarian on each curriculum committee is a must, since one of the values of committee action is the opportunity for the members to grow in background information.

All complete curriculum guides will contain bibliographies of book and nonbook materials for both teachers and
children.   Here the professionally trained librarian can show
the committee appropriate book lists and recommended sources
for nonprint materials.

The new guide has been developed.   We have helped
it on its way with a well-planned meeting for all the teachers who will be using it in their instruction of children.
But what is the key to the correct interpretation of this newly developed set of concepts?   Again we say, "the librarian."
For now he emerges in an increasingly important role--the
interpreter of curriculum.

It goes without saying that if there are central staff
specialists or generalists in the school district, the librarians work closely with them.   Contacts on the Curriculum
Coordinating Council and on subject area subcommittees, of
course, bring about some of this, but a deliberate plan for
effective working relationships is necessary.   When the librarians meet regularly as a group, central staff members
meet with them on problems of common interest, e. g., the
gearing up of the library collections to support curriculum
change.

The new guide which outlines the strands of mathematical ideas for the district reads, "The pupils should be
led through a sequence of steps or questions which result in
discovery rather than follow a prescribed series of directions. "   This is a cue for the librarian to work with teachers in reevaluating the references, filmstrips, and other library materials used in the teaching of mathematics.   A
filmstrip which emphasizes drill rather than discovery may
be removed from circulation, or the staff may decide on a
new use for this material as a supplementary aid rather than
as a prime teaching tool.

If the new mathematics courses emphasize the theory

of sets, the associative and other laws of mathematics, the mathematical sentence, informal logic, and the like, the library will need to find and stock related materials for both teachers and students.

The social studies for the fourth grade has been re-designed with an emphasis on comparative world economics and geography. The guide reads under objectives: (1) "an understanding of basic likenesses among peoples; (2) their needs for food, clothing, shelter, and recreation; (3) an appreciation for the value of differences." But what happens to these objectives if the library continues to circulate an old filmstrip showing children in an Asian home with a caption, "The floor is nothing but the ground itself"?

If the library shelves are not responsibly culled of out-of-date or slanted books describing Africa, how can we avoid situations where children will read about a meal with the Bedouins and compare their habits unfavorably with ours? Librarians will not retain in circulation an old science book which describes the atom as the "smallest irreducible particle of matter." Neither will they continue to expose children to books which describe all racial, economic, philosophical, and other differences among people with an emphasis on our superiority.

Again, let us consider what might be the situation if the study of literature is the subject for the curriculum change. The committee designs a program in which children are exposed to literary content through creative dramatics, through listening to recordings, through choral speech, and through other varied aural-oral experiences as well as through reading. How is such an ambitious program encouraged? Of course, the administration shares some responsibility to teachers for in-service, but think what the librarian does for such a literature program.

The recommended recordings are purchased and some listening sessions planned for teachers. Articles and books on choral speech and creative dramatics are purchased and put on display to tempt the staff. Because the librarian has had training in storytelling and creative dramatics, he offers to demonstrate these techniques for new or inexperienced teachers.

If the literature program recommends the reading of myths or of biographies at a certain grade level, the librarian checks the book collection in the school library to see if the supply of such types of reading is adequate. As a new program is tried during the year, he checks with teachers and plans his next purchases to support the newly revised curriculum.

On what premises does this argument for the librarian as a curriculum consultant depend? It has assumed that the librarian has a broad education to give him a working knowledge of various subjects. Equally it has assumed a thorough up-to-date training in librarianship, as well as in the multimedia field. Added strength would be experience as a classroom teacher so that he can identify with other teachers when they describe instructional problems.

Besides this varied education and experience for the librarian, a second factor emerges--that of clerical assistance to release him for the more important duties as consultant for the teachers. Even if the district has central cataloging, there are myriad tasks such as assembling bibliographical data, slipping books, and so on which are clerical work. If the library operates as an instructional materials center, much of the compiling and charging of the nonbook materials can be done by a competent clerk.

Let us go further and consider making this clerk an "instructional secretary." In this capacity she not only would be of help to librarians (and indirectly to teachers), but also might learn to make visuals for overhead projectors, operate a dry mounting press, and in such ways expand the collection of instructional materials available for children and teachers.

Weigh the costs--a few thousand dollars for a team of topflight librarians and instructional secretaries will ensure basic staff in-service education and reliable curriculum change.

16. Personalized Learning and Accountability

Reprinted by permission of the American Library Association, from School Activities and the Library, 1971.

"It is my belief that the chief school administrator and his staff not only determine the scope and the dimension of the educational program, but in very large measure, they determine the precise quality of the educational endeavor. It is the administrative staff that sets priorities, allocates funds, provides facilities, staff, and resources. If the administrative priorities are out of balance with the priority needs of the educational program, then the educational enterprise will be weak and ineffective.

"Because a quality education demands that learning go beyond the content of the textbook; because an optimum education demands that teaching and learning be individualized, an educational program of excellence must expand from the classroom into the library. Therefore, I believe that the administrative staff must assign a top priority to developing and supporting a functional, quality school library program both on the district and on the building level. This I believe to be an administrative imperative, for, in my judgment, a quality library program is the 'keystone of quality education.'"

Dr. Edward K. Kruse

This quotation from Dr. Kruse, the 1970 recipient of the AASL Distinguished Library Service Award for School Administrators, sets the stage for this issue of school activities--personalized learning, accountability and library-media services.

As school librarians, our hidden agenda is to get school administrators, faculty, and students to realize that personalized learning activities are not new but something that we have always believed in and tried to implement. Materials and services for students and teachers are our bag-- media is the thing. We look to you, our colleagues, for help, support, and constructive criticism. The guideposts on our road are the needs of students, of teachers, of citizens, and one odometer to measure progress is the consideration of where each school library media program is in relationship to those goals outlined in Standards for School Media Programs.

The school library-media program is not a thing but a permeating concept. This concept, fully implemented, is our commitment to maintaining our heritage of inquiry and challenge.

> Roberta E. Young, President
> American Association of
> School Librarians
> November 1970

For years school librarians have talked about administrative support of the instructional materials program in terms of what was needed. We have worked for better standards, more space, more funds, more personnel, more materials-- and, through administrators' support, all of us have gained.

An effective library program will never have enough of what is needed to meet the constantly changing needs and demands of teachers and students. This must be accepted --perhaps frustratingly so, by the librarians--but, whether or not we like it, the day of accounting is here.

School administrators whose educational philosophies recognize the importance of the school library have supported --yes, even fought--to help us establish national school library standards. They have supported the Elementary and Secondary Education Act and, most importantly, they have made an earnest effort to learn what a creative instructional materials program means to the overall modern and effective school program. They have assisted us in interpreting the library program to faculty members so that the latter see its relationship to curricular program.

Administrators have provided more time for teachers and librarians to plan together, and elementary principals have wisely administered the instructional program so that children have time to use the library. At the secondary level, rules and regulations have been relaxed to encourage the maximum use of library facilities.

Personnel administrators carefully seek librarians who are creative, dynamic leaders. They actively include librarians in curriculum planning activities within the school, and in faculty meetings, and they curtail extracurricular activities that will conflict with the honors of library services. Cooperation has been at its maximum in using in-service training to help the faculty become actively aware of the services of the school library program and how this program can be used as an effective aid to teaching.

Most libraries have had their staffs increased so that the best library program possible can be planned and executed. School librarians have more time to work with students in small groups and entire classes both in the library and outside the four walls of the instructional materials center. This additional staff also enables librarians to give individual guidance to students.

In short, school administrators have given us the opportunity to provide educational leadership. Now the effectiveness of administrative support, added funds, more adequate staff, more space, and greater collections of quality materials is up to us.

The same school administrators have every right to expect now that we interpret the library program so that there is an interfusion of instructional materials between students, faculty members, and librarians. The Standards for School Library Programs (1960) states: "School board members and school administrators, however, have the greatest responsibility and opportunity for making certain that schools have libraries with functional programs and excellent resources. These educational leaders are not only primarily responsible but ultimately accountable for the presence or absence, success or failure of libraries in the schools; and no individuals are more influential than they in determining the status and nature of school library programs." In a system of accountability the "ultimately" comes on down to the school librarian.

Librarians should consider generalities first in looking at their programs. What has been done to provide multimedia services? Are listening and viewing centers with collections of corresponding materials close at hand? We often answer that there is no room for such equipment. No matter how crowded the library facility is, there must be room for this important service. Are librarians using the extra staff members as a processing staff and as an opportunity to get more cards filed and new materials cataloged? In the long run, this does not improve library programs or services. The professional who likes working with students

and teachers should move his desk immediately to the center
of the library so that he can serve as a partner in teaching
and learning. He needs to be where the action is. If the
library staff cannot find one of their members who likes
working with students better than anything else, perhaps it
is time to change completely that library's image! Do we
really work at public relations? Do students and teachers
come away from a library experience with the feeling that
someone really cares?

Looking specifically at school library programs concerned with actual accountability to the faculty, to the students, and to the administrator--how do you rate in this
"Accountability Assessment?"

1. Do you fuss, fume, and constantly correct so
that patrons call you the materials specialist,
media specialist, or media programming en-
gineer? Or are you more concerned that a
student knows that a warm human being who
works with books and audiovisual media CARES
that the slides that he took for a Tower of Lon-
don report came out well and that the report was
well received by his teacher and fellow students?

2. Do you join in the controversy at professional
meetings about what the library facility should be
called? Or do you care more about what kind of
program exists and grows in that facility?

3. Do you actively read professional journals to keep
up with educational changes and do you actively do
as much visiting and listening to what students
have to say?

4. Is the library comfortable? Is it attractive? Is
it an academic center for learning?

5. Are you serving as an educational leader giving
direction to teachers and making use of every innovative idea that will promote the use of the library materials, services and program?
(See the table opposite from The School Library:
A Force for Education Excellence by Ruth Ann
Davies, which shows the school library program
in transition to a more accountable state.)

Table from The School Library:
A Force for Education Excellence

FROM TRADITIONAL PRACTICES	TO INNOVATIVE PRACTICES
From the library as an auxiliary service	To the library as an integral component of the total educational program
From the library as a study hall	To the library as an educational force
From the library as a materials distribution center	To the library as a learning laboratory
From the library limited to a printed collection	To a library providing all kinds of instructional media
From the incidental use of library facilities, staff, and collection	To the planned, purposeful and educationally significant use of library facilities, staff, and collection
From the librarian serving as study hall monitor	To the librarian serving as an educator
From the librarian as a curator of books	To the librarian programming for the most effective and educationally rewarding use of all types and kinds of instructional media
From the librarian as an impersonal dispenser of material	To the librarian as a learning expediter personalizing the services of the library
From the librarian working in isolation	To the librarian serving as a cooperating and/or team teacher
From the librarian working incommunicado	To the librarian directly involved in the curriculum planning, revision, and development

6. Do you take time to realize that students and
teachers are individuals? As such, they have
individual needs in working with materials. Do
you arrange the facilities both human and physical, to give each person the opportunity to work
alone? Are the learning materials accessible?
Does the library staff <u>assume</u> that its business
is to be helpful?

7. Does a strong, <u>practical</u> professional library
help the library <u>staff show</u> the leadership that
is terribly important in bringing a meaningful
interfusion of students, teachers, and materials?
What leadership have you shown recently in improving services and materials for the business
education department, the home economics classes, or the vocational training courses? Have
you provided leadership as new ethnic courses
are developed?

8. Have you used an Eckiographic Kit and made a
slide set? An accompanying tape? A multi-
media kit? It's hard to give others direction in
what we have not done ourselves.

9. Do you believe that full library programs can be
carried out in any school, under any physical or
academic condition, if the librarian is creative,
imaginative, and has plain "guts"?

10. Do you firmly believe that a school librarian can
help bring about some meaning, some beauty,
some purpose, some dignity, some sense in a
too often violent, ugly, purposeless, and sense-
less world?

If most of your answers to the "Accountability Assessment" are yes, or if you are vowed toward working toward
a yes answer, then you are accounting to your administrator,
to your faculty and, most importantly, to the students in
your schools. You are alive in the Age of Accountability,
the Age of Aquarius and you've let some sun shine in.

Mike Printz, Librarian
West High School Library
Topeka, Kansas

Personalized learning is one of the big goals of today's education. "The right experience for the right student at the right time," its exponents are saying in many different ways.

If you are one of the rare persons against this trend and want someone to blame, the librarian is your scapegoat. Learning experiences unique to each student are nothing new to the library media center. They were its modus operandi back in the days when classrooms knew nothing but the daily recitation and the weekly test. And lest you think I'm claiming undue glory for my former compatriots, I remind you of the signs in every library insisting upon silence at all times. How else could students work but individually? And remember, too, the classrooms were rigidly controlled.

Yet, even in this unnatural environment of enforced decorum, individual research was taking place when the student used the library. Gradually it became evident to teachers and administrators that there was considerable value in students individually using multiple sources to seek information and to organize it for further use.

To be sure, early assignments were often dull. They required students to look up references and make reports with little attention to individual needs and abilities, and rebellion was a natural reaction. I remember a blonde Adonis in my high school who responded to a dull teacher by analyzing the middle names of past Presidents, and I myself once wrote a term paper on the life of the white ant in Tanganyika, mostly to check on a teacher I suspected of never reading what her students wrote. But if these activities were wasteful, they were also individual and authentic. My handsome friend, now a lawyer, may find some modern proof to his contention that Presidents with longer middle names tend to be less liberal than those with shorter ones, and when Jack Paar showed a movie of those African white ants, I was one step ahead of him all the way.

And what stood by us when we got to college? Invariably it was our library experiences that had taught us how to work alone effectively. Even our friends who never went further than high school often carried some degree of individual learning into adult life by using the facilities of the local public library.

It is small wonder that the big idea of individual experiences caught fire. Teachers began to recognize what librarians had long known--that learning is indeed a personal thing. I can't learn for you and you can't for me. Both my purposes and my prior knowledge differ from yours as well as the speed with which I can accomplish my task. It is frustrating and inefficient for us to try to learn together.

There are other obvious advantages. When I learn on my own, I experience pride in my performance and I develop self-discipline. Yet the school can serve my needs in an economical fashion. With a wide spectrum of print and nonprint sources plus my own individual place to work, the library media center affords me the best possible opportunity for success.

As with any innovation, the stress on individualized learning in the library media center has its critics. On the one hand, traditional teachers are still reluctant to depend largely on personalized experiences for their students. On the other, those who espouse programmed learning say that in library media centers research, students may make choices without an adequate basis for their selection and they may pass judgments without sufficient evidence. These behavioral exponents want individualized learning experiences in which the learner acts exclusively on the expert's decision as to what he should learn and how it should be ordered.

I would remind both groups that the library is not designed to be the school's nerve center of original thought. In my high school days, our library was called the Tomb, and the title had an element of truth. Even today, students visit at our centers not so much to express new ideas as to gather and substantiate existing ones. Our birthright is to provide documentation, authority, and proof; and to suggest that the library fosters simplistic generalizations or unwarranted judgments denies its existence. The most hated footnotes, op sits, ibids and bibliographies of student reports were, and still are, library inventions and with the many types of new media joining books, disc recording, and filmstrips, the bibliographical expertise is even more crucial.

Ours is a middle course in the pursuit of personalized learning. The good library media center offers the means for the traditional teacher to experiment with greater student individual participation. It also provides the implementation or branching that can save programmed learning from being a mass invention. Ultimately, the school library media center will support innovation, experimentation, and realization for all instruction and for those who dare.

Readily, we recognize today's goals of increased individual learning experiences. They are all we, as librarians, have ever known.

Lu Ouida Vinson, Executive Secretary
American Association of School Librarians

17. Behavioral Objectives:
    Panacea or Holocaust

by Larry Frase

Reprinted by permission of the Association of Educational Communications and Technology, from Audiovisual Instruction, March 1971.

Behavioral objectives are rapidly growing as a major tool in curriculum and instruction. Workshop and seminar instructors are often found training participants in the writing and use of behavioral objectives. The majority of university classes, graduate or undergraduate, offer instruction in the development of skill in the use and writing of behavioral objectives. The present trend toward use of individualized instruction has extended and increased the use of behavioral objectives. Many types of materials written specifically for individualized instruction such as LAPs, TLUs. Contracts, and BIPs make use of behavioral objectives.

The behavioral objectives used in the previously listed materials, and those presented to teachers or pre-professional teachers in seminars and workshops include the first three and sometimes the fourth of the following elements: overt behavior, performance standard, conditions, and the doer.

The overt behavior is considered as evidence of the learner's accomplishment of the objective. The performance standard is the quality or quantity of the behavior expected. The conditions are those imposed upon the learner while he or she is expected to demonstrate the behavior. The doer is the person (individual student or teacher) or group (students, teachers) for whom the objective is written. As an illustration, the elements of the following behavioral objective are identified:

> The student will list on paper the name, years in office, and birth date of the four presidents preceding President Nixon within five minutes and with no errors.

116

1. Overt behavior--list (on paper)
2. Performance standard--no errors
3. Conditions--within five minutes
4. The doer--student

The overt behavior is the element that gives the behavioral objective its power and uniqueness--it makes the behavioral objective "behavioral." But when teachers continually use verbs such as identify, list, name, label, match, and
reproduce to identify the desired behavior, the behavioral objective ceases to be an improvement on the selection and
statement of objectives.

The verbs identify, list and name are nearly always
associated with memorization. For example. "List four
types of birds, " "Name six eastern cities, " and "Label the
parts of a flower, " all connote memorization. A review of
Bloom's (1956) taxonomic analysis of the cognitive domain
reveals that objectives of this nature (memorization) are
first-level cognitive objectives. Further review of the
taxonomy reveals that there are also the following five
levels in the cognitive domain: comprehension, application,
analysis, synthesis, and evaluation. All of these levels indicate skill more useful and sophisticated than that implied
by the first level. The acquisition of knowledge is not
wrong, but in large doses it is stifling to students and does
not allow time for the development of the more valuable
skills found in levels 2, 3, 4, 5, and 6.

This case also holds true for behavioral objectives
written in the affective domain. The five levels as indicated by Krathwohl (1964) are: 1) receiving-attending particular phenomena or stimuli; 2) responding-reacting to particular phenomena (usually under teacher direction); 3) valu-
ing-internalizing a particular set of values and behaving in
accordance with them; 4) organization-resolving conflicting
values; and 5) characterization by a value or value complex
--living over a number of years in accordance with an in-
ternalized value or value complex. Because they are easier
to write, the teacher must be careful not to limit all objectives to the first or second level. Behaviors implied by
these two levels indicate little more than receiving and responding like a robot. Surely, to be able to listen (receive)
attentively and respond as directed is of value. Students
must, however, learn the more sophisticated behaviors implied in the affective domain--such as the ability to choose
between conflicting values--and to live by these values if

they represent their finest thinking on the subject.

"How do we write behavioral objectives at different
levels of sophistication?" It must first be realized that
some verbs imply a behavior that coincides with some levels better than with others. For example, the verb list is
more useful and proper for use in the first level (knowledge
recall) than at the synthesizing or evaluating level. To
match verbs with the various levels is a voluminous task,
but some work has already been done. Gronlund (1970), in
his book Stating Behavioral Objectives for Classroom Instruction, has identified many verbs with the six levels of the
cognitive domain and the five levels of the affective domain.
For instance, he indicates that generate implies behavior at
the synthesis level. Teachers sensing student needs for development in synthesis could then state an objective such as:
"The student will generate a hypothesis from his observation
of a scientific phenomenon. To be acceptable, the student
must be able to relate to the teacher the relationship of the
hypothesis to the observed phenomenon. "

Many materials now in use are related to objectives
derived from only the first level of the cognitive domain.
Very few are written from the more sophisticated levels of
either the cognitive or the affective domain.

As a result of this practice, our schools are training
students to memorize and then to promptly forget facts, and
to blindly accept ideas without question. When these students become members of adult society their minds are
molded like clay, never having been stimulated to judge
and weigh.

The challenge to teachers using behavioral objectives
is to write objectives at all levels so their students gain a
variety of knowledge and skill--both cognitive and affective.

18.   Devising Instructional Objectives

by Robert Beacon

Everyone who teaches must know just what it is that he expects his students to learn.   He must know that what he is teaching is worth learning, and must be able to demonstrate that his students have learned it.

Teachers are found not only in schools.   Every person at some time plays the role of the teacher.   Parents constantly show the favored path to their children; industry trains its employees; the librarian teaches the new page the local variety of a universal shelving skill.

Everything taught results in a change in behavior.   A page may not realize that the nonfiction books are shelved on the decimal system during his first hour on the job, but he must learn to replace the volumes on the shelf in proper order so that the public can locate each one from the catalog. His demonstrable change in behavior is proper shelving.

This process can be generalized by stating that learning must result in some new form of observable behavior in the student.   That new behavior is the objective of instruction. Learning to construct and write instructional objectives helps each teacher, parent and librarian to pinpoint the goal of his efforts.   Objectives also aid the student in directing his own efforts in his studies.

Therefore, an instructional objective must state what new action is to be learned and demonstrated by the student. The more specific it is, the easier it is for the teacher and learner to focus their attention on it.

Let us consider our first objective.   Which of these two alternatives is more easily demonstrable?

a.   The new page will learn the principles of shelving.

b.   The new page will shelve one hundred books.

Statement 'a' offers "learn the principles." Statement 'b' mentions "shelving." Which of these two statements contains an observable behavior?

"Learning the principles" is a mental activity, unverifiable until it can be proven by some overt action. Shelving, on the other hand, is easily observable. So, in this case, statement 'b' is easily the better of the two instructional objectives.

This objective is fine so far, but it is not yet complete. There are many ways to shelve a book.

Books replaced on shelves are said to be shelved, but they must be in the proper place, for the purpose of shelving them is their quick and easy retrieval by library patrons. Therefore, some element of quality control must enter the picture. Consider these two objectives:

    b.   The new page will shelve one hundred books.

    c.   The new page will shelve one hundred books with only two errors.

Without question, objective 'c' is a better objective, since it makes an instructional goal more specific and easily measurable. It introduces the factor of quality control into learning in such a way that both student and teacher can see progress toward a previously defined goal. So far with our instructional objective, so good.

A little thought shows that the construction of this instructional or educational objective is not yet complete. Experience with new personnel will bring to mind vast differences in performance by pages in replacing a cartload of books to their proper places. Some will dispose of them in minutes, while others take all day. Therefore, some condition of time is indicated. Let us expand the language of our educational objective to make it more specific, and compare it with what we have to date.

    c.   The new page will shelve one hundred books with only two errors.

    d.   The new page will shelve one hundred books with only two errors within a period of ten minutes.

Obviously, limiting the time of achievement to a specific period more completely defines the job to be done. Statement 'd' is therefore a definite improvement over 'c.'

We have introduced into our instructional objective several factors so far. The terminal behavior has been made observable and measurable in terms of time and achievement. Yet one more factor remains to be added.

Consider two pages, each in similar library structures, with one hundred books to shelve. On one cart are only juvenile fiction; on the other, the first one hundred returned by patrons that morning. It is easy to see that covering one small physical section of the library in shelving will be a much faster operation than trying to restore books to shelves that are located in spread-out sections of a large physical plant. Therefore, one more factor must be added to make the instructional objective complete--the conditions under which the terminal behavior is to be performed:

d. The new page will shelve one hundred books with only two errors within a period of ten minutes.

e. The new page will shelve one hundred books of juvenile fiction with only two errors within a period of ten minutes.

The new objective is obviously superior to the old, since it includes another element that more clearly defines its scope. This objective is now complete, and readily applicable to a training program. It can be applied, with slight alteration, to any library situation. It is a good training tool.

The provisions for a good instructional objective include several factors:

--the terminal behavior which is desired (shelving books correctly),

--conditions under which the performance is to take place (100 books in ten minutes, limited to juvenile fiction),

--level of performance (with only two errors).

There should be little difficulty in writing good,

practical instructional objectives if these three factors are kept in mind. Teaching will be made easier, as it is simpler to prepare a well defined lesson than one which is not. But, more important, clearly understood educational (instructional, learning) objectives help eliminate a common cause of learning failure among students: an all-too-frequent vagueness about what they are required to do.

19. Federal Legislation for School Libraries

by Clem M. Hall

Reprinted by permission of the American Library
Association and the author, from School Libraries,
Spring 1971.

Title II is a "household word" to school media specialists all over the United States who have upgraded their
libraries with grants from the Elementary and Secondary
Education Act. The Title II ESEA program for acquisition
of school library resources, textbooks, and other instructional materials is the only piece of federal legislation exclusively designed for the improvement of school libraries.
But many other sources of financial aid for school libraries
lie obscured in the welter of federal education legislation.

In some cases, libraries or library materials are
specifically named as one component of a larger project; in
other instances, libraries are not mentioned at all, but ag-
gressive school librarians can nevertheless offer the services of the library and sometimes receive federal grant
money for this purpose.

The following compilation presents both well-known
and little-known national programs which can benefit our
elementary and secondary school children through strengthening the school media center. Opportunities for training
of school librarians have been omitted (with one exception)
because at the time of writing, legislation for training of
education professions personnel under the Higher Education
Act is in the process of being amended by Congress.

ELEMENTARY AND SECONDARY EDUCATION ACT--Title I
--Financial Assistance... for the Education of Children of
Low-Income Families (PL 89-10, as amended by Pl 89-
750, PL 90-247, and PL 91-230)

Authorization: Extends through fiscal 1973; based on "low-
income factor" formula.

Purpose: To aid the states in devising special education programs to solve the problems of underachievement, disadvantage, and deprivation.

Uses of Federal Funds: Local educational agencies may use federal funds for staff inservice training and other activities designed to provide effective educational services in schools with higher concentrations of low-income children, including Indians, migrants, and children living in institutions for neglected and delinquent youth.

Purchase of equipment and materials is limited to the minimum required to implement these programs. However, many school libraries have benefited substantially since library materials are an important factor in improving education for low-income children. The hiring of additional library staff and library aides also may be financed with Title I money.

Federal Contribution: 50 percent

Administering Agency: State education agency through plan approved by Division of Compensatory Education, Bureau of Elementary and Secondary Education, U.S. Office of Education, Washington, D.C. 20202.

ELEMENTARY AND SECONDARY EDUCATION ACT--Title II --School Library Resources, Textbooks, and Other Instructional Materials (PL 89-10, as amended by PL 89-750, PL 90-247, and PL 91-230)

Authorization: $200,000,000 for fiscal 1971; $210,000,000 for 1972; $220,000,000 for 1973.

Purpose: To assist elementary and secondary schools to improve the quality of education offered through acquisition of library materials and resources, and textbooks.

Uses of Federal Funds: Local educational agencies may apply for grants to acquire printed or published (including audiovisual) library materials and texts. These materials may also be loaned for use by children and teachers in private schools.

Federal Contribution: Nonmatching.

<u>Administering Agency:</u> State education agency through plan
   approved by Division of State Agency Cooperation, Bureau
   of Elementary and Secondary Education, U.S. Office of
   Education, Washington, D.C. 20202.

<u>Current Funding Status:</u> $80,000,000 was appropriated for
   fiscal 1971.

ELEMENTARY AND SECONDARY EDUCATION ACT--Title III
   --Supplementary Education Centers and Services (PL 80-
   10, as amended by PL 89-750, PL 90-247, and PL 91-
   230)

<u>Authorization:</u> $550,000,000 for fiscal 1971; $575,000,000
   for 1972; $605,000,000 for 1973; in addition, "such sums
   as may be necessary" for the administration of state
   plans, activities of advisory councils, and evaluation and
   dissemination.

<u>Purpose:</u> To make grants for "supplementary educational
   centers and services to stimulate and assist in the provision of vitally needed educational services not available
   in sufficient quantity or quality, and to stimulate and assist in the development and establishment of exemplary
   elementary programs to serve as models for regular
   school programs, and to assist the States in establishing
   and maintaining programs of testing and guidance and
   counseling. "

<u>Uses of Federal Funds:</u> Local educational agencies may ap-
   ply for grants for purposes including 1) establishment or
   expansion of exemplary and innovative educational programs to stimulate the adoption of new educational programs; 2) establishment, maintenance, operation, and expansion of programs or projects, including the lease or
   construction of necessary facilities and the acquisition of
   necessary equipment, designed to enrich the programs of
   local elementary and secondary schools by providing supplementary educational services and activities. Some instructional equipment may be acquired under this program, but the emphasis is on effective application of
   technology (including television) and better utilization of
   manpower. Funds for guidance and counseling programs,
   formerly under ESEA V-A, are now contained in this title.

<u>Federal Contribution:</u> 100 percent.

<u>Administering Agency</u>: State education agency through plan
    approved by Division of Plans and Supplementary Centers,
    Bureau of Elementary and Secondary Education, U. S. Of-
    fice of Education, Washington, D. C. 20202.

<u>Current Funding Status</u>: $143, 390, 000 was appropriated for
    fiscal 1971.

ELEMENTARY AND SECONDARY EDUCATION ACT--Title V
    --Grants to Strengthen State Education Departments and
    Local Educational Agencies (PL 89-10, as amended by
    PL 89-750, PL 90-247 and PL 91-230)

<u>Authorization</u>: Part A--$80, 000, 000 for fiscal 1971;
    $85, 000, 000 for fiscal 1972; $90, 000, 000 for fiscal
    1973; Part B--$20, 000, 000, for fiscal 1971; $30, 000,
    000 for fiscal 1972; $40, 000, 000 for fiscal 1973.

<u>Purpose</u>: To stimulate and assist states and localities in
    strengthening the leadership resources of their educational
    agency and in establishing and improving programs to
    identify and meet their educational needs.

<u>Uses of Federal Funds</u>:
        Part A--Grants to Strengthen State Departments of Edu-
    cation--State departments of education may use federal
    money for statewide educational planning; comprehensive
    processing of state and local educational data; educational
    research and demonstration programs; improving the
    quality of teacher preparation; studies concerning the
    financing of public education in the state; statewide pro-
    grams designed to measure the educational achievement
    of pupils; consultative and technical assistance and serv-
    ices to local educational agencies; programs designed to
    encourage the full and adequate utilization and acceptance
    of auxiliary personnel (such as teacher aides) on a per-
    manent basis; etc.
        Part B--Grants to Strengthen Local Educational Agencies
    --Local educational agencies may apply for grants to pro-
    mote the purposes of this Part, including but not limited
    to educational planning on a district basis; providing sup-
    port or services for comprehensive handling of educational
    data; conducting, sponsoring, or cooperating in educational
    research and demonstration projects; programs designed
    to encourage full utilization of auxiliary personnel on a
    permanent basis; providing consultative and technical as-

sistance relating to academic subjects and other aspects of education.

Programs must involve an expenditure of at least $2, 500.

Federal Contribution: 100 percent.

Administering Agency: Part A--Division of State Agency Co- operation, Bureau of Elementary and Secondary Education, U. S. Office of Education, Washington, D. C. 20202; Part B--state education agency.

Current Funding Status: $29, 750, 000 was appropriated for fiscal 1971 for Part A. Part B, a new program, was not funded.

NATIONAL DEFENSE EDUCATION ACT--Title III--Financial Assistance for Strengthening Instruction in Science, Mathe- matics, Modern Foreign Languages, and Other Critical Subjects (PL 85-864, as amended by PL 88-210, PL 88- 665, PL 89-329, PL 89-752, and PL 90-575)

Authorization: Part A--$130, 000, 000 for fiscal 1971; Part B--extends through fiscal 1971 with amount of appropria- tion left up to Congress.

Purpose: "To provide substantial assistance in various forms to individuals, and to States and their subdivisions, in order to insure trained manpower of sufficient quality and quantity to meet the national defense needs of the United States. "

Uses of Federal Funds: Under Part A, state educational agencies may apply for project grants for 1) "acquisition of laboratory and other materials and equipment, and printed and published materials (other than textbooks), suitable for use in providing education in academic sub- jects in public elementary or secondary schools, or both, " and for 2) "minor remodeling of laboratory or other space used for such materials or equipment. "
      Loans (totaling 12 percent of the annual appropriation) at low interest rates may also be made to private nonprofit elementary and secondary schools for the same purposes as above.
      Under Part B, local educational agencies may apply for grants for acquisition of equipment and materials (as in Part A) to be used for "programs and projects designed

to meet the special educational needs of educationally deprived children in school attendance areas having a high concentration of children from low-income families. " The local educational agency must also provide services (such as educational TV or radio, mobile equipment, etc.) to educationally deprived children in that district who may be enrolled in private elementary and secondary schools.

Federal Contribution: 50 percent for Part A; 100 percent for Part B.

Administering Agency: State education agency, through plan approved by Division of State Agency Cooperation, Bureau of Elementary and Secondary Education, U.S. Office of Education, Washington, D. C. 20202.

Current Funding Status: $50,000,000 was appropriated in fiscal 1971 for Part A; no funds for Part B.

BILINGUAL EDUCATION ACT (Elementary and Secondary Education Act, Title VII) (PL 89-10, as amended by PL 89-750, PL 90-247, and PL 91-230)

Authorization: $80,000,000 for fiscal 1971; $100,000,000 for 1972; and $135,000,000 for 1973.

Purpose: To aid "local education agencies to develop and carry out new and imaginative elementary and secondary school programs designed to meet [the] special educational needs" of children of limited English-speaking ability.

Uses of Federal Funds: Local educational agencies (or institutions of higher education in cooperation with the former), which have a high concentration of low-income children of limited English-speaking ability, may apply for grants.   Elementary and secondary schools operated by Indian tribes or by the Department of Interior for Indian children are also eligible.   Funds may be used for 1) planning and developing special bilingual educational programs, including the preparation and dissemination of instructional materials; 2) preservice and inservice training for teachers and "ancillary educational personnel" to work with bilingual projects; 3) acquisition of necessary teaching materials and equipment, etc.
    Applicants must indicate that they will make "optimum

use" of the community's educational and cultural resources, such as libraries and museums.

Federal Contribution: 100 percent.

Administering Agency: Bilingual Educational Programs Branch, Bureau of Elementary and Secondary Education, U. S. Office of Education, Washington, D. C. 20202.

Current Funding Status: $25, 000, 000 was appropriated for fiscal 1971.

LIBRARY SERVICES AND CONSTRUCTION ACT--Title III-- Interlibrary Cooperation (PL 84-597, as amended by PL 88-269, PL 89-511, and PL 90-154)

Authorization: $15, 000, 000 for fiscal 1971.

Purpose: To promote interlibrary cooperation for greater efficiency and effectiveness of service through the systematic use of funds and the elimination of overlapping and duplication.

Uses of Federal Funds: All types of libraries, including public, school, academic and special, may participate in the establishment and operation of systems or networks of libraries to better serve a community, metropolitan area, state, or multistate area. The funds can be used to set up teletype or facsimile transmission systems for interlibrary loan or reference service purposes. Small public, school, or college libraries, for example, might draw on the resources of the state library, or a large university or metropolitan area library.

Federal Contribution: 50 percent.

Administering Agency: State library agency, under state plan approved by Division of Library Programs, Bureau of Libraries and Educational Technology, U. S. Office of Education, Washington, D. C. 20202.

Current Funding Status: $2, 281, 000 was appropriated for fiscal 1971.

EDUCATION OF THE HANDICAPPED ACT--Part B--Assistance to States for Education of Handicapped Children (PL 91-230)

Authorization: $200,000,000 for fiscal 1971; $210,000,000 for fiscal 1972; and $220,000,000 for fiscal 1973.

Purpose: To assist the states "in the initiation, expansion, and improvement of programs and projects for the education of handicapped children at the preschool, elementary school and secondary school levels."

Uses of Federal Funds: Local educational agencies may apply for grants to carry out the purposes of this Part. Such programs must be designed for the special educational needs of handicapped children, and must be "of sufficient size, scope and quality... as to give reasonable promise of substantial progress toward meeting those needs." Private school children are eligible to participate.

Federal Contribution: 50 percent.

Administering Agency: State education agency under plan approved by Division of Educational Services, Bureau of Education for the Handicapped, U.S. Office of Education, Washington, D.C. 20202.

Current Funding Status: $34,000,000 was appropriated for fiscal 1971.

EDUCATION OF THE HANDICAPPED ACT--Part C, Sec. 623--Early Education for Handicapped Children (PL 91-230)

Authorization: For all of Part C--$36,500,000 for fiscal 1971; $51,500,000 for 1972; and $66,500,000 for 1973.

Purpose: To aid "the development and carrying out... of experimental preschool and early education programs for handicapped children which... show promise of promoting a comprehensive and strengthened approach to the special problems of such children."

Uses of Federal Funds: Appropriate public agencies and private nonprofit agencies and organizations may apply for grants to conduct programs as above. Among other aims, services shall be designed to "facilitate the intellectual, emotional, physical, mental, social and language development of such children. "

Federal Contribution: Not to exceed 90 percent.

Administering Agency: Aid to States Branch, Division of Educational Services, Bureau of Education for the Handicapped, U. S. Office of Education, Washington, D. C. 20202.

Current Funding Status: $7, 000, 000 was appropriated for fiscal 1971.

EDUCATION OF THE HANDICAPPED ACT--Part D--Training Personnel for the Education of the Handicapped (PL 91-230)

Authorization: $69, 500, 000 for fiscal 1971; $87, 000, 000 for 1972; and $103, 500, 000 for 1973.

Purpose: To assist in training and recruiting persons to teach or provide educational services for handicapped children.

Uses of Federal Funds: Institutions of higher education (or nonprofit institutions or agencies in cooperation with the former) may apply for grants to train personnel engaged in or preparing to engage in providing special services for the education of handicapped children, or conducting research in fields related to education of such children. Grants may be used to cover the cost of courses of training or study and for awarding fellowships or traineeships.

Federal Contribution: Unspecified.

Administering Agency: Division of Training Programs, Bureau of Education of the Handicapped, U. S. Office of Education, Washington, D. C. 20202.

Current Funding Status: $500, 000 (for recruitment and information purposes only) was appropriated for fiscal 1971.

EDUCATION OF THE HANDICAPPED ACT--Part F--Instructional Media for the Handicapped (PL 91-230)

Authorization: $12, 500, 000 for fiscal 1971; $15, 000, 000 for
   1972; and $20, 000, 000 for 1973.

Purpose: To promote the general welfare of deaf persons
   by providing them with the enriched educational and cultural experiences to be gained through films; and to promote the educational advancement of handicapped persons.

Uses of Federal Funds: Libraries "directly involved in activities for the advancement of the handicapped" may
   make use of the U. S. Office of Education's loan service
   of captioned films and educational media.   Distribution
   of materials and equipment is through designated local
   or regional centers such as state schools for the handicapped.

Federal Contribution: Not applicable.

Administering Agency: For address of nearest distribution
   center contact Media Services and Captioned Films
   Branch, Division of Educational Services, Bureau of
   Education for the Handicapped, U. S. Office of Education,
   Washington, D. C. 20202.

Current Funding Status: $6, 000, 000 was appropriated for
   support of this program for fiscal 1971.

PART III

MEDIA--EVALUATION, SELECTION,
ACQUISITION, AND ORGANIZATION

20. Policies and Procedures for Selection of Instructional Materials

Approved by the Board of Directors of the American Association of School Librarians at the ALA Midwinter Conference, Chicago, 1970. Reprinted by permission of the American Library Association.

The following statement of policy-making with regard to instructional materials selection for the school library media center is offered as a guide for the formulation of a policy. It is believed that such a policy should be formally adopted by each school district as a basis for consistent excellence in choice of materials and as a document that can be presented to parents and other citizens for their further understanding of the purposes and standards of selection of these materials.

Patterns of Policy Making

The governing body of a school is legally responsible for all matters relating to the operation of that school. It is recommended that assumption of responsibility and the delegation of the authority for the selection of instructional materials should be adopted by the legally responsible body and then stated in a formal policy to the professionally trained personnel employed by the school.

Selection of Personnel

The responsibility for coordination of the selection of instructional materials for the school library media center should rest with the professionally trained media personnel. Administration, faculty, students and parents should be involved in the selection process. Final decision on purchases should rest with the professional personnel in accordance with the formally adopted policy.

Types of Materials Covered

Criteria for evaluation and selection of all types of

instructional materials should be established. Such criteria should be available in written form.

Criteria of Selection

The primary objective of a school library is to implement, enrich and support the educational program of the school. Criteria for instructional materials selection should implement this basic objective.

Criteria for the selection of all instructional materials are both general, as found in the professional literature, and specific in terms of the needs of each school community.

General criteria are stated in terms of significant descriptors of the subject; integrity of treatment; and quality of the medium-style, clarity, originality, etc.

Specific criteria are determined by a study of the characteristics of the school's instructional program and the needs of students as affected by the community, as follows:

Needs of the individual school program

a. Based on knowledge of the curriculum
b. Based on requests for administrators and teachers.

Needs of the individual student

a. Based on knowledge of children and youth
b. Based on requests by parents and students.

Needs from these several sources will require a wide range of instructional materials for an acceptance level of quality, on all levels of difficulty, and with a diversity of appeal; and the presentation of different points of view--ethnic, religious, political and cultural.

Selection Tools

Reputable, unbiased, professionally prepared selection aids should be consulted as guides.

Challenged Materials

A procedure should be established for consideration

of an action on criticism of materials by individual or
groups. An example of such a procedure is included in the
sample statement of policy included in this publication. The
American Association of School Librarians endorsed the
School Library Bill of Rights for School Library Media Programs basic to this procedure at the Atlantic City Conference, 1969.

School Library Bill of Rights
for School Library Media Programs

The American Association of School Librarians reaffirms its belief in the Library Bill of Rights of the American Library Association. Media personnel are concerned
with generating understanding of American freedoms through
the development of informed and responsible citizens. To
this end the American Association of School Librarians asserts that the responsibility of the school library media center is:

To provide a comprehensive collection of instructional materials selected in compliance with basic, written selection principles, and to provide maximum accessibility to
these materials.

To provide materials that will support the curriculum, taking into consideration the individual's needs, and the
varied interests, abilities, socio-economic backgrounds,
and maturity levels of the students served.

To provide materials for teachers and students that will encourage growth in knowledge, and that will develop literary, cultural and aesthetic appreciation, and ethical
standards.

To provide materials which reflect the ideas and beliefs of
religious, social, political, historical, and ethnic groups
and their contribution to the American and world heritage
and culture, thereby enabling students to develop an intellectual integrity in forming judgments.

To provide a written statement, approved by the local Boards
of Education, of the procedures for meeting the challenge
of censorship of materials in school library media centers.

To provide qualified professional personnel to serve teachers
and students.

A Sample Policy Statement*

POLICIES FOR SELECTION OF
INSTRUCTIONAL MATERIALS

I. Objectives of Selection

The primary objective of the school's educational media center is to implement, enrich and support the educational program of the school. It is the duty of the center to provide a wide range of materials on all levels of difficulty, with diversity of appeal, and the presentation of different points of view.

To this end, the Board of Education of _____ reaffirms the objectives of the Standards for School Media Programs, prepared jointly in 1969 by the American Association of School Librarians and the Department of Audiovisual Instruction, and asserts that the responsibility of the library media center is:

To provide materials that will enrich and support the curriculum, taking into consideration the varied interests, abilities, and maturity levels of the pupils served

To provide materials that will stimulate growth in factual knowledge, literary appreciation, aesthetic values, and ethical standards

To provide materials on opposing sides of controversial issues so that young citizens may develop under guidance the practice of critical analysis of all media

To provide materials representative of the many religious, ethnic, and cultural groups and their contributions to our American heritage

To place principle above personal opinion and reason above prejudice in the selection of materials of the highest quality in order to assure a comprehensive collection appropriate for the users of the library media center.

---

*Reprinted in part by permission of the North Carolina Department of Public Instruction.

II. Responsibility for Selection of Materials

The _____ Board of Education is legally
responsible for all matters relating to the operation of
_____ schools.

The responsibility for the selection of instructional
materials is delegated to the professionally trained personnel employed by the school system.

Selection of materials involves many people; principals, teachers, supervisors and media specialists. The
responsibility for coordinating the selection of instructional
materials and making the recommendation for purchase rests
with the professionally trained media personnel.

III. Criteria for Selection of Instructional Materials

Needs of the individual school based on knowledge of
the curriculum and of the existing collection are given first
consideration.

Materials for purchase are considered on the basis of:

overall purpose
timeliness or permanence
importance of the subject matter
quality of the writing/production
readability and popular appeal
authoritativeness
reputation of the publisher/producer
reputation and significance of the author/artist/
     composer/producer, etc.
format and price

Requests from faculty and students are given consideration.

IV. Procedures for Selection

In selecting materials for purchase, the media specialist evaluates the existing collection and consults:

reputable, unbiased, professionally prepared selection
     aids;

specialists from all departments and/or all grade levels;

the media committee appointed by the principal to serve in an advisory capacity in the selection of materials.

In specific areas the media specialist follows these procedures:

Gift materials are judged by basic selection standards, and are accepted or rejected by these standards.

Multiple items of outstanding and much in demand media are purchased as needed.

Worn or missing standard items are replaced periodically.

Out-of-date or no longer useful materials are withdrawn from the collection.

Sets of materials and materials acquired by subscription are examined carefully, and are purchased only to fill a definite need.

Salesmen must have permission from the superintendent's office before going into any of the schools.

V. Challenged Materials

Occasional objections to a selection will be made by the public, despite the care taken to select valuable materials for student and teacher use and the qualifications of persons who select the materials.

The principles of the freedom to read and of the professional responsibility of the staff must be defended, rather than the materials.

A file is kept on materials likely to be questioned or considered controversial.

If a complaint is made, the procedures are as follows:

1. Be courteous, but make no commitments.

2. Invite the complainant to file his objections in writing and offer to send him a prepared questionnaire such as the one prepared by the National Council of Teachers of English, so that he may submit a formal complaint to the media committee.

3. Temporarily withdraw the material pending a decision of the media committee.

4. Inform the superintendent and the media supervisor.

5. The media committee will

   a. Read and examine materials referred to it.
   b. Check general acceptance of the materials by reading reviews.
   c. Weigh values and faults against each other and form opinions based on the material as a whole and not on passages pulled out of context.
   d. Meet to discuss the material and to prepare a report on it.
   e. File a copy of the report in the school and administrative offices.

(See Appendix for list of aids in selection: "Selecting Materials for School Media Centers.")

21. Evaluation Techniques?
First, Some Fundamental Questions

by Hilda Taba

Reprinted by permission of the Association for Educational Communications and Technology, from Audiovisual Instruction, May 1964.

I am glad that this conference was devoted to evaluation because I have the impression that we have hurried into innovations without sufficient provision for evaluation. Even the very adequately funded innovations, demonstrations, or experiments have spent a very small fraction of their money and effort on evaluation.

I feel that the media are trying to figure out a curriculum by themselves and for themselves in place of acting as media. Somehow the trend of thought in the afternoon meetings suggests that you are more concerned with how to run media than with what the media are for.

I would like to start, therefore, with a few general comments that may apply to all kinds of media. Each of the media comes to us invested in a certain kind of learning theory, and we ought to know what this theory is, because only by examining ideas about learning can we determine the legitimate application of whatever technology we use in teaching. For example, certain concepts of learning are imbedded in the teaching machine. Among these are the concepts of linear learning and of bite-size steps. The idea that there are sequences of steps by which a person learns is a creditable one. Yet, the teaching machine converts these into linear, single predetermined sequences, and thereby excludes the possibility of autonomous, individual, cognitive development.

Further, the linear process of thinking which assumes a straight line from the question to the right answer, may not be equally applicable to all areas of learning. Try to apply this process to social studies. What is the reason

141

for the death of President Kennedy? What is the reason for
our difficulties with Russia or with India? Linear thinking
has very little to do with this aspect of our social studies.

Errorless learning is still another principle of programing for teaching machines. Learning is assumed to be
better if it is errorless. I wonder what happens to creativity and the experimental attitude under conditions in which
all learning is purified of error?   ⁕

Questions such as these suggest that in using any
medium of learning we must determine what its proper function is, and what other types of learning experiences must
be combined with it to achieve proper balance in learning.
To do either, we need to be aware of the kind of learning
theory that underlies the essential conception of the medium
and of the kind of program a given medium offers.

We must look at other media in the same way and
ask the same kind of questions; namely, what kind of learning theory is imbedded in it? How can we free ourselves
from the imposition of the medium upon curriculum and, instead, make it a servant of curriculum?

Within any technology lies a compulsion for "packaging, " for mechanizing, and rationalizing. Educational
technology involves a similar danger. For example, in the
physics films and the packaged series of mathematical materials, someone has figured out all the sequences for all
the American children of all the American people. Someone has assumed that these sequences that are good today
will also be good five years from now. The idea of packaging means that something is fixed, finished, and put into
order; it is something with which the schools should not
tamper. The idea of packaging also suggests that the
schools should not take the products of scientific thinking
and devise ways for students to handle and recombine them.

The central question, then, is what particular objectives of education does a particular medium serve and what
function does it need to perform in order to serve that kind
of objective?

There are four areas of objectives: (1) knowledge,
(2) thinking, (3) values, attitudes, and sensitivity, and
(4) skills. Each one of these objectives requires a different kind of teaching strategy, different materials, and dif-

ferent ways of using media.   Knowledge is the only objective that can be implemented by the choice of content.   The
other three large areas of objectives can only be implemented through the ways we teach and learn.   In the past, in
curriculum development and the use of media, our attention
has been largely concentrated on the use of media to improve communication of knowledge.   We have done little to
find out what kinds of learning experiences are needed to
serve these other three objectives, when actually the strong-
est contribution of the media lies in their service to the development of thinking and attitudes.

We have done enough for the passing on of knowledge.
We sorely need more sophisticated techniques for such areas
of behavior as the development of concepts, of the capacity
to compare and contrast sharply.   We need sophisticated
techniques to help children begin to project what they know
to predict consequences, to hypothesize consequences of described conditions, and to begin to use the principles they
acquire for explaining things they have not learned directly.

The media have larger potentiality than we are now
using, so we need to explore the ultimate potentiality for
any medium and exploit it optimally rather than minimally.
Evaluation should therefore always include the question,
"How can we push the potentiality of the medium itself further than we are now doing?"   It is no enough to ask
whether, as a result of using new media, students perform
as well as under older methods in acquiring information.
When reports on the use of new media claim that information achievement went up a bit, I always wonder what else
went down.   This becomes, then, one of the questions to
be asked.   One might, by a certain packaged series, increase the body of historical and geographical knowledge,
but it is quite possible that actually the capacity and the
inclination to think actively about the information might decrease at the same time.

Finally, the total consequences of using a medium
must be evaluated also.   Each medium enforces a certain
organization of mind and materials.   This organization needs
to be examined for its total consequences.   This is especially needed in the use of mass media because they make a
mass impact.   Therefore, because of their very efficiency
they also magnify errors on a larger scale.

22. Acquisition of Materials in the School Media Center

by Mildred L. Nickel

Reprinted by permission of the American Library Association and the author, from School Activities and the Library, 1970.

The word acquisition may be defined as "the act of getting." This connotation is extended here to include those operations which deal with the ordering, receiving, and keeping of records of all materials added to the school media center. Budget planning as well as selection, which precede acquisition, and cataloging, which follows it, are not included here.

For many school media specialists, having little or no responsibility for the acquisition process allows them more time to work with children and teachers. To have some one or some thing produce all needed materials by what may seem sheer magic or by the clicking of a machine saves energy and time. And it often makes the difference between chaos and efficient operation of the media program. Students sometimes seem to have the impression that a wand is waved and the materials they want appear in the media center and then in their hands. But we know better. Instead of a magic wand acquisition procedures require time, organization, patience, efficiency, accuracy--and money, of course.

The school media specialist may have a one-man operation; he may have a supervisor who assumes all the responsibilities for acquisition; or all operations may be done by some form of automation. Whatever the degree of responsibility, certain basic principles apply. The person charged with acquisition of materials must be knowledgeable about publishing, the book trade, and the principles of good business; procedures must be efficiently and systematically organized; processes should be charted to avoid wasted motion; needs and budget must be coordinated; vendors are to be evaluated for service as well as cost;

144

and acquisition must be viewed as a service seen in relation to the total program of service to students and teachers.

Regardless of the number of service agencies involved, operational procedures have many common characteristics; they vary only in complexity. After the needs are determined and the budget is established, the actual development of procedural policies will depend on what is economically feasible in the local situation. School media specialists are trained in the selection and use of materials, but they are not always experts in budgetary matters, or in cost analysis, or in time-and-motion studies. Every school district, however, has someone in its employ who can be called upon for advice or who will assume part or all of the responsibility for acquisition: a purchasing agent, a director of budget and finance, an accountant, an auditor, a systems analyst. In addition to its being good business to consult with such persons, rapport is established and a better understanding of the media program is developed.

Local regulations may also affect these operations. For example, bids must be taken on all purchases or on those amounting to more than a stated figure; local merchants must be patronized whenever possible; all bills must be submitted in triplicate; materials may be ordered only once a year or at specified intervals; funds must be encumbered in time to have all bills paid by the end of the fiscal year. When such regulations exist, it is of course taken for granted that they will be followed--unless it can be demonstrated that they impede service or are unnecessarily expensive. A recommendation for change of policy should be well documented.

Automation must be reckoned with today as a means to better service, especially where there is a large volume of routine tasks to be done. Its usefulness has been demonstrated; it is no longer just a gadget. In those school districts which already have such equipment being used for other purposes, it behooves the school media specialist to find out what it can offer. A computer can be programmed for acquisition, as well as for other media-oriented operations such as cataloging, circulation control, and compiling bibliographies. The professional literature contains much information about automation and libraries, but school districts seem to be the followers rather than the leaders up to this time. School media specialists need not be concerned about how these machines communicate with each

other or why bells ring and lights flash on them.   They
must, however, be willing to surrender their responsibility
for all the time-consuming minutiae they have traditionally
considered their own private domain if the end result is to
be a faster, cheaper, more efficient process.

Manual, or personal, handling of acquisition routines
is still the general practice in most schools and school districts.   Since acquisitions is really a business operation, it
should be organized in a business-like way, with accurate
records being kept at each step.   The steps in the process
follow a logical sequence; receiving requests, compiling and
placing orders, and receiving materials.   In each of these
steps there are mandatory decisions as well as value judgments to be made, some of which follow.

1.   Receiving requests.   Requests for purchase originate with the individual school media specialist.   They may
then be sent directly to a vendor (in a one-man operation)
or to the person responsible for the acquisition process; a
supervisor or someone in the central or cooperative purchasing office.   These requests are usually one copy of an
order slip, with a carbon copy retained at the place of origin.   The central office will then consolidate all of them, on
order slips or as typed lists.   Multiple-copy order slips arranged by main entry are easier to handle and more functional, although some jobbers prefer a typed list arranged
by publisher.   This slows the process and does increase
the cost.   Even though jobbers prefer the list arrangement,
they will fill orders sent on three-by-five cards or slips.

2.   Compiling and placing orders.   Before orders can be
placed, and if bids are not required, a decision must be
made to determine the source of purchase.   Experience is
the best basis for such decisions.   But in these days of
conglomerates and company mergers, it is imperative that
one keep up to date about what is going on.   This can be
done by checking commercial mailings carefully, by reading
professional periodicals regularly, by examining commercial
exhibits at professional meetings, and by talking with other
media specialists about their experiences.

Orders for books, magazines, and most pamphlets
are usually placed with a well-established wholesaler or
jobber, but nonprint, or audiovisual, materials must for
the most part be ordered directly from the producer.
Direct orders usually prove to be time-consuming and

expensive in terms of clerical work and bookkeeping, while orders sent to one jobber simplify all procedures. In the latter, for instance, only one account is maintained, and checks are written to only one company. Several words of caution should be inserted here: Buying under pressure or directly from a company just because that is the only way the salesman gets his commission is to be avoided, as are package deals or lease-purchase plans. Discussions with salesmen are helpful, however, as an excellent way to keep abreast of what is being published and produced--but as information only, not as a sole basis for selection.

Since everyone wants to get the most for his money, the word discount many times looms large as a factor in purchasing, but the word service must parallel it in importance or even precede it as a factor in determining the vendor. The amount of discount usually depends on the total amount to be spent in a given fiscal period, but there are always some exceptions. For example, no discount is allowed for books in library binding, and short discounts are allowed on many highly technical books. Rarely are discounts given on the purchase of audiovisual materials, although this practice does vary. If there is a local bookstore or jobber, it is good public relations to buy there. It is easy to contact the local dealer personally or by phone if any problems arise; there will be no transportation charges; but he may stock only current materials. If, therefore, he cannot supply what is ordered because he does not maintain an adequate stock, he will not be able to give service.

There are also some companies and societies that do not sell through trade channels, which makes it necessary to order directly from them. The National Geographic Society, the Superintendent of Documents, and publishers of encyclopedias are good examples. If a local regulation requires that bids be taken on orders, there is no problem about deciding on a vendor--the lowest bidder gets the business. Some dealers are now refusing to bid unless the orders are large, with many duplicate copies included. They have found that it is not economical to prepare bids for thousands of dollars worth of individual titles. Experience has shown that in some school districts where bids are required, service has been poor or inconsistent, but this is not always the case.

Regardless of the vendor, it is a good policy to have

a written agreement with the company. Will it replace imperfect copies? Can all the materials ordered on the same purchase order be boxed together? Can the invoice be included in the box of materials listed on it? Who pays transportation costs? If the vendor is a jobber, what publisher or producer's materials can he furnish? How long are outstanding orders kept before they are reported out of stock? These and similar questions should be answered and mutually agreed upon before any orders are placed.

The last step in placing an order is to obtain an authority to purchase (usually a purchase order), which is sent to the vendor along with the actual order. Each school system will have its own form, and each will have a policy about who signs it. This form should also include where materials are to be delivered. This is especially important in a large school system.

3. Receiving materials. Receiving room procedures do not require sustained professional attention. The actual checking in can be done by clerks or para-professionals, with supervision from time to time. As the boxes are opened, the most expedient practice seems to be to arrange the materials on shelves in the order in which they are listed on the invoice. It does help if the invoice is in the box with them. Producers of nonprint materials seem to fail to include it more often than do publishers of books. When it has been determined that at least the correct titles have been received, they must be checked against the order slips, recording the date received and the actual cost of each item. Accuracy in checking at this point is most important, because errors which can easily be spotted here do occur. The wrong edition may have arrived, or even the wrong book may have been sent, but in the jacket of the one ordered! If there is adequate staff, each item should be collated, but if materials are later found to be imperfect, most vendors will replace them. The invoice is then approved for payment and forwarded to the proper authority and the materials are sent on their way to be processed. A copy (or copies) of the original order slip should be enclosed in each one.

In addition to the general acquisition procedure, there are a number of miscellaneous policies, practices, warnings and suggestions that will be helpful.

Several categories of materials essential to a well-rounded collection are not acquired in the usual way. Serials, including both periodicals and continuations, can be (and usually are) ordered from one agent. In this way a discount can be received, all subscriptions begin at the same time, and only one company need be contacted regarding discrepancies.

Most pamphlets, too, can be ordered from one source. Exceptions would be those from the Superintendent of Documents and free ones. In the case of the latter, it is a good practice to use postal cards which have been preprinted, with just the necessary information to be filled in.

Paperback books may be ordered from a local dealer who has a large stock or from some of the regular book jobbers. If it is desired to have these arrive in any one of the available kinds of reinforced covers, there are companies that provide them. Some firms sell paperbacks in the original and/or reinforced bindings. Again it is important to know these companies, and it is a good idea to examine the workmanship of each before ordering.

Many elementary school library books are purchased prebound, especially those which are used in the primary grades. The justification is that these books receive hard wear and neither trade nor publisher's binding will survive long. The cost of prebound books is greater than those from the publisher, but devotees of them are convinced that they are worth the extra cost and that it is still less expensive than rebinding the book when it gets worn. Again, it must be stressed that experience is the best basis for judgment. Small trial orders will be an excellent way to evaluate the workmanship of the bindings. Each of these companies publishes a list of books available, which naturally is restrictive to a degree. Generally, the companies do have a good reputation for prompt delivery and for reporting very few titles out of stock.

It is probably safe to say that every library and every media center in existence get frequent offers of gifts. Has anyone escaped a call from a well-meaning citizen who has finally decided to get rid of all those National Geographics which have been piling up for years and years? Or a teacher who no longer needs his college textbooks? It will be difficult to refuse such offers unless a policy has been established. The usual practice is to accept gifts with the understanding that only those will be added to the collection

which will be useful; the others will be discarded. Most
bearers of such gifts are glad to get rid of them, but others
may have their feelings hurt. The only position to take is
to stand firm with the adopted policy. Memorial gifts are
not quite the same as donations of materials because they
are usually for just one specific title, and the giver speci-
fies that title or suggests a general category. A special
account should be set up for these funds, and it is usually
a good practice to order them separately, not with a regular
order.

Should duplicates and replacements be included with
orders for new or first copies of books or other materials?
The answer to this question will depend on the local situation. If the order is placed separately and all at the same
time, say just once a year, the cataloging department or
the individual who does his own processing will find the work
easier because new cards will not have to be made for the
entire order. On the other hand, some people report that
it really makes no difference. Their only plea is that the
order slip indicate that initial cataloging need not be done.

Accusations of unfair trade practices have been
charged in recent years against some publishers and the
jobbers who stock their merchandise. These companies
place one fixed price on a book which is available in one
binding only, and no discount is allowed. The decision
whether or not to buy from these firms is the kind of decision which should be made by the purchasing agent or by
the board of education--not by the individual school media
specialist or by the supervisor.

To keep up with newly published materials and to assure a steady flow of materials arriving at the media center
throughout the school year, it is a good practice to space
the orders at regular intervals. There should be more than
one a year; four or five has proved to be a good practice.
Placing several orders a year also makes it possible to provide materials for new curricular offerings which may not
have been anticipated. The work load of the acquisitions
and processing staff will also be more evenly distributed
throughout the year.

The physical requirements of an acquisitions department are few: space for receiving and storing materials
and supplies, as well as desks, chairs, tables, typewriters,
and a calculator. Within the area the furniture and equip-

ment should be arranged in such a way that there is little moving back and forth or wasted motion as the materials travel from one step to another--from input to output in a logical sequence.

The total acquisition process seems complicated to the uninitiated. If, however, it is systematically and efficiently organized and operated, it can be exciting and fascinating to those who are involved in it. A deep sense of satisfaction can result from knowing that one has contributed to a vital service to children and youth.

23. Streamlining for Service

by Richard L. Darling

Reprinted by permission of the American Library
Association and the author, from School Activities
and the Library, 1965.

Changes in American education have increased the
demand for more and better school library services. To
provide library programs adequate to support instruction,
school districts have devised special services to schools
so that librarians, freed from routine and repetitive tasks
associated with the organization and circulation of materials,
can devote more of their time to work with pupils and
teachers.

Centralized Processing

Probably the most important school district service
needed to eliminate duplication of effort in school libraries
is the centralized ordering, cataloging, and physical preparation of materials for use. Centralized cataloging includes
only the classifying of books and the supplying of full sets
of catalog cards. Centralized processing includes both the
cataloging and the physical preparation of books, i.e., marking call numbers on the books and putting cards and pockets
in the books. The only step to be done at the local library
is the filing of catalog cards. A complete centralized processing system includes ordering as well.

Several school districts have cataloged centrally for
their schools for many years. Since 1944 the Georgia State
Department of Education, through its State Catalog Card
Service, has offered catalog cards to both school and public
libraries in Georgia at nominal cost. In the 1963-64 fiscal
year, 4 school districts and 1,413 individual schools participated. In a few states public libraries and area processing centers have offered similar services or more extensive ones, including ordering and physical preparation of

books, to school libraries. More frequently, however, school districts have organized their own central cataloging or processing centers to serve all schools within their jurisdiction. In 1960-61, according to a U.S. Office of Education study, 467 school districts in the United States were providing centralized processing of school library materials for elementary schools, and 239 for secondary schools. [1] No doubt the number of school districts with this service has increased since the study was made.

Practices in centralized processing differ from district to district. In some school districts centralized processing is supplied to elementary schools only. In others processing is done only for new schools; during the summer vacation; or for special materials, such as those purchased with National Defense Education Act funds. Some school districts provide only central ordering and cataloging, and leave full processing to the schools. Many now, however, are providing complete processing for all library books.

A few school districts also process nonprint materials, such as filmstrips, slides, and recordings. The Montgomery County Public Schools, Rockville, Maryland, for example, began by processing books only. As a second step the district started processing all films in the central office inventory and depositing complete sets of cards in each school library for interfiling in the card catalog. Now cards are being prepared for filmstrips, and soon recordings and other instructional materials will be fully processed. This development is probably typical of that in many school districts.

Use of Machines for Processing

Early in the development of centralized processing for school libraries, librarians administering the service turned to machines to increase output and economy of operation and to assure a standardized product. Most processing centers use pasting machines, call-number lettering machines, one of a variety of duplicating machines, and photographic equipment for producing duplicating masters. A few processing centers have added photocopying machines which will copy a full set of commercially printed or locally typed catalog cards for each additional copy of a book.

Commercial Cataloging and Processing

Other school districts have turned to commercial sources for cataloging or processing. For many years school libraries have depended upon the Library of Congress and the. H. W. Wilson Company for printed catalog cards for books. Some publishers now supply sets of catalog cards with their books. Some school districts are buying their books from suppliers who deliver them ready for use, completely processed. Several firms now process books before delivery, either according to a standardized procedure or tailored to fit customer specifications. One large eastern school district pays only 85c per book to receive its purchases preprocessed, and was able to contract at 65c per book for a large order for new schools. Ordinarily most schools would have to pay from 70c to $1. 70 per book for this service, depending upon the type of material involved and the kind of processing demanded. The availability of printed cards and preprocessed books has great advantages for small school districts, for which the cost of equipment and the difficulties of employing staff for processing centers may be too great.

Cooperation among School Districts

Whether each school district should set up its own processing center is doubtful, for an effectively administered processing center can easily serve more than one district. A state school library supervisor from a state where four large school districts operate central processing centers has indicated that she feels these four are probably sufficient to serve the state's smaller school districts, and is urging them to extend their services to the rest of the state's schools through cooperative arrangements.

In other states, particularly those with large numbers of small school districts, central processing centers to serve several districts might be organized as cooperative ventures and administered by one school district for all of them or by an intermediate unit of school administration. Support for these centers would have to be apportioned among the cooperating school districts, and legislative action could be sought to secure state assistance. It has also been found feasible for schools and public libraries in an area to cooperate in a processing endeavor.

Data Processing Equipment for Ordering and Processing

As school districts adopt the use of data processing equipment, they will be able to process a far greater volume of school library materials more efficiently than they do now. Punched cards on which essential data have been coded make it possible to reduce the number of routine procedures to be done manually. Several school districts already use data processing equipment for acquisitions, and at least one school district has proposed to handle all processing of books by such machines, including the preparation of book catalogs.

Montgomery County, Maryland, has begun a data processing program which will be used throughout the various steps involved in providing materials to schools. Though much of the plan remains to be implemented, it provides an outline of ways in which data processing can assist in streamlining procedures of evaluation, selection, ordering, and complete processing.

When the school district requests copies of instructional materials for evaluation or receives complimentary copies for its review program, punched cards are prepared for each title, including cards for control purposes, for reviews by members of the professional staff, for use in preparation of approved lists, and for ordering. After reviews have been written, additional data from them are punched into the cards, and masters are prepared by machine from which lists are duplicated. Orders submitted from schools are entered on punched cards so that the machines can produce combined purchase orders with materials correctly listed for each vendor, and can provide lists with the necessary information to expedite the processing and delivery of materials to each school.

Printed Book Catalogs

A logical future step in planning might be the printed book catalog prepared by machine methods. Some public libraries have abandoned card catalogs in favor of book catalogs. Before school districts transfer their card catalogs to books, however, there should be a careful study made of their value for schools. Individual school libraries do not have the same relationship to the district central office that public library branches have to the main library with its large supporting collection. Nor has the exchange of materials, common within public library systems, become widespread in school districts. The book catalog facilitates this exchange. School districts also need to determine whether such exchange of materials is desirable for improving school library services. The answers to these questions are the important factors in deciding on book catalogs. Compared to these questions, technical problems are minor.

Data Processing Equipment for Information Retrieval

Some schoolmen have proposed the use of data processing equipment for information retrieval systems for school libraries. The value of such retrieval for school libraries should be seriously questioned, since the consensus at present is that the mechanical storage and retrieval of information hold little promise for libraries with general collections.

Undoubtedly there are other ways in which school districts can streamline routines, such as by centralized production of some kinds of instructional materials. School librarians should explore innovations which promise greater efficiency. The sure test of the value of such innovations is that they free librarians for selection of materials and for service to students and teachers. The goal of streamlining must be improved instruction through better school library service.

Note

1. Mary Helen Mahar and Doris C. Holladay, Statistics of Public School Libraries, 1960-61: Part I, Basic Tables (Washington, D. C. : U. S. Dept. of Health, Education, and Welfare, Office of Education, 1964), p. 69.

24. Cataloging and Processing Non-Book Materials--
A True Instructional Resources Center Concept

by Robert A. Veihman

Reprinted by permission of the Association for Educational Communications and Technology, from Audiovisual Instruction, December 1970.

It is almost normal procedure for a new junior college to organize an instructional resources center (IRC) rather than the more traditional library and audiovisual department. Since most educators realize that learning may result from watching a film or filmloop as well as from reading a book, it is only logical that all media be housed together in one central location. This is the first step in organizing an instructional resources center. Steps two and three follows--intershelving all media and interfiling cards into the central card catalog. In order to accomplish this, it is necessary that all materials be cataloged and processed. Why not catalog and process filmloops, transparencies, filmstrips, and study prints on oceanography and place them on the shelves next to the books on this subject?

Providing the means to learn is the main objective of an instructional resources center; every possible step should be taken to accomplish this. A physical education student or faculty member looking for material on gymnastics should find not only books on the subject but all other available materials. Filing all cards in one card catalog would make all materials easily retrievable.

Here at the College of DuPage we are taking all three steps and are thrilled with the results. It is most rewarding to walk through the IRC and see students reading at tables, watching a motion picture at a carrel, or listening to a tape. To observe students checking out books, films, filmstrips, tapes, phonodiscs, slides, study prints, filmloops, transparencies, and kits makes our work all the more worthwhile.

The concept of our IRC was formed three years ago
when the college was originated, thanks to a director who
was able to foresee the advantages of an instructional resources center and a president who shared the ideas. Our
staff consists of 9 professionals (all with advanced degrees)
and 15 full-time classified personnel members, serving over
6, 000 students and a faculty of approximately 300. To serve
the students and faculty the IRC staff is divided into four
divisions: Utilization and Distribution; Production; Acquisition and Preparation; and the Developmental Learning Laboratory. Each division is headed by a director who in turn
is under the direction of the Associate Dean of Faculty, Instructional Services. Each division is dependent upon the
others.

Little information is available on the cataloging and
processing of nonbook materials. Because of this our Acquisition and Preparation division has prepared a processing
manual for book and nonbook materials. The paragraphs
that follow are a summary of this manual.

Tapes: There are usually no Library of Congress
cards available for tapes; therefore, original cataloging is
done. Catalog cards are typed on dark green banded cards
and filed in the central card catalog. The tape is then processed. Two labels are typed and affixed to the reel and to
the text. The LC classification number is the only information given on the label. A card and pocket are typed and
pasted inside the box top. The title of the tape and the
classification number are typed on both. A label giving the
title and classification number is prepared and affixed to the
spine of the tape box.

Phonodiscs: Fewer than 3 phonodiscs are housed in
commercially-produced plastic record jackets. Multi-volume
recordings are housed in their original containers. Library
of Congress cards are available for most phonodiscs. After
the classification number has been typed on the dark blue
banded catalog cards they are filed and the phonodisc is processed. A label giving the classification number is typed
and affixed to the record jacket in the lower left hand corner. A card giving the title and classification number is
prepared and inserted into the pocket of the plastic record
jacket. If the phonodiscs are kept in their original box, a
card and pocket are typed and pasted inside the top of the
box. Two labels, giving the classification number, are typed
affixed to the center of the disc and to the text.

Filmstrips: All filmstrips are housed in boxes which we purchase, be it one filmstrip or a set of 30. If there are no Library of Congress cards available, original cataloging is done and the cards are typed. Banding for filmstrips is black. When the cards are ready for filing, the filmstrip is ready for processing. A round label is typed giving the classification number. Before it is affixed to the top of the filmstrip can it is cut in half so that the title is not covered. If there are two copies of the filmstrip, "c. 1" and "c. 2" are added after the classification number. This also applies if there are several parts in the set, "pt. 1, " and "pt. 2, " etc. is added to the classification number. Two labels are typed giving the classification number. One is affixed to the side of the filmstrip can and the other is affixed to the text. A label is prepared giving the classification number and is affixed to the front of the filmstrip box. Another label is prepared and affixed to the front of the pamphlet folder which houses the text. A card is prepared giving the title and classification number; it is then placed in the filmstrip box. Another card and pocket are prepared and pasted inside the folder which houses the text.

Motion Pictures: Library of Congress cards are usually available for motion pictures. The classification number is typed on cards which have a red band. The cards are then filed and the motion picture is processed. A card and pocket are typed giving the title and classification number. These are then attached inside the lid of the film can. If the film has a text, a label is typed giving the call number. The text is then placed inside the film can. A label is prepared giving the title and classification number. This label is then affixed to the perimeter of the film can.

Because of the size and shape of motion picture storage cans, we have not intershelved motion pictures. Nevertheless, the cards are filed in the card catalog.

Slides: We have two means of housing slides: more than 40 slides on one subject are processed in carousel trays; fewer than 40 slides are processed in plastic slide holders which are then inserted into pamphlet folders. Each slide is identified by its title, classification number, and its number in the set. This information is typed on a label and cut to fit the slide or the information is printed on the slide. Even though this is a time-consuming process; it assures that each slide will be returned to its original set when removed. Since few slides have Library of Con-

gress cards, original cataloging is done. The information
and classification number are typed on a light blue banded
card, the cards are filed, and the slides are processed.

    More than 40 slides: A label is typed giving the call
number and affixed to the carousel tray. Two title labels
are prepared. One label is affixed to the carousel tray, the
other to the spine of the box. A card and pocket are typed
giving the title and classification number which are then
pasted inside the top of the carousel box. A label is typed
giving the call number and then affixed to the spine of the
carousel box.

    Fewer than 40 slides: A label is typed giving the
classification number and then affixed to the text. The text
is taped inside the back cover of the folder. A card and
pocket are typed giving the classification number and title.
The pocket is pasted inside the front cover of the folder.
A label is typed giving the title of the slides and is then
affixed to the front of the folder. A label is prepared giving classification number. It is also affixed to the front of
the folder.

    Filmloops: Filmloops are processed in their own
boxes. Library of Congress catalog cards are usually
available; if not, original cataloging is done. After the
classification number has been typed on yellow banded
cards, the filmloop is processed. A card is typed giving
the title and classification number. The card is then placed
in the filmloop box. A label is typed giving the classification number. This label is affixed to the filmloop cartridge.
If there is a text, another label is typed and affixed to the
front of the text. A label is typed giving the call number
and affixed to the spine of the filmloop box.

    Kits: There are usually no Library of Congress
cards for kits. They are processed and shelved in their
own boxes. After the cards have been typed on orange
banded cards, the cards are filed and the kit is processed.
A label is typed giving the classification number and affixed
to the front of the box.

    Study Prints: Study prints are processed and housed
in their own containers. After the cards have been typed
on purple banded cards they are filed, and the prints are
processed. A label is typed giving the classification number and affixed to the text. A label for each print is typed

giving the classification number and the print number. These labels are affixed to the prints. A card and pocket are typed giving the title and classification number. The pocket is either pasted inside the box or placed loose in the folder. A label is typed giving the classification number and affixed to the front of the box or folder.

Transparencies: Each set of transparencies is cataloged and processed in a commercially prepared box. After the cards have been typed on brown banded cards, they are filed and the transparencies are processed. A label is typed for each transparency in the set giving the classification number and its own number then affixed to the transparency. A card and pocket are typed giving the classification number and title. The pocket is either pasted inside the box top or placed loose in the box. A label is typed giving the classification number and is affixed to the front of the box or folder.

Combinations (Filmstrip/Phonodiscs, Filmstrip/Tapes, Slides/Tapes, etc.): Whenever we process such a combination, the rules are used which apply to each medium. The only difference would be that each item would have the same classification number to be shelved side by side.

In the three years of operation, our collection consists of 32,000 books, 600 filmloops, 1,200 filmstrips, 6 kits, 370 motion pictures, 2,300 phonodiscs, 24,000 slides, 440 study prints, 2,300 tapes, 900 transparencies. Even though it has been a long, difficult and expensive task to catalog and process all these items, we feel that it is the only way to make all materials easily accessible and retrievable to faculty members and students. We do not hesitate to shelve a small book next to a large book. Why should it concern us to shelve a small filmstrip next to a large book? Because we at the College of DuPage feel that learning may result from numerous means, we are trying to make all materials available to everyone. After all, this is our main function.

25. A Notched Card System for AV Libraries

by John G. Vogeler

Reprinted by permission of the Association for
Educational Communications and Technology, from
Audiovisual Instruction, September 1969.

Sooner or later, almost every AV library reaches a
point where the work load demands a "systems analysis, "
with a view to improving the overall effectiveness of operations. This was the situation at Southeast Suburban Audio-
Visual Library in Wayne, Pennsylvania--an AV cooperative
that serves 103 schools with a total of 68, 000 students. The
library has over 3500 films, plus special filmstrips and
slides. Last year over 31, 000 films were lent to member
schools.

Increased demand for films had exceeded the capacity
of the small staff to cope with it, even working overtime.
Further, there was no efficient way to draw off statistics
from requisition copies. At the suggestion of one of the
directors, a notched-card system was investigated and installed. It has proved to be extremely effective for requi-
sitioning, scheduling, dispatching, and usage analysis of the
library's audiovisual materials.

The new system revolves around the use of a three-
part Keysort Requisition set. Keysort forms come with a
series of holes around the perimeter. When notched, these
holes become coded data, which can be quickly sorted and
arranged via the Keysort method. Requisitions are prepared
in batches for each member school. The name of the school
can be imprinted, using a metal Addressograph plate, or
left blank for the school to fill in. In all cases, however,
holes representing the school and district number are grooved
(notched) in the margin of the forms. Prepared forms are
sent to each school.

To order, the teacher selects the desired AV material from the library's catalog. He creates the requisition by
filling in the AV catalog number, date requested (and alter-

162

nate), name of requesting teacher, and title of AV material. He also checks the type of material; area of usage; and latitude that can be used in scheduling delivery. The top copy is retained as a control by the school, and the balance of the set is forwarded to the library.

All requisitions received at the library are first notched for catalog number, type of material, and subject area. They are then sorted by the Keysort method into catalog number sequence. This greatly facilitates checking the reservation file to determine whether or not the item is available for the week requested. If it is available, the school number is posted in the applicable week box on the reservation file, and the confirmed week number is entered and notched on the requisition.

If the item is not available for the date requested, but delivery can be made at an acceptable alternate date, this date is used instead. In some cases, the item cannot be delivered. The second copy (Confirmation of Delivery or Notice of Non-Delivery) allows the library to merely circle the reason for nondelivery.

Confirmed and Non-Delivery requisitions are sorted (by the Keysort method) by school each day. The top copies are removed and sent to their respective schools. The last copies (on card stock) are sorted by delivery week and filed.

Daily, cards for items to be shipped are pulled and given to the shipping department. Here they are sorted into catalog number sequence for picking materials from the shelves (stored in catalog number order). After the items have been bagged for delivery, the card requisition copies are filed by delivery week.

Incoming AV materials are first matched with their control copy before being inspected and placed back in the racks. Unmatched cards are followed up to learn the reason for nonreturn.

It will be noted that these procedures involve sorting the requisitions at almost every step. This is where the Keysort facility for sorting or arranging in sequence a large number of requisitions in seconds saves a great deal of time. This facility really comes into its own, however, in the preparation of usage reports.

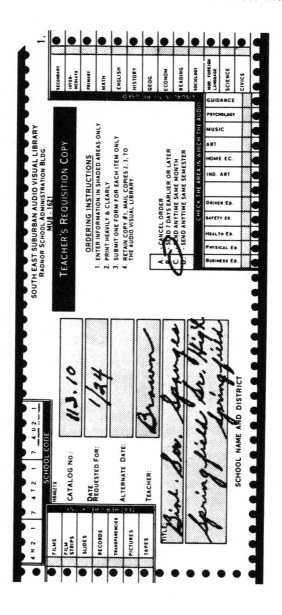

This 3-part requisition speeds handling of materials and provides a built-in facility retrieving information and compiling statistics.

Each year, the library prepares a usage report for each school, listing AV materials supplied by subject area and by type. In addition to this annual report, the library is in a position to prepare such usage reports at any time, if requested to do so. Another analysis report--a "not available" report by catalog number--helps the library decide when one or more extra prints of a given film should be ordered. Conversely, a periodic usage report by catalog number will spot "out of favor" items that can be eliminated from the library.

Florence Blank, director of the library states that the system has substantially reduced the amount of staff time required to process a requisition. Use of the multiple-part set also saves teacher time, and improves communications between the library and the member schools.

26. Computers in School Libraries

by Elfrieda McCauley

Reprinted by permission of the American Library Association and the author, from School Libraries, Winter 1971.

A yawning gap exists between developments of electronic data processing (EDP) in education and the use school librarians have made of this potentially great tool of the academic information explosion. For the most part, the school librarian has dealt with the educational challenges of the 60s with little more than a typewriter and a Potdevin paster. Scientific management practices have rarely affected school libraries. Even computers and schools are rather new acquaintances.

However, in even moderately innovative schools teachers are meeting their classes with computer print-out class lists. Computers assemble and organize into neat, modular time slots a bewildering mass of large-group small-group teacher relationships. Report cards are delivered in long sheets of perforated print-outs. Complete attendance records for an entire school are on hand before ten in the morning. There's a teletypewriter hooked up to a computer center in the Math Department, and down the hall, business students are learning to keypunch and program in COBOL.

A confrontation with the electronic age is imminent. The unwary school librarian is in for a rude awakening. The educational environment with which she has been comfortably familiar will have moved into the computer age-- and will have left her behind in the technological backwaters of the 1920s.

If she is a school librarian who began her professional career stretching out a miniscule book budget with free and inexpensive vertical file materials--her success largely measured by her effectiveness in shepherding a crew of library helpers through an apprenticeship course in library housekeeping--she has already survived some teeth-jarring

166

changes of fortune. Since the first federal aid for school library resources, she has seen her collection grow in number of books per pupil and is reaching toward the goal recommended in the 1969 Standards. By these standards, she is
vested with specific responsibilities for incorporating her
school's slides, films, tapes, videotapes, kits, dioramas,
and realia into her collections and bibliographies. She is a
department chairman sharing in curriculum decisions.

The school's textbook system (she's responsible for
that too, according to the new Standards) is in chaos since
the single-textbook-per-student-per-course system that made
life so simple in the old days was abandoned. Her multi-
media faculty, inspired by federally funded summer workshops, wants the new media in abundance, and close at hand,
in decentralized resource centers.

At the same time, the librarian realizes from past
experience, the additional staff members, professional and
supportive, recommended by the Standards are still some
fiscal years away.

What does the school librarian do, then, who realizes
that there is a computer in the Board of Education Office or
Town Hall that is doing good work issuing payroll checks,
attendance records, class schedules, and report cards?
Professional literature will give her little help; the literature
of education even less. What has been accomplished through
KWIC and KWOC indexes, though impressive, offers little
help. Nor do MARC tape accomplishments, MEDLARS,
SYMBIOSIS, or the published plans of interuniversity cooperative cataloging via bibliographic data banks. College libraries and special libraries have found uses for computers--
school libraries rarely. EDP is pioneering territory for
school librarians.

What Kind of Computer?

Having read everything there is to read on computer
applications to librarianship in general, the school librarian
must conclude that academic librarians--indeed, librarians
of any kind--rarely go shopping for computers of their own
choosing. The time will probably come when the librarian
or library supervisor may share in determining the characteristics of a new installation. In the meantime, to get the
benefit of what's available, she must plan her uses of a

computer to fit the capabilities of the existing equipment.

Following specifications painstakingly gleaned from
her reading, she'll hope for a computer with tremendous
storage capabilities, high level language capability, and re-
spectable memory. When she looks over what's available,
she'll find it's one superbly efficient in accounting operations. It has small memory, limited storage--limited perhaps to the deck of cards being manipulated.

She will hope to have connection with the computer
by remote console. She may have to settle for an easily
accessible keypunch. She may hope for something attractive in the way of print-out typeface. If the computer is a
new model, she may be lucky. The chances are she'll
have to do without some essential punctuation and without
lower case.

Since the Board of Education foots the bill, she
won't ask about relative speed of the machine components--
but that's important, too.

And there's the amount of time she'll need for the
school library jobs. She won't know at first, but will soon
find out that it's wise to schedule her jobs around payroll,
tax bills, income tax time, and other regular fiscal visita-
tions. The librarian will be bumped as surely as a half-
fare student on a fully booked flight. Beyond that, she'll
probably get the go-ahead signal to use the computer as
best she knows how.

What Will It Do?

Having discovered the capabilities and ground rules
for using the computer, the school librarian will have the
job of deciding what part of her library routines can be
safely and profitably turned over to this beast of higher
intelligence.

It is possible that a school librarian, considering
the advantages of a computer in her professional life, may
dream of having a book catalog of her collection. No school
librarian who has ever had a class of thirty children close
in on a single card catalog during a 40-minute class research
assignment can fail to see the advantages of a book catalog
for a school library. To put a copy of one's total instruc-

tional resources in the hands of every teacher and every student, is a noble dream. Unfortunately, this is likely to be the last fruit of her relationship with the Board of Education's computer. Very large systems are required to do meaningful bibliographic jobs in this area. She must save that dream until she has money in her account for an outside job, and concentrate, in the meantime, on assigning to the computer those housekeeping chores whose disposition will give her time to be the type of librarian that the 1969 Standards expect her to be.

Shifting from the third person to the second, at this point: what can a computer do for you, then--even the most run-of-the-mill, punched-card-input, minimum-storage electronic workhorse, purchased with no thought to library requirements? Quite a few things, if you will think through the library jobs that correspond in some way to those repetitive routine tasks for which the ordinary business machine was designed in the first place.

Do you type a weekly or monthly new acquisitions list? Having typed it once do you use it to update, separately and manually, your various subject bibliographies? Just suppose you were to keypunch that new books list, keycoded to signal which books are to be included in what bibliographies. At the end of a year you'll have a sizeable deck of punched cards representing your recent titles. Do you want a list of the new books on civil rights? On oceanography? Retrieve on the key code and get a print-out by subject.

Do you want a subject guide to your new titles? Interfile your acquisitions by Dewey number and arrange the titles under subject heading cards. It's not a book catalog, but it will do until such a time as you are on line to a data bank where Books in Print titles are stored by Standard Book Number, and you can order, receive catalog cards, and get a print-out for books received, with no more effort than it now takes to type out your book order on multiple copy order slips. In the meantime, even an IBM 360/ 20 with an 8K memory will do the job described above. If the installation at your disposal can do more, you can do more with it.

Remember that the computer equipment you are proposing to employ has been designed for fast, efficient processing of business data. Expect, therefore, to find your

greatest advantage in using data processing equipment in
four major areas of school library management: ordering,
payment, and budget control; listing operations; serials record keeping; and, perhaps, handling circulation. All of
these are adaptations of office management routines which
business machinery has been handling mechanically for at
least thirty years.

Think through your manual procedures. How many
times do you type a title that you order? How many times
do you file a card and search for it again--manually, of
course? The chances are that you can--in a single operation, with the simplest EDP equipment--record all information you need about that book once and thereafter, list and
relist, arrange and rearrange mechanically, and print out
in a variety of acceptable forms any of that information according to your requirements. If you can find a way of assigning a class number to a book you are ordering, you can
plan your system so that your original order will generate a
spine label, the book pocket information, a punched card
shelflist card, and a circulation card (which you can use for
reordering if the book is lost or chewed up by the family
dog). That original deck of your order cards can be sorted
by publisher and its financial information can be totaled and
posted against your account. It can generate checks for payment, and, in the end, produce a new acquisitions list.

If you run a library with an elaborate circulation control system, and your computer is reasonably accessible,
data processing equipment, combined with a machine-readable
borrower's identification card, a machine-readable book card,
and a time recording device, can automate that system and
keep a record of your circulation statistics. However, most
school libraries are looking for ways to relax rather than to
elaborate the structure of their circulation systems, and so,
undoubtedly, are you.

In most libraries, school and otherwise, the check-
ing-in of periodicals and the reordering of issues that fail
to appear when due is a chore fraught with wearisome detail. It's possible to design a punched card slotted to register all expected issues so that notices regarding missing issues are automatically printed out.

Computers and Systems

Thus far I have considered computer applications to single library situations.

In business, the computer is causing a recentralization of operations,[1] and in library management, the trend is toward application of larger and larger computers to larger and larger library management jobs. The tendency to combine single library units into systems for greater efficiency and better service is likely to continue as central computer services become available. One such program, which will provide total information services for a seven-county metropolitan area around Minneapolis, is planned for St. Louis Park, Minnesota. A similar center in Hobbs, New Mexico, will supply EDP services for school libraries of five cooperating districts of Lea County. Los Angeles has already computerized its school library ordering operations. In Schenectady, a regional center is automating acquisitions, cataloging, and some of the steps in the processing of materials. In Yonkers an EDP Center is serving upwards of sixty public and twenty parochial schools with a staff no larger than that of a well-staffed high school library.

Business Management, Not Information Science

For the most part, data processing services for school libraries are not examples of sophisticated information handling--except in the broadest sense--but simply good business management techniques. School librarians and library administrators are setting out to do what any business office handling purchase orders, customer accounts, and merchandise processing has done with business machinery, with increasing efficiency, ever since Hollerith invented the punched card in 1888. They are techniques for handling routine jobs that need doing quickly and well if only to free school librarians from the drudgery of library housekeeping long enough to be school librarians.

This is not to say we must put aside our dreams of automated libraries. They are persistent dreams that will not die, either in library literature or in librarians. Such dreams may, indeed, be closer to coming true than we think, based on the projections made by C. Walter Stone for Columbia City, Maryland,[2] by J. C. R. Licklider,[3] and by William T. Knox.[4]

A more realistic appraisal of what the future holds
for school libraries is implied in an account of a conference
attended by 181 university communications leaders at Boulder, Colorado, in the summer of 1966. According to the report published a core staff of EDUCOM, an interuniversity
communications council, is presently at work planning a pilot educational network, EDUNET, with switching centers in
Denver, Chicago, Pittsburgh, and Boston. If compatibility
between local and regional networks and already existing
computer facilities can be achieved, it's possible that a full
range of communication experiences, voice and video, via
digital and analog computer, will be nationally accessible to
the university community. National ETV, shared computer-
assisted and programed instruction, telelectures, telecon-
ferences will be possible. Through EDUNET, also, libraries will be on line to bibliographic and data banks.

Here again, participation of school systems is not
specifically mentioned, but the implications are there, nevertheless. Ties between local schools, ETV, and regional
networks already exist. Interaction between universities
and their dependent communities is present and growing.
The provinciality of local schools and local school libraries
is surely in jeopardy.

So then, is there a telephone jack for a computer installation in your school library? Are you ready for the
teletypewriter console, cathode ray tube, and electronic
stylus? It could be that by the time you have learned to
eyeball-read your deck of keypunched book orders, the network node that connects your local, state, or regional sub-
network with EDUNET or its equivalent communication network will put you, by interconnecting interface, directly on
line to the moon!

Notes

1. Don D. Bushnell and Dwight W. Allen. The Computer
   in American Education (New York: John Wiley and
   Sons, 1967).

2. C. Walter Stone. A Library Program for Columbia
   (Pittsburgh: University of Pittsburgh, 1965).

3. J. C. R. Licklider. Libraries of the Future (Cambridge, Mass.: M. I. T. Press, 1965).

4. William T. Knox. "The New Look in Information Systems," in Edgar L. Morphet and Charles O. Ryan, Designing Education for the Future, vol. 1: Prospective Changes in Society by 1980 (Cambridge, Mass.: M. I. T. Press, 1967).

27. A Slide Classification System*

by Edward Kazlauskas

All instructional research materials need organization for retrievability by instructors, students, or any library or media center patron. Access to book materials has traditionally been via card or book catalog, with their intellectual content indicated by subject headings and classification schemes.

Book and book-related classification schemes, such as the Dewey Decimal and Library of Congress Classification Schemes, also index the shelf location of the material. Other classification schemes and specialized subject headings have been developed to handle other types of materials, such as the ANSCR Scheme, or the alphanumerical system for classification of recordings. The majority of these classification schemes were developed prior to the advent of the computer and thus are basically manual. Now, however, a number of new systems have been developed which utilize fully the power of the computer for information retrieval. A Slide Classification System[1] describes one of these new computerized systems.

Slides have always been an important medium in the fields of art and art history. Recently the use of slides has become widespread in other instructional areas, such as theatre arts, architecture, the biological and health sciences, and every other area of instruction where visual representation is important.

A number of manual classification systems had been developed in these subject matter fields, most of them originally specifically for cataloging art slides. The classification schemes of the Fogg Museum and the Metropolitan Museum of Art are good examples. When any institution attempted to use a slide classification system to cover the full breadth of knowledge of curriculum, it either had to

---

*Reprinted by permission of the author.

adapt an art slide scheme or develop its own system. The usual results were not satisfactory. A new method was mandatory.

Thus, when the field of slide classification was investigated by the University of California at Santa Cruz through a grant from the Council on Library Resources, the following points were deemed to be of utmost importance:

(1) that the classification scheme should be universal in nature, covering all knowledge areas;

(2) that user browsability through the slide collection be considered in its development.

Using these concepts and the utilization of computer technology, a new classification scheme was designed. This system has been implemented by the University of California, Santa Cruz; the California Institute of the Arts; Mount San Antonio Community College, and a number of other institutions.

A Slide Classification System--general view

The main objective in classifying pictorial images according to any slide classification system is visual content. Visual content of pictorial images is categorized into three broad areas:

(1) a representation of an historical event, person, etc.

(2) a representation of a work of art;

(3) a representation of a scientific or technical concept, principle, etc.

All pictorial images are classified into one of these three broad areas--with history reserved as the field for those items which cannot be classified specifically.

Each image is cataloged and the following information is gathered:

(1) a call number;
(2) descriptive information about the slide;
(3) location of the original image;
(4) source of the item.

This information is typed on a label and placed on the
slide as in the example.

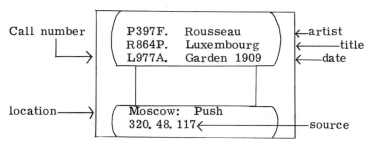

Call number
P397F.   Rousseau   ←artist
R864P.   Luxembourg   ←———title
L977A.   Garden 1909   ←——date

location——→
Moscow: Push
320. 48. 117←————————source

The same information is used to create machine
readable data by input onto punched cards.   Each card contains fifteen fields of data.   These fields are used to create sort tags, allowing computer sorting for order variations in computer-printed indexes.   Typical examples of
both a key punch card and a computer produced index from
many such cards are reproduced on page 177.

Slide Classification System--Specifics

The example chosen for classification is a slide of a
painting entitled "The Luxembourg Gardens" by Henri Rousseau, the fourth item found in the sample computer produced index.   The book, A Slide Classification System, contains the correct classification numbers; however, other
sources may also be required in order to obtain necessary
subject, pictorial, or biographical information.

The first consideration is to determine into which of
the three broad subject categories the pictorial image would
fall.   In this case it is obviously art, since the slide is a
representation of a work of art.   The classifier would turn
to the "Art" classification section (see the summary copy of
the classification schedule that appears at the end of this
article).

There are eight general chronological periods for art
classification.   The appropriate chronological period for
Henri Rousseau (1844-1910) is the 20th century, represented,
according to the tables, by the letter P.   The next numbers,
reflecting the country and geographical division--397 for
France--are obtained from a table of countries and geograph-

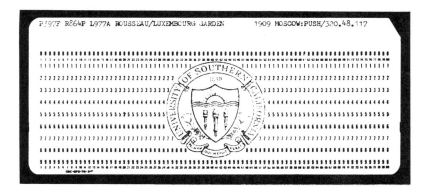

[Sample computer produced index*]

P397F.	R864P.	P232A.	ROUSSEAU	PARIS BRIDGE
P397F.	R864P.	M645A.	ROUSSEAU	MILL AT ENFORT
P397F.	R864P.	L977A.	ROUSSEAU	LUXEMBOURG GARDENS
P397F.	R864P.	L265A.	ROUSSEAU	LANE
P397F.	R864P.	L263A.	ROUSSEAU	LANDSCAPE:MAN FISHING

continuation	1898-	PARIS:PC	320.61.89
of original	1902-	NEW YORK:PC	320.65.99
index line →	1909	MOSCOW:PUSH	320.48.117
	1905-	PC	320.44.79
	1897	PARIS:PC	320.59.83

*In sequence by artist according to country and chrono-
logical period

ic areas. The medium is a painting by a known artist--
coded as the letter F. Therefore, the first line of the
classification numbers is the field P397F.

The next field reflects the origin of the art work; in
this case the work is attributed to Henri Rousseau, an individual. A four-character Cutter number (a numbering
system used to place similar authors and artists together)
is assigned from the Cutter tables, also located in A Slide
Classification System. The appropriate Cutter number for
this particular artist is R864. A letter places the pictorial
representation into a subject area--in this case, P, since P
is the code letter for a painting of a landscape, seascape,
or cityscape--the Luxembourg Gardens being a visual representation of actual gardens in the city of Paris. Thus the
second line of the classification is R864P.

Another four character group is obtained from the
Cutter tables to represent the title, L977. The last numbers to be assigned are used to denote the view or views
represented by the art work. In this case the letter A is
assigned from the tables, signifying an exterior site or general view. Thus, using the classification and Cutter tables
in A Slide Classification System, an appropriate and unique
classification number has been developed for the slide--
P397F. R864P. L977A.

The artist's name and title of the work are also
part of the classification scheme. These two items, plus
the date of its completion, are typed in the upper right
hand corner. The date of the work, the city, and a code
for the location within the city are gathered; e. g., 1909,
Moscow, and Push for the Pushkin Museum. The last information gathered is a code for the commercial source of
the slide. This information will probably be unique to the
institution classifying the slide. After all of the necessary
information has been gathered about the slide, labels are
typed and placed on the slide.

The same information that is typed on the labels is
used to create indexes by computer. The data is keypunched onto keypunch cards, sorted according to the various sort tags, thus producing the several needed indexes to
the slide collection. The slides are filed in appropriate
storage units and are then available for the user.

Conclusion

This slide classification system truly utilizes the power of the computer. At present, the system operates on a batch processing mode, with retrieval by visual search through a printed index. Since the data is in machine-readable form, the system can be developed into an on-line input and on-line search with visual CRT (cathode-ray-tube) display.

An institution has the option of specifying the sequence of the indexes; a few main indexes can be provided and specialized indexes can be prepared upon user demand. It is also of interest to note that this system is equally adaptable to picture collections. Truly, we have seen developed a universal slide classification scheme.

Note

1. Simons, Wendell W., and Tansey, Luraine C. A Slide Classification System for the Organization and Automatic Indexing of Interdisciplinary Collections of Slides and Pictures. Santa Cruz, Calif.: University of California, Santa Cruz, 1970.

CLASSIFICATION SCHEDULE SUMMARY

HISTORY

Field 1.	Chronological period
Field 2.	country
Field 3.	subject
Field 4.	subdivision by subject
Field 5.	primary keyword
Field 6.	format
Field 7.	-
Field 8.	secondary keyword
Field 9.	detail number
Field 10.	additional detail number

ART

Field 1.	Chronological period
Field 2.	country
Field 3.	medium
Field 4.	style
Field 5.	origin (artist or city of origin)
Field 6.	subject
Field 7.	subdivision by subject
Field 8.	title
Field 9.	detail number
Field 10.	additional detail number

SCIENCE

Field 1.	Science group
Field 2.	country
Field 3.	subject
Field 4.	subdivision of subject
Field 5.	primary keyword
Field 6.	-
Field 7.	-
Field 8.	secondary keyword
Field 9.	format
Field 10.	detail number

PART IV

SELECT NONBOOK MEDIA--
PREPARATION AND USE

28. Toward Media Competence:
     An Experiment in Multi-Media Education

     by James J. Higgins

Reprinted from Media and Methods, April 1970,
by permission of the publisher and the author.

Perhaps the movement toward media based instruction is not a revolution, and perhaps its opponents are not
inclined to issue such sweeping indictments. It sometimes
seems, however, that the misuse of media is a calculated
machination designed to discredit any but the pencil and paper approach. Educational television and its big brother,
the instructional film, provide the most glaring examples,
but this misappropriation often exhibits itself in the use of
all the vehicles which have been parked under the banner,
educational media.

Take a boring, 6'2" math teacher, stuff him into a
24-square inch box and what do you get? Nothing more
than electronically proliferated boredom, reduced to scale.
This "shrink it and spread it approach" is somewhat like
tacking wings and propellors on a space ship. Not that
making a master teacher available to greater numbers of
students is a poor objective, but it is valid to join Miss
Lee in asking, "Is that all there is?"

Much of what is happening is directly traceable to a
case of elliptical logic. Someone, somewhere along the
line discovered that outside of school the kids are subject
to seven trillion inputs (whatever that is) per month, while
in school the kids receive less than half an input per year.
Since kids are energetic out of school and lethargic in
school, it was easy to conclude that increasing the in-
school input count to a zillion trillion would immediately
electrify the kids. It is true that the kids were shocked.
It used to be that the hallways belonged to them. These
were the only places in the school where they could speak
and be heard. Now they have to compete with the audio-
visual aide who pushes his clinkety-clank projector cart

from room to room during class change.

The film titles often tell the story, especially when they range from Telephone Manners Matter to How to Eat a Banana Without Peeling the Skin, or the omnipresent This Is Your City, winner of countless Academic Awards. No matter what city or town this film concerns itself with, it always has a hypnotic, dreamlike effect. After five minutes, even the most suspicious viewer begins to imagine he has drunk one too many holiday toasts and has zonked out on the model train platform, right under the fountain in the center of Plasticville's town square.

So what can the machines do to help? Can the machines teach? It is equally as absurd to ask if a teacher can teach, because neither teacher nor machine can do anything more than facilitate learning. Going back to prehistoric times, even before the coming of the Carousel projector, the role of the teacher was to stimulate the students, cause them to question, then help direct them as they searched for answers. Mass education has helped eliminate the first two steps and limited the third to providing a textbook page number. It is still the teacher's responsibility to find the most effective method of performing all of his services. If a multimedia approach is to be a part of this method; it must move in two directions. It must first become quality rather than quantity conscious. Secondly, it must help free the kids from their desk-prison and make it more possible for them to investigate their world.

As to the first, David A. Sohn, in the February, 1969 issue of this magazine, suggested a "Multi-Sensory Approach to Writing, Reading and Discussion. " He was concerned in his article with only one medium, "sensitive, imaginative film art, " but his method is applicable to all media since what he advocated was: (a) stimulating the kids with a powerful aesthetic experience, (b) allowing them to react dynamically, then, (c) helping them to respond creatively. This is an example of the movement away from the tendency to use films, filmstrips, slides, etc. only as information dispensers and as rewards. To be totally effective, however, this kind of approach must be joined with one that will allow the machines to facilitate a two-communication process.

Imagine if the telephone operated in such a way that only one-way communication was possible. In other words, the caller could speak but not be answered, and the receiver of the call could listen but not speak. Now imagine that, instead of being gradually exposed to it, growing as it grew, you were born into the world of instant information. From the day you were born you were inundated with sounds and images. How do you respond to your environment? Man prefers to respond in an eye for an eye kind of way. In the old days, a student would read a book and respond with a poem, story or essay. The pace of his world was slow, his response was slow. How does today's kid respond to his EasyRiderAgnewMansonLennonPeaceDraftWarWallace CleaverJonesSupremesMyLaiPillCancer kind of world? He might speed up his responses with LSD or slow the world down with marijuana, but he won't look for help in school. He could. And he should be able to. But the surest way to choke off a kid's interest in the learning to respond process, is to bind his hands and feet, imprison him in a desk and tell him to keep his ears open while all the information he will need for the rest of his life is funnelled into his brain, very slowly. When print was an only child it was sufficient for the schools to prepare kids to respond by teaching print literacy skills, but it is time someone tells educators that the stork has paid numerous calls on the communications family. Kids today require new kinds of literacy. They need to learn the how behind the howl.

Does this mean the schools should relax in their effort to teach reading and writing? Not at all. In fact, by expanding teaching approaches to include many media, the teaching of these skills could be made easier. Students must see reading and writing as tools, not products. In a multi-media situation they can be made aware of this reality since these skills are used to write a radio play, a TV commercial, or a script for a slide-tape or film. This is language in use rather than language usage.

(1) 600 students; up to 35 students per class
(2) Three teachers and one student-teacher
(3) Up to six periods per week--one period four days with one double period
(4) 22 Instamatics
(5) 2 Super-8 movie cameras

(6)   8 portable cassette tape recorders
(7)   1 stereo tape recorder

     The above broth, concocted at Philadelphia's Vaux
Jr. High School, went by the name of "Communications."
The teachers sought to discover if in-class multi-media
learning could be implemented under conditions which face
all teachers in overcrowded schools.   They classify their
program as a tremendous success, but readily admit to
moments of horrendous failure.   They did not discover a
panacea for all of education's ills, but they did learn some
things which might be helpful to others who are experiment-
ing with multi-media learning processes.

     First off, the structure of the classroom had to be
changed.   It had to be possible for the students to move at
their own chosen speed, and the large group structure in-
hibited this.   Each class, consequently, was divided into
sub-groups of four.   This small group structure also made
it easier for the teachers to individualize their instruction
but they had to abdicate their position as dictatorial dispensers of information and assume instead the role of guide.

     The initial activity aimed at getting the kids involved
in mediating information in some way other than with the
mouth--which they knew how to use--or the pen--which they
were often afraid of or confused by.   It was important to
help them discover the inter-relatedness of the media at
their disposal.   Each team was told to pick a topic about
which they knew something that they could communicate to
others.   They were given a series of steps to complete in
preparation for their first experience with a multi-media
project.

(1)   Decide what topic your team will investigate.

(2)   Write a list of at least 25 ideas, opinions or
facts about the topic.

(3)   Compare fact sheets.   Make a master copy
listing the 20 best ideas.

(4)   Make a list of pictures, describing one picture
which you think best explains each of your twenty statements.

(5)   Write an original poem, play, short story or

song which in some way deals with the topic you have chosen.

The students were given absolute freedom in their choice of topic they wished to explore, but since each group was allowed only one topic, arriving at a consensus provided them with insights into the machinations of back room decision-making. A lot of important deals were swung. One girl, obviously tuned in to the fine points of compromise, traded her vote for a date to a Halloween party. The final choices covered a wide range of subjects, from Fashions, to Sports to Gangs to Race. Not one group picked sound distortion as their topic, which was surprising given the sound level in the room.

It was not unusual on a given day to have one group in a corner rehearsing the fight scene in its play about gangs, and another group role-playing fashion models. The teacher rotated from group to group helping the students clarify their direction by keeping the topics in focus.

The photograph and taping followed the written work. The ideas were taped first. Each member of the group was given the responsibility for getting five of the twenty pictures. These were later matched to produce a rudimentary slide-tape. The poems, plays, short stories and songs were recorded as the group performed or read them to others in the class. If it was a play, stills were taken during the performance and later synchronized with the tape. For a poem, story, or song, visuals which matched the meaning or feeling had to be created and photographed.

Each group had a folder into which all completed written work was to be placed. No member of the group was permitted the use of any equipment until each member of the group had completed his assignments. This requirement produced some interesting side-effects. There was a tremendous amount of peer pressure, relieving the teacher of the responsibility of establishing and enforcing a deadline. It wasn't even necessary to impose time limits. In most groups a spirit of teamwork developed. Students who were embarrassed about spelling or other reading or writing skills were helped by the more literate members of the group with little of the usual teasing or scoffing. And, not least important, the students were able to get a preliminary evaluation of their work before handing it over to the teacher. These peer evaluations were usually more direct, yet less threatening, than those of the teacher. The most serious problem was the need to maximize the availability of the limited amount of useable hardware.

29. Photography and the Instructional Media Center

by Robert Beacon

Librarians at all levels have begun to discover the many diverse ways that photography can serve their needs. It can be a teacher of library skills, an introducer of books and a recorder of library activities. It can transmit information and produce attitude changes. Its every use in the Instructional Media Center (IMC) can make the job of serving its public much more effective, more simple, and more attractive to its patrons.

The elementary librarian can show a film demonstrating simple shelving or the use of the catalog; filmstrips of books to motivate reading; or slides, photos or 8mm movies of some special activities as a culmination of things past and motivator for the future. Secondary librarians can produce more detailed lessons on filmstrip and/or Super 8; can leave filmed instructions to operate simple IMC machines; or can use film to record special exhibits for their own use or for other librarians to add to their permanent collections.

The primary problem that IMCs encounter when they first decide to use photography in their program is the choice of camera.

The question asked most often by people new to photography is: "What camera shall I buy to take slides" (pictures, color, black and white, etc.)? The answer is simple. Pictures or slides, color or black and white results are determined only by the film that is used in the camera. This simple concept is so important, and the common knowledge about it so incorrect, that this statement bears repeating.

Whatever kind of film is put into a camera will determine whether the results will be slides or prints, color or black and white. Any reliable dealer will help a neophyte. But no help is really needed, for each box of film will state "slides," "prints," or whatever its special use might be.

The choice of camera is usually limited by the library budget.   But there is no need to spend more than $100. 00-125. 00 for a camera that will do almost anything necessary for a good library program.

The first camera for a beginning picture-taker might well be a drop-in-load type automatic camera using size 126 film, the Instamatic type.   Film cartridges drop in; the lens needs no focusing; the shutter speed is adjusted to the film.   Almost every snap yields an acceptable picture. Ignobly named "idiot" cameras, they are extremely popular with many because of their dependability.   These range in price from $10. 00, for a very simple mechanism, to $150. 00 for a very good one.

The most convenient size film to use for general purposes is 35 millimeter, producing the popular 2" x 2" mounted slide.   More kinds of film are made for this size camera than any other.   Any kind of still photography is possible with a good 35mm camera.

The simplest 35mm camera is the range-finder camera, which can also be the "idiot" type camera: aim and shoot.   Simple automatic models are available in all price ranges.   More complex models permit the photographer options on determining lens opening and shutter speed. However, this extra skill is not necessary for most uses.

There is one job for which a range-finder camera is not suitable if used by a neophyte: close-up work.   It can be done, but it is complicated by parallax and by the inability of the photographer to focus upon his objective correctly without careful and time-consuming measurement.   A single lens reflex (SLR) camera makes close-up work simple.

An SLR will show in its viewfinder exactly what comes in through the lens.   Covering the lens prevents light from entering the lens, of course, so that the viewfinder will show the photographer the same--no view at all. This prevents the frequent experience of inexperienced camera handlers--getting blank negatives or slides because the shutter was snapped when the lens was covered.   Focusing is simpler, too, because no matter what supplementary lenses may be added to the camera, the operator of an SLR can focus on the picture he sees in the viewfinder.

Supplementary lenses that are of great help in photographing typed or printed copy, or pictures or objects that are very small, are portrait lenses. These, either in a set of individual lenses or one zoom lens, enable the camera to take a picture of an object 1" x 1 1/2" on a piece of film the same size.

Anything else about photography may be more than a beginner really wants to know. The best advice to anyone just beginning is to use an inexpensive idiot camera, one that will cost no more than a couple of rolls of color film, and snap. If the results are satisfactory, fine. If not, then the best possible advice to find out about ASA, shutter speed, F stops, light meters, copy stands, interchangeable lens, behind-the-lens metering, needlematching, and lots more. Then, the next step, modified by budget, will soon shape itself.

Photography can be art, just part of a job, and/or great fun. Whichever, it is, for any librarian, it will contribute to a good job better done.

30. Local Production with 35mm Photography

by Otis McBride

Reprinted by permission of the American Library Association and the author, from School Libraries, Winter 1971.

There is a clear call for local production of materials to supplement what is available commercially. Local production may involve anything from a flat picture to a sound film. One of the simplest types, and yet most satisfying in result, is the process of 35mm photography. You may want one slide, several dozen slides forming sets, or a film strip from the camera.

Now hang on while we go into one or two technical aspects. Photography in the time of Matthew Brady, who took Civil War pictures that were surprisingly good, was not for those who gave up easily. It was a rugged and complicated business with a heavy percentage of trial and error. In contrast to all the heavy equipment that had to be lugged around, the slow emulsion, the necessity for immediate processing after the picture was taken, the chance for spoilage or for overdevelopment with crude equipment, the photographer of today "has a breeze." Nearly everything is done for you:

The camera. Small, light, easy to carry. Inexpensive (about $35 and up), unless you want to get into the mad whirl of the camera bugs.

The film. Choice of black and white or color. Results beautiful, unbelievable in both cases.

The rangefinder. Convenient but not essential. This device tells you how far you are from the subject, so your pictures will be in needle-sharp focus.

The exposure meter. Essential. This uses the magic of the photo-electric cell (referred to for years as

191

the electric eye) to analyze the amount of light and indicate
to you exactly how to set the camera.

The viewfinder. Essential. This is as necessary
as sights on a rifle. In the viewfinder the picture appears
exactly as it will show if photographed. In a regular camera, this is at the top or on one side. In the more convenient "single lens reflex," you look through the lens at
the subject. No matter if it is only an inch away, you will
have it centered in the picture.

Focus. Only the cheapest cameras have fixed focus.
Don't get one of those. Nobody likes a picture out of focus,
blurry, indistinct. By turning the lens, on practically all
cameras from about $35 up, you can have a very sharp
picture. You want that.

The shutter. Only a very cheap camera will lack a
controlled shutter. Obviously if your camera is set to take
a picture in bright sunshine, it will be wrong for a cloudy
day. So part of your pictures will be bad, under- or over-
exposed--or you will sit around and wait for just the right
kind of day. Not much fun! You should be able to take a
picture at a tenth of a second, a fifteenth, a thirtieth, a
fiftieth, etc.

Stops. The "iris" diaphragm. An adequate camera
will have a movable or controllable iris diaphragm--called
that because it resembles the iris diaphragm in our own
eyes. If you look into a mirror in a semidark room and
turn on the light, the pupil will rapidly become smaller.
That is the iris diaphragm working. In an adequate (not
expensive) camera the diaphragm works the same way.
The settings are called stops. So we "stop" down or
change the setting to f. 2, f. 3. 5, f. 4. 5, f. 5. 6, f. 8, f. 11,
f. 16. Most 35mm cameras go down no farther than f. 16,
at which stop the lens has an opening behind it about the
size of the head of a match. There is another good result:
the iris diaphragm not only controls the amount of light but,
at f. 16, makes all the light go through the center or fat
part of the lens. Refraction is not so great, the rays are
bent less, and things are in focus from nearer the camera
to much farther away. This characteristic is called "depth
of field. " I usually stop down as much as the amount of
light will allow me to--and have great depth of field.

So, these are some of the main things about the

camera. I trust it did not sound too complicated. Here is one more idea, very important to you if you put your camera to work at school.

The standard, regular 35mm camera uses film that has a width of 35 millimeters or 35/1000's of a meter. On that film the camera when the shutter is opened, will put a picture that is about 1" x 1 1/2". The cardboard mount of your slide is 2" x 2"; but, count on it, the picture itself will be 1" x 1 1/2". Now that size is fine for slides. You may want to prepare many slides and slide sets. And they will all be 2" x 2" slides (cardboard mount) with a picture area 1" x 1 1/2".

What if some fine day you want to make a filmstrip? This may come as a surprise, but go measure the picture size of a commercial filmstrip. You will find it is 1" x 3/4". It is only half as big as the picture area of a slide. Your roll of film has 36 exposures. The same length of filmstrip will have 72 exposures.

So how do we make a filmstrip with "single frame" pictures, size 1" x 3/4"? Technically and actually, we can't. But we can fake it, very handily, to look as if we took single frame pictures. Suppose we prepare mounts or flats for a slide set on Chaucer's Canterbury Tales. Let us pick a convenient size of our mounts, in proportion of 2:3. A convenient size, allowing space for captions, might be 8" x 12". We prepare forty mounts that size, with appropriate captions; and we could make forty slides. But we want a filmstrip. Put several of the pictures (flats, mounts) down, with about one inch between mounts. Then photograph two mounts at a time. To the camera, that makes up one picture: to you it will appear to be two, single frame pictures.

Caution: Stand over the pictures so as to take vertical shots, in relation to the whole row of mounts. And be sure the film, when you turn to the next shot, moves opposite to the way the mounts go. If the first mount is placed so you can read it as you face east, the second mount under it, etc., then be sure that the film, when you roll it for the next picture, moves west. If you don't care much for east and west, use opposite ends of the yard or the sidewalk.

What about light for all this? If you have had considerable experience, take care of lighting any way you choose. I've had some experience, but I still prefer the sun. If you put your work on the garage driveway, sidewalk, or shuffleboard court, you can use your light meter in the usual way--and lighting from the sun will do the job, without changing the color, getting reds too red, yellows a little sick, etc. The best time of day is from about 9:30 A. M. to 4 P. M. The sun is bright and at an angle so that when you shoot straight down your shadow will not fall on the material being photographed. When there isn't any sunshine, wait awhile. It will be worth it.

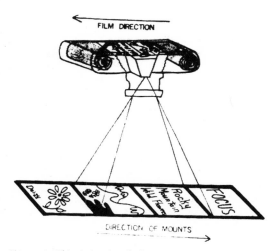

Figure 1. This is a detail, but a *very* important one. You remember that the lens *inverts* (reverses) everything. Look closely at the picture. "Focus" on the copy is on your right. But in the camera it is on your left. Be *sure* your camera is positioned like this in relation to the copy. Otherwise, when you get your filmstrip back, it may be a beautiful strip, but the order will be 2,1,4,3,6,5, etc., instead of 1,2,3,4,5,6, etc.—very bad for your sequence.

Working with 35mm photography is uncomplicated. After a few trials you will find it fast and easy. The guesswork has been taken out. Another important fact is that 35mm photography is comparatively inexpensive. You can produce a 72-frame filmstrip or a 36-exposure slide set for very little more than the cost of the film. And it will be yours--exactly the way you want it.

Bear in mind that it doesn't really matter who does the actual "shooting." Your worry is to set up exactly what you want: flat pictures in a series, live action, mounted material, etc. If you don't care for photography, you can easily find a neighbor, colleague, or student who is a "camera bug" and who will enjoy helping you out.

You will enjoy materials you have produced for yourself, in "living color," exactly as you want them. Reach up and get the "do it yourself" kit.

31. How to Use a Copy Stand

by Robert Beacon

Anyone using photography in a media center for instructional or motivational purposes will find it necessary sooner or later to make copies of print or nonprint materials, either for projection as slides or for pictures for display purposes.

Copying either type of material is a simple process, but it may be frustrating. Unwanted reflections, limitations of equipment, and lack of experience at times may make the process costly in wear and tear on the nervous system, and in wasted film. But there is no need for despair, for in copywork, as in other skills, "practice makes better."

The best advice one can give a beginner is: "take it easy." Unlike live photography, the subject will not run away. If the attempt comes out badly, there are always opportunities for the shot to be repeated.

The procedure outlined below lists the step-by-step operations for production of successful slides and pictures of copy material. If the results are consistently too dark or too light, adjust the lens opening or exposure accordingly. If they are inconsistent, check your meter and camera; if the problem is still not solved, consult an expert. But keep trying!

1. Gather the following materials together before any copywork is begun:

> copystand
> film for slides or pictures
> lights which color match the film
> camera
> supplementary lenses, if needed
> gray card
> light meter
> cable release
> bubble level
> lens tissue

glass sheet, 9" x 12", nonreflecting
copy material.

2.   Load the camera with film.   Clean the lens with lens
tissue only.   Ordinary tissue can scratch valuable lenses.

3.   Set both meter and camera at the proper ASA number.
This number can be found, for each film, on the film roll
or cassette, or on the box it comes in.

4.   Mount the camera on the copystand.   Make sure that it
is level, pointing perpendicularly down to the copy.   Use a
bubble level if one is available.   Shooting copy at even a
slight angle will produce distortion.

5.   Attach the cable release to the camera.   Its use will
minimize camera movement at the moment the shutter is
released.

6.   Place the copy material on the copystand.   Place a
glass sheet over the material if there is need to keep it
flat.   Adjust the lights so that there is no glare or unwanted reflections; they should be at an approximate angle
of 45 degrees to the copy.   Focus.

7.   Measure the light falling on different parts of the copy
material with the light meter.   For best results, the meter
should show the amount of light falling on all parts of the
picture to be the same.   Adjust the lights to eliminate
glare and reflections that may arise through moving the
lights.
     If the copying is done outdoors, it should be done in
the shade, away from any structure which might reflect a
strong color.   Changes in lighting are accomplished by
moving the copystand.

8.   Refocus the camera on the copy as sharply as possibly.

9.   Frame the copy in the viewfinder so that it appears
exactly as it is to appear as a slide or picture.

10.   Place a grey card on the copy stand as though it were
the material to be copied.   Take the exposure reading for
this card.   The light-meter reading will usually be more
accurate if taken from the gray card than if the reading is
taken from the copy material itself.   Read the values for
exposure and f-stop on the meter, (or through the built-in

meter of your camera) and set your camera (if it isn't automatic).

11. Release the shutter by slowly squeezing the cable release.

12. Advance the film, and begin again with the next exposure.

Notes: Use f8 or smaller whenever possible. This will minimize focusing error, especially with close-up lenses. Recheck the focus and the gray card reading whenever the camera, lights or copystand are removed. When an exposure of 1/60 second or more is required, the copystand must be very steady, for a small vibration will cause the slide or picture to lose its sharpness of image.

32. Cassette Tapes: An Overview

by Andre A. Blay & Thomas A. Pegan

Reprinted by permission of the Association for Educational Communications and Technology, from Audiovisual Instruction, September 1970.

It's a small, plastic device, smaller than a pack of cigarettes. Yet it has the capacity for recording, storing and reproducing a full stereo performance of Eine Kleine Nachtmusik without interruption. And when it ends, all the listener has to do is lift it out of the player, turn it over, reinsert it into the slot, and that same marvelous device will play the Divertimento in D.

The item in question is, of course, a cassette tape. Because of its unique features it has been hailed by some as the "ultimate audio recording medium," and pooh-poohed by others as "just a passing fad."

As usual, the truth lies somewhere in between. The cassette tape system has not taken the world by storm. But by the same token, the increase in sales volume of cassette hardware and software items over the past few years has been nothing less than phenomenal. Some statistics can illustrate this point.

Industry sources claim a 1969 sales volume of $25 million in prerecorded cassettes and $125 million in blank recording cassettes. This represents almost a 100 percent increase over 1968. While this growth rate is not expected to continue, forecasts of a 35 percent growth rate over the next three years is expected. In the hardware area there has been a 50 percent growth rate the last two years and a 15-20 percent growth rate is expected over the next three years. On the other hand, sales of open reel recorders have all but leveled off and will probably begin to decline as a consumer item.

This article is intended to give you an overview of

199

the cassette tape phenomenon from the viewpoint of a commercial tape duplicator and producer.

Originally developed by the Philips organization in Holland, it was several years before cassettes found their way into the United States in any numbers. To a great degree, this slow initial growth and acceptance was a deliberate effort on Philips' part. Philips' management rightfully recognized that if they were to enshroud their new development with a cloak of secrecy and a wall of highly restricting patents, a development as significant as the cassette is would have been subject to a plague of imitations, modifications and hybridizations by competitors. This would result in a deadly battle of competing systems with no beneficial resolution. And the effects such a standards battle would have on consumer confidence would have been disastrous.

What Philips' management did was to obtain strong patents on the cassette system, and then offer complete blueprints to anyone who had a qualified interest. In exchange for this valuable information, Philips requires its licensors to conform exactly to their standards--and not to introduce any modification or improvement in these standards without Philips' consent.

With these wise and sobering guidelines to follow, the growth of the cassette system has been methodical, deliberate and highly successful. In a sense, the cassette revolution has been a well-planned behind-the-scenes battle. It is now about to come into its own.

Tape recording has, of course, been with us since World War II. But there always were some problems inherent in the process which have restricted its wide acceptance. Threading the machine is a cumbersome process, the machines are typically expensive and heavy and operating controls are usually complicated for the uninitiated.

The cassette system solved these problems by enclosing the tape in an integral plastic case. The tape always remains within this case and is never touched. Tape speed is fixed at 1 7/8 inch per second and four separate tracks can be recorded across the .150 inch wide tape. The track format is so arranged that the stereo pairs are adjacent to each other, thus facilitating stereo-mono compatibility. A stereo machine will record two narrow tracks side by side along the bottom half of the tape, a mono ma-

chine will record a single track across this combined area
and then can playback a stereo tape by reading across both
tracks.

The low tape mass and simplified dynamics involved
allow the cassette recorder/player to be much smaller and
less complicated than its reel-to-reel counterpart. Thus,
for the first time, one can have a truly self-contained full
feature tape recorder smaller than many transistor radios.

The cassette's small size and ease of operation are
deceptive. It is actually a very sophisticated piece of plastic. There are no reels inside to support the fragile 1/7
inch wide tape. Instead, the tape is connected at each end
to a molded plastic hub which is driven by the player during operation. The tape is supported and guided by the actual walls of the cassette with special lubricated shim materials to reduce friction.

When the tape is in motion, it is driven by a capstan and pinch roller from the supply hub, past a turn-
around guide, past the head and integral pressure pad as-
sembly, and around another guide to the take-up hub. Some
very subtle forces are occurring at this time. Friction and
static cling are fighting to slow the tape down. The accumu-
lating turns of tape around the take-up hub can exert great
pressure on it. Irregularities in the hub can cause creas-
ing or distortion of the tape, or greatly increase wow and
flutter.

Because of these not always obvious forces which are
in play, the good cassette is actually a precision molded
item. Slight tolerance errors can cause failure or drasti-
cally shorten the normal life expectancy of over 1, 000 plays.

Unfortunately, this need for high precision in molding
and assembling of the raw cassettes has become a serious
problem in the industry. Despite Philips' attempts to maintain rigid standards in cassette technology, the inevitable
has occurred. In recent months, the sudden upsurge in demand for cassette software and hardware has spurred many
to enter the market with hastily contrived and manufactured
wares. There are now more firms molding cassetts than
one can keep track of. The consumer is being deluged with
a flood of low grade blank cassettes and recorders. These
cassettes usually contain inferior tape which can perma-
nently damage the delicate head in the machine. The cas-

settes can bind, stick, or jam up--sometimes damaging the player in the process. The result is a wave of negative sentiment and disenchantment with the cassette system.

The old cliché, "caveat emptor" holds true here. Don't expect discount tapes to be anything more than discounted in quality. Buy from a reputable dealer and expect to pay a fair price for the cassette. C-90s and C-120s, which run for 45 minutes and 60 minutes per side respectively, are made with ultra-thin tape and are always a compromise. That's not to say that there aren't some acceptable long play cassettes. But they are stretching some tolerances and many players cannot handle them effectively.

In quantity production of prerecorded tapes, there are two generally accepted methods: in-the-cassette duplicating, and bulk tape duplicating. In-the-cassette duplicating, as the name suggests, involves the recording of the program material onto a preloaded blank tape cassette. Such duplicators generally transport the cassette tape at four times normal speed and will have four or more cassette slots. The program material can be supplied by either a reel-to-reel transport or another cassette, and this also operates at four times normal speed.

In bulk tape duplicating, the process is more complex and requires more equipment. The original program tape, called the source master, is rerecorded onto a 1 or 1/2 inch wide tape called the duplicating master. Compression, limiting, and equalization are performed during this process as the need arises.

The duplicating master, much like a photographic negative, now becomes the source from which the mass-produced copies will be derived. It is placed into a special high-speed tape transport and the two ends are connected together to form a loop. Called the "loop transport," this machine stores the slack tape in a special bin rather than on reels. In operation, the duplicating master runs through this loop transport continually at rates of up to 32 times normal speed. This can mean an actual tape speed of up to 240 inches per second.

The signal from this duplicating master is amplified, processed and fed to a bank of interconnected recording transports called "slaves." These machines look much like a regular reel-to-reel tape recorder and carry large 5,000 foot reels of cassette tape.

The completed reel of tape, after it leaves the slave, contains many copies of the program along its length. This reel is now placed on a tailoring machine which separates the segments as it winds the tape into the cassette.

There are inherent advantages and disadvantages to both systems. In-the-cassette duplicating requires less expensive equipment and less involved preparation, and is quite sufficient for producing limited numbers of cassettes. But attempting to guide the tape through the cassette and across the recording head at four times normal speed often results in poor tape motion and a resultant loss of quality. The use of substandard cassettes often compounds this problem. Also, the fact that a preloaded blank cassette is used means that one usually winds up with several minutes of blank tape at the end of the program, (unless the trouble is taken to produce the original master with the exact timing of the stock blank cassette).

Bulk tape duplicating, because of the superior electronics and tape handling involved, results in consistently good audio and physical quality.

At the same time, a bulk tape duplicating system, although it is more capital and labor intensive, has a much higher production capacity. Tens of thousands of cassettes can be produced in one shift.

Aside from the obvious use of cassettes for prerecorded music, the system's ease of operation, portability and the ability to record as well as play back, have extended the powers of magnetic recording to whole new areas. The cassette system has become a viable new medium of communications in business, industry, education and religion.

Sales managers are talking to their salesmen while on the road, ministers are sending their sermons to shut-ins, executives are dictating to their secretaries while driving to work, conventions are being experienced by those who couldn't attend, and separated lovers are whispering in each other's ear through the mails.

In education, the cassette is rapidly becoming ubiquitous. Students are taping lectures. They can check out or even duplicate their own individualized instruction tapes from learning resource centers. They are learning languages from them and watching synchronized slidetape presentations.

"Talking magazines," or audio publications are rapidly gaining favor in professional fields. Like closed circuit radio programs, these cassettes are mailed regularly to subscribers, just as a print magazine is distributed. Designed as a method of inservice training, there are programs now available for lawyers, doctors, EDP managers and many others.

Just recently we contracted with the NEA and AECT to produce two cassette periodicals: Today's Education Forum and AV Forum. The first program is directed toward inservice training and professional advancement of school teachers. The second one is directed to audiovisual communication specialists.

Audio publications such as these take up where print leaves off by presenting the actual sounds, and voices of roundtable discussion, guest speakers, interviews with authors and soundtrack excerpts. This new communications medium extends the data assimilation capacity of listeners by allowing them to use otherwise nonproductive time more effectively. They can be listened to privately or with a group, while driving to work, and while doing routine tasks such as housework, sewing or while in the workshop.

What can we expect from the cassette cartridge and player manufacturers in the future?

It must be remembered that the cassette is not a great invention. It was developed because open reels of tape could not fully utilize the comparative advantages of magnetic tape. In other words, there were uses that industry, education and consumers wanted to put magnetic tape to but couldn't because of packaging limitations.

We can expect that the manufacturers will continue to innovate and adapt the cassette for as many uses as the market demands. We will soon have automatic reversing cassette machines for continuous replay. We will even have continuous loop cassettes. Better changer mechanisms will be built for multiple cassette selection. Players will be built smaller, better and less expensive.

On the other end of the scale, electronic design will enable cassettes to compete more actively in the home stereo market. We will find cassette mechanisms integrated into all types of communications equipment for record or playback features, as in telephone answering equipment or burglar alarm devices. Intensive research is underway to perfect them for computer use. There are already manufacturers using certified cassettes in desk-top computers.

Magnetic tape provides information in a way that no other medium can. It is the development of the cassette that has finally brought to fruition all the inherent advantages of magnetic recordings.

The same will be true with videotape recordings. All the advantages of videotape will not be fully realized until the emergence of video cassettes, which are just over the horizon.

33. How to Choose a Portable
Cassette Tape Recorder

by John J. Chalmers

Reprinted by permission of the Association for Educational Communications and Technology, from Audiovisual Instruction, September 1970.

The portable, battery-powered, transistorized, cassette tape recorder is here to stay! However, if you're in the market for a cassette tape recorder, which one do you buy? Aside from the pros and cons regarding the cassette tape recorder, the teacher who has decided to buy one is faced with a proliferation of models and a difficult choice. The buyer will find himself confronted with an array of tape recorders ranging in price from under $20 to over $100.

According to one source, there are over 200 models to choose from which use the popular "Compact Cassette" developed by the Philips Company and adopted by most manufacturers. The recorders on the market range in quality from junk to fine machines that can be used for everything from a swinging beach party to rugged educational applications.

Choice will probably be limited to some degree by the amount of money you are prepared to spend. However, the advantages and limitations of such a recorder should be considered so that its need can be carefully assessed. Such tape recorders are compact, portable, easy to operate, perform well and will do most things that a reel-to-reel tape recorder will do.

But aside from cost, purpose and use of the recorder must be considered. For example, it might be used only to play back pre-recorded commercially-available tapes through a headset in an individualized study program. If the machines are signed out by students for use only in carrels in a library, then recorders may not even be necessary--perhaps $20 playback units are all that is required.

However, if the teacher wishes to buy his own, to use as a verbal notebook, to prepare materials on cassettes for students and to record lectures and visiting speakers, then a $50 tape recorder may suffice. It will likely be used only by the owner as a personal machine, and will be well taken care of so that good performance may be expected from the recorder for a long time.

But if the recorder is to be located in an instructional materials center where it will be on loan to anyone who needs it and will consequently be handled by a lot of people, then a prime criterion will be ruggedness and dependability. To get that kind of quality it might be wise to invest $100 in a top-of-the-line model. It is not the purpose of this article to discuss the "cassette vs. reel" argument that began when cassette tape recorders hit the market in large quantity. Rather, let's consider some criteria for selection of portable cassette tape recorders by looking at some desirable features.

The following 20 criteria should be considered in selecting a cassette tape recorder. No attempt has been made to list them in order of importance, as all are necessary and available in good models at reasonable price. Common sense helps, but these are specifics which can be considered before purchase.

Does the machine have or accept:

* The "Compact Cassette" cartridge tape

* Adequate recording time on battery power; e. g. , one model records for only seven hours on a set of batteries, while good competing model records 36 hours

* Built-in AC adaptor, or is it available as an option, to allow 110 volt operation when desired

* Capstan tape drive, which assures more constant tape speed than reel drive, and less tendency to stretch tape

* Remote control microphone, convenient for frequent start-stop work, when using recorder as audio notebook

* Recording level meter which also serves as a battery condition indicator

* Automatic recording volume control and/or manual recording level control

* Cassette access with hinged lid rather than lift-off removable lid which can become misplaced or lost

* Rugged shoulder carrying strap to permit freedom of both hands in field work

* Carrying strap anchored in strong metal mounts, not just screwed into the side of a plastic case

* Strong, well-constructed carrying case

* Built-in or separate microphone case, preferably with room for extra cassettes

* Push button controls; these are usually the easiest to operate, but one school for handicapped children uses recorders with a "gear shift" control because many of the children lack the coordination needed to operate "piano key" controls

* Tone control for playback, in addition to volume control

* Two-track recording capability on monaural recorder

* Earphone for private listening

* Availability of other accessories if desired; these may include rechargeable battery packs, adaptor for use with automobile battery, foot switch for secretarial use, or a telephone pick-up

* Auxiliary input jack for off-air recording, record taping and tape duplicating

* Frequency response capability of approximately 50 to 10,000 cycles per second

* Backed by warranty and service through a reputable dealer.

Now a couple of hints for use. Good tape of known quality is perhaps more crucial to good recording with cassettes than reel tapes. Good tape will cost more, but will be stronger, will resist stretching, and will probably be

silicone lubricated. Furthermore, actual construction of
the cassette case will be superior.   Most makes of tapes
come in sizes referred to as C-30, C-60, C-90, and C-120
to indicate how many minutes of recording time can be obtained from the tape.   For example, a C-60 tape will provide a total of 60 minutes' recording time by recording for
30 minutes on each track.

It must be remembered that since the dimensions of
each tape cassette are the same, i. e. the actual plastic
cartridge, additional recording time is obtained by including
more tape within the cassette, and this is accomplished by
using thinner tape.   Thus a C-120 tape uses extremely thin
tape which will wrinkle or break much easier than a stronger tape.   For general use, a 60-minute tape is a good size
to work with.

Another thing to consider carefully is the type of
battery which will be used.   Alkaline batteries should be
used, not cheap carbon-zinc varieties.   It's amazing how
many "leak-proof" batteries spill their insides all over the
electrical connections of flashlights, radios, tape recorders,
etc. , with seriously damaging results caused by corrosion.
Alkaline batteries cost more, but they give more power and
last longer, as well as providing protection for your invest-
ment.

Battery capacity can also be considered.   When buying a tape recorder, note the kind of batteries used and
how many.   Most common are the size C and D.   For example, four size D batteries are more powerful than four
size C batteries.

The foregoing criteria are intended as a guideline
only.   Before you decide to buy, read the technical information in the booklet that comes with the recorder.   There
are a lot of good recorders on the market and final choice
will be determined by price, quality and purpose for which
the recorder is intended.   Remember, too, that luxuries
such as a built-in microphone or digital counter are nice
to have, but be prepared to pay for them.   Regardless of
the model you select, try it out first before you buy it.
Quality control on some models is not very rigid, and one
unit may be perfectly fine, while the one beside it on the
shelf is full of bugs.   Be sure that your choice is backed
up by warranty.

Recently a medium-priced tape recorder was assigned to a number of schools. The recorders bear one of
the best-known names in the electronics industry and were
to be supplied with microphone, carrying case and five empty cassettes. As soon as schools started receiving them, a
complaint came in. The tape recorder had been received
without a microphone, only one empty cassette, and the recorder didn't work! The supplier was called immediately
and he promptly assured us that everything would be set
right, and reminded us that for the first year the recorders
carry an unconditional 100 percent warranty.

At times like that, you appreciate good service!

34. The 8mm Film Loop

by Joan R. Forsdale

Reprinted from Media and Methods, November 1969, by permission of the publisher and the author.

"Primary attention ... is governed by an almost involuntary attention to changes in the visual field, to movement, to brightness and the like." That sentence sounds like commercial puffery. It isn't though; it's a quotation from Jerome S. Bruner's Studies in Cognitive Growth. The distinguished Harvard psychologist is citing the distinction in the psychology of learning long ago established between primary, secondary and derived primary attention.

It is easy to recognize that controlled changes in the visual field can frequently be best achieved for educational purposes with the media of film and television. Why have the schools, then, neglected so long to capitalize strongly on the educational value of the moving image? Was it the usual resistance to change in a profession too often accused of a conservative bias? Let's look at the implications of the Bruner quotation itself for a hint of the answer to that question.

Before the advent of instant-load rear- and daylight-screen projectors, the cumbersome procedures necessary for film showing were themselves so interesting, so full of visual changes, that they distracted the learner from full concentration on the film images from which he was expected to learn.

And, in many cases, the conventional classroom film made very little use of the teaching power of visuals, for it tended to rely heavily on its sound track to convey information.

The easy-to-use projectors and screens have not only placed the image itself in a newly powerful position, but also they have allied that image with the teacher, instead of replacing the teacher with the movie, which has been the traditional practice.

211

Another reason that the new hardware permits a change in the power of the moving image available for educational purposes is film's heretofore overwhelming richness as a medium: there is enormous information contained even in the most simple glimpse of dynamic reality. The amount of "unpacking" of information from the image should be ideally defined by the purpose and skill of the learning group and its teacher. Instead, too often it has been the mere logistics of the viewing situation which are in control, resulting in inefficient exploitation of the medium's potential and therefore only minimal instructional gain.

In the face of all these arguments for the short accessible film, why has the twenty-or-thirty-minute-long "instructional" film ("Safety in the Laboratory") persisted? It has, of course, many legitimate uses, but as the norm, it is highly suspect. It is suspect first of all because it is likely to be a concession to very clumsy projection hardware: can you ask a teacher (plus the A-V team?) to show a film that takes less time to run than to set up for? In addition, it is suspect precisely because it is so firm a standard, perhaps based on a trivial marketing convention, rather than based on the requirements of subject matter and/or learning characteristics of students. In contrast, however, if one thinks of a single cartridge loop not necessarily as the total length of presentation but as a module of length, viewing experiences may be made up of as many of these modules as is appropriate. Great flexibility may thus be gained, for these film modules may be arranged in whatever order, and with whatever distribution of repetitions, as optimizes learning for that group at that time for that purpose. The conventional film cannot easily be used in this fashion--and one of the wisdoms of modern technology is that people tend to do with objects those things that are convenient to do, and leave undone those things which are awkward and inconvenient.

What are the specific educational advantages of the loop?

(1) It is currently the easiest, fastest access to the moving image. It makes film as easy a medium to use as any other medium which requires hardware, and far easier than most. No normal four-year-old needs more than a minute of instruction before he is on his own with a cartridge projector. He can't put the cartridge in wrong; there is no loose film to drop on the floor, or to get

dirty; there are no reels he can struggle to fit on a spindle, correct side out; there are no leader ends to trim.

(2) It is a "no nonsense" form, especially in its silent version. Stripped of the portentous baggage most films carry, it must get down to business fast or it won't get there at all. The short loop by its very nature tends to begin where many other films only struggle to reach after long wandering through the dreary land of inflated production values mistakenly borrowed from Hollywood-Movieland. It reflects the fact that when a child is learning what he is ready to learn, extrinsic motivation is irrelevant--and insulting to the learner's seriousness of purpose.

(3) The fact that the film loop does not require rewinding, but continues to re-play until it is turned off, has profound educational implications. Its built-in predisposition to repeat encourages not just second but third and more showings of the film. Students are not forced to choose between two equally undesirable alternatives: trying to catch all the information as it goes by; or, retreating into passivity. And passivity has been the most serious charge consistently leveled at film as an educational medium. Since people become passive when they cannot cope, when they are overwhelmed, the accessible film, by its quality of being under the control of the learner, can escape this charge. The passivity charge, however, legitimately can be leveled at many conventional classroom films which are overloaded with information. Repeated viewings of an accessible film can help even the youngest child "unpack" a great deal of information from film; knowing that he can show the film to himself later, as often as he wants and needs, permits him to engage himself with it and not be tempted to retreat. The student need not even realize that the film is re-playing until he has reached at least the recognition level of learning.

Repetition also means a single film may be used for several different purposes: e. g. , a documentary showing scenes from a foreign culture can be viewed first for the action, then for the clothing, then for the setting, then for the insights into relative rank and power of the persons portrayed; and the same film can be used for several different class levels as well.

Another value of repetition, both subtle and exciting, is its consonance with a conviction stated by Jean Piaget,

the Swiss psychologist widely regarded as preeminent among
the scholars providing us with new insights into children's
learning processes.   He states in Play, Dreams and Imita-
tion in Childhood that repetition is of basic importance in
the assimilation of experience to the self.   We intuitively
understand that it is the experiences we repeatedly encounter
which most profoundly shape us; we make them our own, and
we make ourselves out of them.   A persuasive and familiar
example of this phenomenon is the child's demand to be told
his favorite stories over and over again in exactly the same
form.

Carl Bereiter and Seigfried Engelmann, specialists
in curriculum research and development at the University of
Illinois, in their influential Teaching Disadvantaged Children
in the Preschool also emphasize the need for repetition in
their plea for consistent presentation of new material.   They
point out--in reference to the teaching of techniques to increase verbal skills, but their argument may legitimately be
generalized to other matters and other modes of presenta-
tion--that if variety is prematurely introduced, the child becomes confused and cannot focus on the matter to be
learned.

They say, "Initial uniformity is extremely desirable,"
and suggest that we educators often too soon "amplify and
enrich" more for our own needs not to be bored or to seem
stupid than to assist the child in his mastery of concepts and
skills new to him.   The cartridge loop has built-in biases
in the direction of these newly formulated widespread learning predispositions.

Similarly, Peter Drucker, giant of the management
consultants, in his recently published The Age of Discon-
tinuity, states that learning requires repetition: the only
things we truly and solidly know are those that we practice
over again.   He points out that few of us retain our ability
to do logarithms but most of us can add, multiply, divide,
subtract.   This is not because those operations are intrin-
sically easier, but that they are used daily and therefore do
not fall into disrepair.   Drucker also reports recent research which reveals that different students require a far
greater range of repetition to learn a segment of material
than had previously been suspected.   If students from a
variety of backgrounds and with a variety of learning styles
are to learn effectively, each of them must have free access
to the amount of repetition he needs to master that particular

curriculum item. The modular, endless loop form serves well this need for intensive individual or group study and drill. With correctly designed films (for no hardware has value unless there is a proper "fit" between it and its software programs), the short cartridge loop seems "bite-size" for the learner's mind.

One frequently overlooked learning "bonus" that the loop yields is its cyclical nature. Many phenomena have a fixed beginning and an end, and in those cases films would appropriately employ attention-gaining titling techniques at their beginnings which signal where the viewer should "come in." But many phenomena, both in the natural world and in the formulae of instruction, have neither a beginning nor an end; or, if they do, it is in short episodes within an endlessly repeating cyclical total pattern. Two widely diverse examples are the seasons (which have a time direction but no one season represents a true beginning or end) and, say, long division problems (each problem has a beginning and end, but the corpus of long division problems is infinite.)

A Guide to Super 8mm Cartridge Projectors

	Technicolor 1000 A	Bolex Multimatic	Fairchild-Eumig 711	Fairchild 70-31	Kodak Ektagraphic 120
Projects	front	front	front	rear	front
Sound Play	yes	yes	yes	yes	no
Price	299.95	229.50	380.00	375.00	134.00
Capacity	200', 600'	six 50'	50', 100' 200', 400'	400'	50, 100'
Lens	20mm, f 1.1	20mm, f. 1.3	17-30mm f 1.3	10mm, f 1.1	22mm, f 1.5
Weight (lbs)	18	22	26	20	15
Speeds (fps)	24	6, 8, 18, 24	18, 24	24	18
Single Frame	no	yes	no	no	yes
Reverse	no	yes	yes	no	yes
Sound Record	no	no	yes	no	no
Lamp	150 quartz	150 quartz	100 quartz	80 quartz	80 DFE
Converts to Reel-to-Reel	no	no	yes	no	no
Cartridge Type	Technicolor	Bolex	Kodak	Fairchild	Kodak
User Inserts Film	no	yes	yes	no	yes
Compatible with Other Cartridges	no	no	no	no	no

Until the loop came along, conventional film modeled itself unconsciously on the structure of print--the linear succession of symbols.

Using Loops--Multiplying Configurations of Instruction Film Use

> The typical child has been reared in an environment of audio-visual electronics. It is natural for him to learn from a variety of media. From their pre-school years most children have been at home with television and radio. It is a major educational asset that for them there is nothing alien about the advanced technical equipment and methods that may be employed in their studies or which may be available to them to bring into their home.
> --Statement on National Policy, Committee for Economic Development, Subcommittee on Efficiency and Innovation in Education, 1968.

Students of all ages--from K on up through the grades--can project the short accessible film by themselves and for themselves. It does not require the teacher or audio-visual technician heretofore necessary to open the gate to the moving image. This fact makes possible many new ways for this medium to be employed as a central learning device in studies at every school level. Which one of the wide variety of configurations of use chosen to best accomplish a particular learning task should be based on the film's subject matter and format, the teacher's pedagogic style, and the characteristics of the student audience--just to mention a few of the major factors. Let's start with an example of the perhaps most typical way of using loops, then go on to consider some of the interesting variations.

A. Teacher As Discussion Leader. The subject is biology; topic paramecia. Several times during the lesson, the teacher shows a film loop to the class which makes clear the characteristics of this protozoan. As convenient as using a wall chart, the film permits the class to see paramecia as they are in their natural environment--moving, eating, etc. Because we assume this is to be a silent loop, the teacher tells the class what he wants it to hear about paramecia--exactly the amount and level of information which he knows the class can handle. He teaches as much or as little technical vocabulary as he deems effective for these particular students, and observes them, as they watch the film, for signs of confusion or especial interest, so he can teach to the ongoing "dialogue" between the film and his class. And not only may the teacher function skillfully as the sound track, but he may, as an effective summary or review device, ask various students to supply the narration, thereby testing their degree of comprehension. A daylight or rear screen, which permits film to be viewed in a lighted room so that the teacher and class members can see each other, greatly facilitates discussion.

B. Source of "Prepared Data" for Study and Discussion. The importance of discovery as a high road to learning is increasingly recognized in the schools. What is discovery? It is to find out something for oneself rather than to be taught it. But how can we expect each child to reconstruct our entire culture unaided? We can't, and so discovery in the school is largely guided discovery, and properly so. (Those teachers who pretend not to guide must beware of prompting their students into "discovery," thus corrupting it into a coy guessing game.) What seems a responsible compromise between pure "laissez-faire" discovery and the rigid administration of information to students is prepared data. A metaphor which may serve to clarify what is meant by prepared data is a mine which has been "salted," so that the learner-prospectors may probe at will, but where the barren areas have been reduced to a minimum. By this preparation, the level of effort realistically to be expected of student prospectors will be rewarded with a "strike." But how to present that data from which discoveries may honestly and legitimately be made?

What better way to present rich chunks of carefully chosen data to be mined and sifted for a multitude of purposes than the moving image? It stimulates life more closely than any other medium--color, motion, time duration--but without life's ephemeral quality. Film can "hold life still" to be studied, or better, present repeatedly to us a good copy of life's dynamic complexity for our ever more close study.

C. Loop as Model. "The classic demonstration lecture is a uni-directional process... it is orderly, tasteful, and well-programmed--and in all these respects, it is replaceable... by a well-made film. This tight coupling [of mind of audience and ideas of lecturer] is indeed exactly

what film or television can achieve better than any other
medium. " This statement is from the chapter "Conveying
Science by Visual Presentation, " by Gerald Holton, M. I. T.
physicist, and appears in the superb collection, Education
of Vision, edited by Gyorgy Kepes. Whether it is a science
experiment which the teacher wants his students to study
again and again in its ideal form, without distracting and
interesting irrelevances such as the personality and appearance of the demonstrator, idiosyncrasies of his movements,
small mishaps, etc. , or the standard procedure for operating a piece of somewhat complex equipment, the loop is an
excellent instructional device. It may be useful to pause
here and deal with one of the relevant Either /Or red her-
rings which often comes up at this point: should the student
have contact with the real world, or should he experience
that world through media? The answer to that "question" is
... both. Have the students work with as many test tubes
and wriggling worms as seems desirable, but also let him
learn from the compressions and abstractions and clarity
which a carefully designed "canned" statement can make.

D. Individual Study Exercises. Simple projectors,
and film-packaging formats that permit near-random access
to the moving image, enable students to move without technical harassment through individual study exercises. With
cartridge modules or any other easily-indexed format, he
may branch from level to level of a presentation as directed.
The study carrel which uses film alone or as part of a multimedia study package is a configuration which is becoming
increasingly familiar. The recently developed types of films
with participation possibilities offer especially exciting new
forms for individualized film assignments, perhaps as segments of Individually Prescribed Instruction programs.

E. Home Study. Small, easily-carried projectors
make home-study of film realizable. Gerald Holton, in the
same article cited above, goes on specifically to note that:
"Film cartridges which the student can use in the library or
take to his dormitory to study with the new closed loop projector are one example of the extension of demonstrations
in lectures. " Obviously films may be of many kinds as well
as the demonstrations mentioned by Holton.

It is apparent from the examples cited above that simple projectors enlarge the function of film so it may serve
both ends of the individual-group learning spectrum: for the
group, it can be the mass-integrating cheer leader or choral

conductor; for the individual it functions to free each learner
to work alone with the medium at his own pace. Heretofore,
print has tended to nourish the solitary learner, while film
was used in the past as only a group experience. Film now
is becoming a major source of instruction for both groups
and individuals.

35. How to Use, Make and Buy
     Overhead Transparencies

     by Philip Lewis

          Reprinted by permission from Nation's Schools,
          November 1967.

          The increasing acceptance of overhead projectors by
public schools is due largely to the wide range of commercially prepared transparencies available to the teacher and
the ease with which she can prepare additional ones by herself.

Sources of transparencies

          1. Very simple visuals can be prepared locally by
lettering or sketching directly on blank acetate sheets.
China marking pencils, felt markers, and ink pens containing acetate solutions all will work.

          2. More finished products can be produced with rub-
on letters and figures, which are applied directly to the acetate. Self-adhering colored tapes add emphasis.

          3. Most schools have spirit duplicators for turning
out multiple paper copies. This equipment is also excellent
for producing transparencies. Approximately 10 sheets of
paper are run through the machine after the normally prepared master has been inserted. An acetate sheet is then
slowly handfed through the machine. After two or three
minutes of drying time, the transparency is ready for projection. It is easy to produce a multiple-color transparency
by using various colored spirit carbons in preparing the
master. Carbons are available in purple, green, red, blue
and black.

          4. Special spirit carbon-master sets incorporate a
sheet of transparent film instead of the usual paper surface.
The master is prepared conventionally and placed on the machine for duplicating. After the desired number of paper

copies is reproduced, the film can be removed and used as an overhead transparency.

5. Blank, heat-sensitive plastic sheets used with appropriate office copying machines, or with special purpose equipment, can produce very clear and usable transparencies. Written, typed or drawn copy--which must be made with carbon-base inks for effective reproduction--is placed in contact with the plastic sheet and passed through the machine for a few seconds. The system's limitation is that the transparency will be reproduced in white or black lines only, although some special plastic sheets offer such opaque background colors as red, green, blue, white and yellow. The heat faxable process is excellent for reproducing newspaper clippings, pages of books, etc. A plastic halftone screen carrier may be used for reproducing photographs.

6. One of the earliest methods of making transparencies was with diazo plastic sheets. These sheets are impregnated with a dye which is developed through an ammonia process to bring out the color. Many different colors and shades are available, although it is necessary to process a separate sheet for each color desired. The diazo equipment generally consists of a light exposure unit and a developer unit, some manual in operation and others fully automatic. Several companies provide products and equipment utilizing this process.

7. The use of appropriate plastic inks makes it possible to produce transparencies through offset printing. A four-color system can produce very attractive visuals. If desired, of course, only black can be used.

8. The color-lift technic is an inexpensive method of producing full color transparencies. Although several variations of this process are in popular use, it consists basically of removing the ink image from a printed sheet-- such as a magazine picture on coated stock--and transferring this ink to an acetate sheet.

Both the acetate sheet and the picture are coated with rubber cement. When the cement has thoroughly dried on both surfaces, press together with a rolling pin or similar object to squeeze out any air bubbles. The whole "sandwich" is then immersed in a lukewarm solution of detergent and water until it is possible to peel off the paper from the plastic sheet, leaving only the ink image behind. It is then

helpful to wash away any clay or similar material that may
cause cloudiness on the transparency.   After the sheet has
dried, it can be used for projection.   It is a good technic,
however, to coat the ink side with acrylic spray.   This
added step will make the visual more transparent and will
also protect the ink from abrasion.

9.   A polarization accessory, consisting of a motor
and a rotating transparent disc, adapts any overhead projector for specially prepared transparencies which produce
an "animated" effect on the screen.   Generally, a basic
transparency is prepared in the usual manner and polarized
materials are attached to the surface where the illusion of
motion is required.   Kits are available containing a variety
of such materials to simulate straight-line motion, radiation
and so forth.   Such technics can, for example, show the
flow of electrons through a circuit, indicate the process of
the water cycle, or illustrate the action in an internal com-
bustion engine or hydraulic system.

10.   Many simple transparent plastic items--protrac-
tors, drafting triangles, French curves, rulers--can be
used directly on the stage of the overhead projector as
manipulative devices.   The creative teacher will adapt many
other items.   For example, toy gear sets, scissors and
pliers, can be manipulated on the projection stage to demonstrate mechanical advantage and the laws of levers.   Commercially produced manipulative items can eliminate the
need to acquire and employ large demonstration equipment
for science and mathematics presentations.

Transparency accessories

There are many varied technics for developing transparency formats.   The following seem sufficiently important
to warrant attention:

1.   Although unmounted transparencies can be projected, they should be framed to protect the acetate as well
as to facilitate handling.   Cutout frames are available to
accommodate different transparency sizes, including 5" by
5", 7" by 7", and 10" by 10".   The latter size is by far
the most popular.

The nature of the optical system in most overhead
projectors generally results in substantial light fall-off at

the corners of the projection stage. For this reason the commercial frames and transparencies (10" by 10") are usually horizontally oriented. The resulting aspect ratio makes allowances for the corner fall-off. Similarly, there are vertically oriented frames that compensate for this phenomenon. Also, frames that accommodate full 10" by 10" transparencies are available and are usually fitted with modified corners.

Some commercial frames only provide sufficient margin for the effective mounting of the transparencies, while others are designed to provide a more generous margin at one side to accommodate notes and other relevant material for the instructor during a presentation.

Frame materials are generally of two varieties -- cardboard and pressed board. The cardboard type is less sturdy and cannot take rough handling. Pressed board is more durable and is recommended for long-term or frequent use. Sturdiness is particularly important with multiple hinged overlays.

Some frames are equipped with register holes. They slip over pins on the overhead and automatically align the transparency for proper projection.

2. A number of manufacturers offer transparency preparation kits. These vary in degree of completeness, depending upon technics to be employed and quantities of transparencies to be produced. Such kits contain a variety of markers, lettering devices, mounting materials, frames and blank acetate sheets, as well as a miscellaneous collection of useful material.

3. It is possible to hinge multiple overlays with conventional pressure sensitive tape. Such adhesive, however, tends to dry out and become brittle. Metallized silver Mylar hinges (usually 1-1/4" square) are recommended as rugged and durable. A proper masking tape should be used for mounting the transparencies within the frame.

4. Special red carbon paper is available for transferring carbon images to a blank acetate sheet. Such carbon transfers are easily smeared, making it necessary to overlay the image side with a protective sheet of plastic.

Special black sheet film, which resembles ordinary

typing carbon, has a special application here. By writing
directly on this film when it is on the projection stage, a
white line is produced on the screen at all pressure points.
This effect can be accomplished with a ballpoint pen, pencil
or any similar pointed object. This film can also be typed
upon, or carefully drawn graphics can be inscribed on its
surface. To preserve such carbons, it is again necessary
to protect them, this time by placing plastic sheets on both
sides of the carbon and taping then in place.

Some publishers provide translucent or opaque paper
sheets with images for making transparencies so the local
consumer can select and produce his own acetates.

Other producers incorporate completed transparencies
for use as either single acetates or as part of sets having
multiple overlays. A recent trend has been the development
of bound "books" of transparencies. These are organized for
sequential projection and they always remain in the binder for
protection and organization.

36. The Current State of the Remote Access
    Audio Video Information System

by David M. Crossman

Reprinted by permission of the Association for
Educational Communications and Technology, from
Audiovisual Instruction, September 1970.

Education, like many other institutions in our culture,
is very easily diverted by novelty. As a profession we find
ourselves, particularly with respect to technology, catering
to obsolescence and irresistably attracted to that which is
new. It is not difficult, then, to understand the importance
attached to innovation as it has spread throughout the education establishment. Our restless need for newness charac-
terizes us as a nation. The ritualistic annual model changes
of consumer goods are symptomatic of this national trait.
In federal education projects of the past 12 years, it would
be difficult to find a guideline criterion more frequently cited
or eagerly sought than that of "innovation" in proposals being
considered for funding.

Perhaps this is because, as we so often have been
reminded, public and private education at all levels has been
extremely reluctant to change. Virtually every major critic
of American education points out the slow speed with which
changes are made. Certainly some professional education
groups have actively sought change. Important changes are
reflected in the new math, the new social studies and science curriculums, black studies programs, work study patterns and particularly in the emphasis that is now being
placed upon independent learning patterns.

The educational technologist almost always thinks of
himself as an innovator, an agent of change and an important vanguard of the profession, introducing his colleagues to
the ways of the future. Frequently he is. Unfortunately,
he is frequently a victim of innovation. In 1960 enthusiasm
ran high for the future of the teaching machine. At last it
seemed that Sidney Pressey's ideas were being shaped into

a useful educational tool. At the Department of Audiovisual Instruction Convention in Cincinnati that year, several hundred companies exhibited so-called teaching machines ranging in cost from several dollars to complex equipment completely out of the purchasing range of most schools and colleges. During the course of that year it was discovered that virtually all of the benefits that could be derived from complex self-instructional consoles could be arranged into the pages of a programed text and sold for the price of a book. By 1961 most of the teaching machines had vanished.

Between 1961 and 1964 several firms undertook the manufacture of automatic response devices designed to provide individual and group feedback data from students in classroom situations. In the case of two manufacturers, equipment supplied was of such poor quality as to render experimentation impossible. In both cases teachers and students using the equipment on an experimental basis became discouraged and disenchanted resulting in the premature termination of the experiments (David M. Crossman, "Fix It So It Will Work," Audiovisual Instruction, 8:8, Oct. 1963, pp. 596-599). The effect of this lack of concern for equipment reliability delayed the development of this innovative idea several years.

A similar situation in the middle and late 1950s threatened to destroy the development of the language laboratory. The persistence with which the audio electronics industry sold consumer quality audio equipment for heavy-duty language laboratory applications cost both secondary schools and colleges millions of dollars in useless equipment and thousands of hours of time in maintenance. It was not until the joint publication of minimum specifications by the U.S. Office of Education and the Electronics Industries Association that sufficiently rugged language laboratory equipment began to appear on the market. Unfortunately, the frustrations of dealing with poor equipment still troubles many schools. Based upon research done by the author in New York State, 80 percent of the first language laboratories purchased by secondary schools in that state (as of 1967) were acquired prior to 1963 when the USOE-EIA specifications were adopted throughout the state. Unhappily, it took five years from 1958 when language laboratories began to be purchased in quantity, until specification standards were established in 1963. In one college situation known to the author, a 40-position language laboratory was purchased by the institution in 1958. In 1963 the laboratory had to be

replaced. The college was told that the used electronics
had no value whatever. The equipment was given away as
scrap.

Perhaps the most conspicuous example of the way the
profession is diverted occurred during the late 1940s and
early 1950s when educational radio was almost totally
scrapped in favor of television. In spite of the fact that the
audiotape-recorder was developed and introduced into the
United States in 1947, its importance clearly took a back-
seat to the video image. On April 14, 1952 the Federal
Communications Commission issued the now famous Sixth
Report and Order allocating 242 television channels for educational use. This new interest in television caused a dramatic decrease in the applications of audio technology and
particularly educational radio broadcasting. The unfortunate
effects of this rush into television technology are still being
felt. While television facilities, equipment and systems
are today very sophisticated indeed, developments in audio
technology, until recently, were comparatively primitive.

Much to the delight of those few faculty members who
still have not purchased a television set, the world of audio
is staging a renaissance. This situation has developed for
two main reasons: the cost of television systems has become so great that other alternatives are being sought and
it has become increasingly apparent that a high percentage
of television programing is being used for purposes far better suited to simple audio technology.

For the better part of the 20th century, learning theorists have attempted to identify general learning characteristics to provide education with data upon which to make decisions relating to curriculum, the arrangement of the
school day, instructional resources and the need for specialized physical facilities.

For many years cognitive theorists have been at odds
with the behaviorist school. Certainly areas of agreement
between these two schools of thought have left the profession
with very little theory that can generally be inferred about
the learning process. This substantial disagreement, however, has stimulated perhaps the most important trend in
America education of the past decade.

We have finally come to the conclusion that it might
be wise to concentrate on the many differences among learn-

ers rather than center all of our attention upon their far
fewer similarities. As a result of this rather dramatic de-
parture from conventional ways of looking at learning patterns and related instructional needs, the idea of individu-
alizing learning has gathered strength.

Because of the flexibility such new patterns provide,
the individualization of instruction has permitted experimentation with an almost unlimited number of learn-resources.
One of the most useful of these is the remote access information system.

Every four or five years a new piece of technology
manages to sweep through the education community carrying
with it excitement, enthusiasm, promise, apprehension and
usually, considerable expense. Such a piece of technology
is the so-called dial access system. The use of the term
"dial" refers to the usual use of a telephone type dial as
the means of access to information stored in the system.
During the past three years, however, the manufacturers
of such systems have introduced push button equipment similar to the common touch-tone telephone, rendering the term
"dial access" somewhat obsolete. A more generic term,
which embraces all such equipment, both audio and video,
is "remote access information system. "

The remote access information system normally is
composed of a number of student carrel positions, each
equipped with a telephone dial or touch-tone pad, volume
control and headphones. Carrel units designed for audio-
active response for foreign language purposes are generally
equipped with a microphone as well. Video systems also
include a television screen. From a centrally located series
of audio and/or video playback machines with associated
switching equipment, an individual, by consulting a directory
at his carrel, may request any program available through
the dial or pushbutton control. Such systems have the advantage of removing audio- and videotape from the hands of
the user. This not only preserves the tape but enormously
simplifies user access. Further, the number of programs
that can be stored in such a system is limited only by the
size of the system purchased. Generally speaking, equipment of this kind handles short programs, from five to 15
minutes, more efficiently than longer programs. Where
long programs are necessary, portable tape (either audio
or video) equipment can be set up without tying up the
switching potential of the remote system.

The remote access information system was developed as an outgrowth of the language laboratory. It was thought that students of modern foreign languages would be well served if the many audio programs which are needed for language laboratory usage could be put into a system by which any program could be available automatically upon request. Under the direction of F. Rand Morton, the first dial access language laboratory was developed at the University of Michigan in 1961 by the Chester Electronic Laboratories. The initial success of this experimental installation has led to a proliferation of both audio and video systems during the intervening eight years. In a recent publication entitled Dial Access Information Retrieval Systems: Guidelines Handbook for Educators, by Gabriel D. Ofiesh, done at the Catholic University of America under a grant from the USOE, it is reported that by the spring of 1968, 121 systems had been installed nationwide with 56 institutions planning to purchase remote access equipment.

One of the interesting changes in direction that has characterized the remote access information system has been its broadened use in a wide variety of subject matter areas. First conceived as a tool of primary use for the learning of modern foreign languages, it grew, predictably, to meet some of the needs of music and speech. What might not have been predicted, however, has been the extension of systems of this type into practically every subject area. Further, the locale of the user carrel has shifted from the language laboratory to the library.

With this change in locus and broadened utility has also come a change in rationale. No longer limited to foreign language pattern drills, the remote access information system is now generally viewed as a means of providing information to an individual student on any subject at any level. It simply provides another medium through which audio and video information can be made available.

One of the rather inappropriate terms that became associated with the remote access information system has been that of "random access." In fact, some systems have become known as "random access systems," suggesting that any program can be made available to any student at any time. Most common of these installations is the four track tape playback system. Utilizing four tracks on each tape machine, four separate programs can be accommodated on each machine. Therefore, the purchase of 10 machines

yields a capacity of 40 programs. This multi-channel utilization of each machine quadruples the program capacity of
any system, but at the same time reduces the random accessibility of each program. Obviously, any program in use
requires the movement of a tape upon which are located
three other programs. Unless a user is satisfied by entering a program at some point distant from the beginning,
each of the three remaining programs are tied up until the
first user has relinquished his program, which automatically
rewinds the tape to the beginning of all four programs. At
that point a second student may select a second program.
In short, only 25 per cent of any system of this type can be
used simultaneously. The problems of accessibility, of
which the multitrack problem is only one example, have led
to at least three different programing arrangements: serial
access, parallel access and scheduled access. Serial access
is essentially an audio or video reference collection. A
series of programs, generally under five minutes in length,
are recorded on a single reel of tape and are indexed for
electronic access, one program at a time. The use of one
program of course renders all other programs on that tape
inaccessible, in much the same way that a reader consulting an article in an encyclopedia renders inaccessible other
articles in the same volume. Parallel access partially al-
leviates the difficulties encountered in the multi-track arrangement described above. By anticipating the need for
certain programs, multiple copies of individual programs
can be placed on different playback machines. In this way
more than one student can be accommodated simultaneously.
Where program needs can be anticipated and where high-
speed dubbing equipment is available, this method of providing multiple copies of the same program is quite practical.
Scheduled access provides yet a third possibility. Where
extremely heavy use of individual programs is anticipated,
timing devices can be installed which automatically play programs on a pre-announced schedule. That is, a program
for which heavy use is anticipated can be preset to be
played repeatedly on any time schedule. In this manner
students come to their carrels just prior to the transmission time and dial the timed program.

     At Ithaca College in Ithaca, N. Y. , a basic dial lan-
guage laboratory has matured into the kind of configuration
described above. Audio lines were run between the lan-
gauge laboratory located in a classroom building and the new
library. There, in a series of carrels, telephone dials
were installed, permitting access by any student in the li-

brary to any program available in the system. A further refinement of this idea at Ithaca has included the installation of microphone lines to a number of classrooms adjacent to the language laboratory area. By a telephone request to the control room, any instructor may record his lecture or presentation, or perhaps record the presentation of a guest lecturer. The recording, made in the control room, is then placed into the dial system for access at a later time in the library by any student who, for any reason, was unable to be present in the classroom. This mode of use has the obvious advantage of providing for students unable to attend class, or for the professor who must be away from the campus. Further, the storage of presentations of this type permits repeated listening for added clarification and understanding.

In 1965, Oklahoma Christian College set perhaps the most ambitious goal involving remote access information systems. Convinced that students study ineffectively in their rooms, Stafford North, Dean of Instruction at Oklahoma Christian, undertook to provide a separate carrel for each student on the second and third floors of the new library. Added to each carrel was a telephone dial which provides access to as many as 136 separate programs. The college now has constructed over 1, 000 carrels and has placed terminals at numerous points throughout the campus including several large group classrooms. Each student carrel in the library, in addition to the dial console, is equipped with a lockable compartment for personal property, a book shelf, typing "L, " and a large work surface. Power outlets are built into each carrel so that projection equipment or supplementary lighting fixtures can be used.

Another elaborate audio system has been installed on the campus of Ohio State University. The Ohio State system to a greater extent than perhaps any other has decentralized its terminals, providing access to the system in a number of different places throughout the campus. Special emphasis should be made here of the Ohio State technique, since one of the main advantages of any electronic distribution system lies in its potential for decentralization.

Other more elaborate systems, some including remote access to video programing have been installed in libraries at Oral Roberts University in Tulsa, Okla. , in the public schools of West Hartford, Conn. , the Beverly Hills Public Schools, Calif. and elsewhere. In more installations visited by the author it appeared that audio equipment, in general, works very well indeed, but that those institutions which have invested in video distribution equipment are limited to very few programs, unreliable operation and expense that far exceeds the utility of the system.

When planning is based upon an installation of approximately 40 audio carrels utilizing an audiopassive mode (listen only), Ofiesh estimates that a reasonably accurate cost can be projected by calculating $500 per carrel position and $500 for each program source. The adding of video capability to any system can be estimated at approximately four to five times the cost of the audio system. Thus, an average audio system of 40 carrels capable of storing 40 programs, audiopassive, would cost approximately $40,000 plus an estimated $6,000 for installation, or a total of $46,000. A video system of the same capability would cost between $184,000 and $230,000--considerably more than most institutions have to spend.

A unique audio/video system is in the final stages of completion at the Oak Park School District in Illinois. Utilizing high-speed duplicating machines, each student requesting a program has it duplicated at high speed from a master tape onto his own tape. In this way no student must wait more than one minute for any program, thus more closely approximating random accessibility than any other system now available. This year the district plans to complete the installation of video discs for the retrieval and display of still television images. These too will be reproducible at high speeds.

In Pennsylvania, pioneering work in remote access audio systems was done at the Abington School District near Philadelphia. More recently new installations have been completed at Marywood College and at Shippensburg State College, both located in library space. At Marywood College the control and switching room is located in a Communication Center adjacent to the library. The carrels are located at convenient places in the stack areas of the library. At Shippensburg the carrels are placed in rows adjacent to the stacks. The control room is located nearby in a non-public area of the library with a glass wall overlooking the carrel area. Fifteen of the 100 carrels in the Shippensburg system are equipped with video capability programed from a videotape recorder designed to store information in a serial access mode.

Other significant installations include Forest Park Community College in St. Louis, Mo.; Wayne State University in Detroit, Mich.; Southern Illinois University, Carbondale, Ill.; Brevard Junior College, Cocoa, Fla.; Bucknell University, Lewisburg, Pa.; and the State University College at Fredonia, N. Y.

If one looks at a fair sample of the various types of remote access systems now in use, several tentative conclusions can be drawn. First, those institutions that have planned carefully and thoroughly on the basis of their needs, and who have written specifications directly around those needs, invariably acquire systems more satisfactory than institutions which permit a vendor to make decisions for them. Second, quality audio systems work very well indeed. Access times for programs not in use are well within tolerance limits, (frequently less than 10 seconds) and audio quality can be excellent. Both Ohio State and Oklahoma Christian handle thousands of dial requests each week and report very high equipment reliability rates. Third, remote access video, while installed in some institutions, does not yet enjoy the reliability of audio and generally is more expensive than can be justified in an automatic retrieval system. The recent development of electronic video recording, which is a new and inexpensive way of recording video information on film, as well as the excitement now being expressed in the video cassette, (New York Times, Sec. 3, p. 1, July 5, 1970), all promise to provide an economic and technological breakthrough in the accessibility of video information. Fourth, it appears that future remote access systems will be combined with other methods of providing both audio and video information. Present systems permit a student to utilize information only at the carrel or terminal position.

Much interest has been expressed in recent months of utilizing the 1/8 inch tape cassette in conjunction with remote access systems. Through the development of high-speed cassette duplication equipment it will be possible for a student to request a program from a central storage bank in the remote access system and have it duplicated on a cassette. A contract for such a system has already been written for one western community college. Further, cassette players are now available in the less than $20 range, making it possible for libraries to lend them and for student book stores to sell them. Such equipment is clearly not suited for music reproduction, but is entirely adequate for

speech. Consumer Reports noted recently that some cassettes now contain audio quality comparable to disc versions
of the same recordings.   Some, they report, were actually
superior to reel-to-reel types (Consumer Reports, 35:7,
July, 1970, p. 397). The increases in cassette audio quality have taken place even faster than predicted by many.

It is clear that remote access information systems
have proved useful to a number of institutions. It is also
clear that carefully designed equipment functions with great
reliability.   However, it is important that any user of this
type of equipment provide himself both with programing personnel and with technical assistance.   Trained librarians can
be taught to handle and edit audio- and videotape without difficulty, but the maintenance of remote access systems requires an electronic technician.   For smaller systems a
technician can be available on call.   But larger installations
ordinarily require the services of a full-time person.   While
a detailed guide to system planning is clearly beyond the
scope of these few pages, a few precautions are in order.

Where a new building is being planned, attention
should be paid to the provision of conduit from control room
space to each carrel location.   Further, if the system is to
be decentralized into other buildings, institution owned cable
or leased telephone lines will be required. Where video
carrels are contemplated, 110 volt AC power should be
available.   In any case, power is necessary in the carrel
for the operation of many types of additional audio and video
equipment.   Care should be taken in the selection of headphone units.   Soft cushioned dynamic headphones provide a
high level of noise reduction and increase acoustic privacy.
This type of headphone is the most practical for use in public service areas.   Control room space for both tape playback equipment and switching equipment generates heat and
noise.   Building planning must provide for adequate power,
air conditioning and acoustic isolation from other spaces.
A false floor similar to the type used in computer rooms
facilitates the wiring of equipment.

A remote access information system is a most useful complement to a developing independent learning facility.
It provides a particularly efficient method for handling audio
collections of all types and will, within the next few years,
be capable of providing for video information at affordable
prices.   It is expandable and can provide unlimited decentralization.   Remote access technology is no longer just an

experiment. In many institutions it is already an important dimension to newly organized independent learning programs.

In the fall of 1970, AECT will publish a new book entitled, Remote Access Audio Video Information Systems, edited by the author. It is designed to assist administrators and educators responsible for purchasing, installing and using such systems.

37.   Pamphlet Collections:
      The Defense Rests

      by Stephanie Goldsmith

          Reprinted by permission of the American Library
          Association and the author, from School Libraries,
          Summer 1969.

          For three years, I, as librarian in charge of the
pamphlet collection at the High School Library of the Laboratory Schools of the University of Chicago, have been de-
fending the value of such a collection, not so much to our
faculty and students who use it extensively, as to visiting
librarians. Several have implied that the development and
maintenance of such a collection is a waste of time, energy,
and money. I have tried to convert these librarians to thinking "pro" pamphlets, and I hope at this time to be able to
convert high school librarians in general to the value of a
pamphlet collection by explaining the practices and procedures
currently employed at U. High. I also hope that with the
publication of this article I will have had to defend the value
of a pamphlet collection for the last time.

          At this time, these questions present themselves:

    1.   Why do we include pamphlets in our library's
         collection?
    2.   What types of pamphlets are found in our collec-
         tion?
    3.   What sources do we have for obtaining pamphlets?
    4.   How do we catalog and display our pamphlets so
         that they are easily available and accessible to
         our users?

          1.   Why do we include pamphlets in our library's
collection? We at the U. High Library believe in the multi-
media approach to learning. We try to make available to
our users, faculty and students alike, all types of materials
--book and nonbook. We do this because our students, Pre-
Freshmen (at the Laboratory Schools the seventh grade and

                              236

eighth grade are incorporated into one year called the pre-
freshman year) through Seniors, have varying interests and
ability levels. Also, we have found that the student requesting a "book" on "air pollution" for example, is actually seeking information which may be better found in reports
of government findings or in magazine or newspaper
articles, and that the student wanting a "book" on
"India" may find the information he needs in a
government prepared pamphlet, in a newspaper or magazine
article, by examining a map or an art reproduction, by listening to a recording of Indian music, or perhaps by viewing a film. Depending on the type of information being
sought, we suggest to the student that he use the Reader's
Guide to Periodical Literature, the New York Times Index,
or our subject card catalog, which is the key to our library's collection of books, filmstrips, films, art reproductions, maps, recordings, music scores, three dimensional
objects, human resources, and pamphlets. In addition, we
include pamphlets in our collection because they often supplement our periodical holdings. They provide up-to-date
information on timely subjects. Finally, they help provide
and make available more information to our users. We may
have only three or four books on "air pollution" in the library, but we have at least fifty or sixty pamphlets including
reprints from scientific journals and the latest facts and findings as reported by federal, state, or even local fact finding committees studying the problem.

     2. What types of pamphlets are found in our collec-
tion? Our pamphlets fit into either of two categories: they
support the school's curriculum or they are of interest to
young people living in today's world. These two categories
are often one and the same. Moreover, to remain in the
collection, the information in the pamphlet must be up-to-
date or it must be of historical value. We have for example, extensive collections of pamphlets on Vietnam, both pro
and con U.S. involvement, and on Chicago, its history, development, and the current scene. Our latest additions to
our "Chicago" collection are reports expressing the differing accounts of the activities surrounding the Democratic
National Convention in Chicago last August.

     For years the collection has been primarily support-
ing the Social Science curriculum in the school, but recently,
with the help of interested faculty members, we have been
able to build up our collection of scientific pamphlets.
These consist largely of reprints from Scientific American

and publications issued by the U.S. Atomic Energy Commission.

3. What sources do we have for obtaining pamphlets? Whenever possible we try to get pamphlets for free. This is not difficult to do. We have learned that certain publishers will give a sample copy of their publications to libraries. For example, we have received a sample copy of each of several articles reprinted from the World Book Encyclopedia. We have also received sample copies of pamphlets issued by the U.S. Public Health Service and other government agencies. By writing to our congressman, we have received at no cost, reports of congressional committee hearings. We are also on the mailing lists for several local and federal government agencies.

Other sources for free materials are listed in:

Sources of Information and
Unusual Services,
Information Directory Company,
200 West 57th St,
New York, N.Y. 10019.

Free and Inexpensive Learning
Materials,
Division of Surveys and
Field Services,
George Peabody College for
Teachers,
Nashville, Tennessee 37203.

Foreign embassies located in the United States and Permanent Missions to the UN also send free literature. Their addresses, from time to time, are listed in an excellent publication entitled Intercom, published by the Foreign Policy Association, Inc., 345 East 46th St., New York, N.Y. 10017.

I have limited myself to listing only free sources of pamphlets. The tapping of these sources alone would provide the basis for a valuable pamphlet collection, but there are endless sources for relatively inexpensive pamphlets. For example, there is the Vertical File Index, ALA Booklist, and U.S. Government publications. Checklists of government publications available for purchase from the Government Printing Office are most valuable. We regularly

check The Selected List of United States Government Publications, a biweekly which gives the titles and prices of the
more important publications on sale at the G. P. O.   This
list can be obtained free from the Superintendent of Documents.   Also available free from the G. P. O. are Price
Lists on specific subjects such as American History, Education, Indians, etc. , which are revised from time to time.

     4.   How do we catalog and display our pamphlets so
that they are easily available and accessible to our users?
Our cataloging procedures for pamphlets are simple.   We
want our students to use them so we make them easy to locate and circulate.   We assign to each pamphlet a subject
heading.   We use the same subject headings assigned to the
other materials in our collection, i. e. , books, films, and
filmstrips, to allow for coordination and consistency with
the rest of the library's collection.   These headings for the
most part are from Sears List of Subject Headings.   When
establishing a new subject heading or cross-reference in the
pamphlet collection, we place cards in both our subject card
catalog and in a separate pamphlet card catalog located near
the pamphlet file.   These cards state that the library has
pamphlets on the subject.

     Each pamphlet has a book card to facilitate its circu-
lation so in addition to a subject heading, a main entry must
be determined for it.   Here again we try to make procedures
simple so whenever possible, we enter the pamphlet under
the name of the personal author responsible for the work.
If the pamphlet is issued by a government agency, a committee, or an organization, then we enter it under the name
of the agency, etc.   The rest of the information needed on
the book card is the title of the pamphlet, its cost, and a
copy number which we assign to it.   The worksheets for
pamphlets include all of this information, and if the subject
heading is being used in the pamphlet collection for the first
time, the worksheet must also include this information so
that catalog cards for it will be typed.   These worksheets
are kept and later used as a shelf list for the collection.

     All pamphlets with the same subject heading are
placed together in a folder in the pamphlet file.   At present we have sixty vertical file drawers with several more
on order.   We like, however, to display all new pamphlets
before they are filed.   Finally, we usually keep no more
than three copies of a pamphlet, but we do have multiple
copies of some pamphlets which we keep in storage.   These

we place on period and overnight reserve when a faculty member requests it or when the needs of a particular assignment demand it.

We do not have all the questions answered nor all the problems solved. Our policies and procedures are still in a state of being evolved, and we never close our eyes to new ideas or suggestions, but the development and maintenance of our pamphlet collection has been neither costly nor a waste of time or energy. It has been rather, a most significant addition to our library's holdings. The time and energy spent on such a collection is time well spent when you see the extensive and profitable use that is made of it by students and faculty alike.

The defense rests!

PART V

HELPFUL HINTS

38. The Librarian's Personality; or,
More Than Scraps of Information

by Pearl L. Ward

Alfred North Whitehead, the philosopher, scientist,
and teacher, once said:

> Culture is activity of thought, and receptiveness
> to beauty and humane feeling. Scraps of informa-
> tion have nothing to do with it. A merely well-
> informed man is the most useless bore on God's
> earth. [1]

Librarians need to be reminded of this statement as
much as, if not more than, any group of professional people. Most librarians are outstanding in the area of specific
or isolated knowledge--the scraps of information of which
Whitehead speaks--but they too frequently fail in the areas
of personality, personal relations, and humane feeling.

The personality of the librarian has concerned administrators, the library public, and library school teachers
for some time. Since it is my professional job to assist
with the preparation of future librarians as well as with many
of those already in the field, I have been acutely aware of
my responsibility in this area. I have given much thought
to the problem and have attempted to find some reasons and
solutions.

Librarianship is a service profession. Most librarians meet the public regularly, others occasionally. We depend on the public for our very existence. And yet too
many of our number treat the public, more frequently than
not, in a disrespectful and discourteous manner.

What basically is the matter with librarians that they
should treat patrons as they so often do--ignoring a patron
who stands and waits for assistance, speaking in a sharp or
a supercilious tone of voice, using technical library terminology, to name just a few examples of behavior often observed. Why are we not more adept at public relations,
more skillful in communication?

242

An analysis of the problem reveals a few possible causes which seem to be worthy of careful consideration.

First of all, librarians fail to recognize mere scraps of information for what they are and are intended for--to help those seeking answers. We make the mistake of substituting the scraps of information for wisdom or understanding that help to make knowledge meaningful and related to the student's needs. By so doing, we let the information we possess make us haughty, self-centered, and disdainful, or appear so to the patron.

The second failure thus results--disregard for the person who seeks the information, disregard for him as a human being with sensitivities, frequently with inadequacies, and often with fears of revealing these inadequacies to the librarian. We fail to recognize that the scraps of information we possess become useful to others or have meaning only if we are approachable, understanding, and willing to share. With all our knowledge, we often lack understanding and concern for people as human beings. We all fall short when it comes to such qualities as consideration for others, genuine concern for the individual, warmth, compassion, kindness, and generosity. We fail as individuals.

This leads to the third point: we can't be better librarians than we are persons. 2 Librarians stand in a very unique position. We are middlemen. We are directly between the individual who is seeking or learning and the information which is available to him. We might say that knowledge is filtered through our minds and characters. If we stand in the way because of our warped personality, we hinder the learning process, the constructive on-going search for truth or for answers.

Fourth, there appears to be something in librarianship which is damaging to personalities. Many librarians become more rude, more sharp-tongued, haughty, smug, or cynical as they get older, or older in the profession. Young librarians do not fit this pattern generally, although this is occasionally the case. Perhaps we have too many pressures on us, or we are overworked, are naturally introverted, or dislike people. Whatever the cause, our personalities too often tend to become warped and thin. We let librarianship keep us from growing as persons.

To analyze and identify the problem is not sufficient.

Solutions or answers are needed. One of the most important answers lies in a deeper understanding on the part of
each librarian of his or her personality, and in an attempt
by each individual to grow as a person, because at the basis of these four points is personality growth and development.

I should like to refer to the work of Professor Pullias again and to consider six of the principles of growth
in being from his book, A Teacher Is Many Things. [3] He
speaks of two kinds of growth: growth in knowledge and
growth in being. Librarians do well in the first of these;
the latter should be of special concern to us. All of these
principles of development of the quality of personality apply
as directly to librarians as they do to teachers. Surely a
librarian, too, is many things, chief among them a growing,
thoughtful, genuine person.

   1. Sensitivity. "The widely sensitive person," says
Pullias, "perceives with increasing rapidity the meaning of
situations involving things and people." He does not need
to know all details in order to assess the situation. A sensitive person is able to put himself in another person's
place and to perceive the other's feelings.

   2. Interest and Curiosity. A personality grows
through "cultivating the roots of wide interests and restless
curiosity." These are interests beyond those needed for the
individual's job. "Narrowed interests mean a narrowed
self.... When routine, fear, illness, or habit destroys interest and curiosity, the vibrant quality of life tends to go
out of the person." We need balanced growth in order to
bring continuing personality development as we meet life's
demands.

   3. Love. [4] The word love seems to be embarras-
sing to some people, or they are afraid of it. And yet,
"many in our world are love-starved and would profit from
a frank discussion of their need." The nature of love is
very complex and has many expressions. But it seems that
"running through all of love is the losing of self and the
concerns of self in a concern for the welfare and happiness
of another." Giving and receiving love is very important to
the growth of personality.

   4. Self-determination. "Growth in this quality
means an increasing ability to feel and behave in terms of

resources which are within the self. " A person who has developed some maturity has built up a philosophy of life which gives him "flexible stability. " He is a self-determined individual and is not concerned with "satisfying an external authority or surmounting what seems to be an artificial hurdle. "

5. Humility. As used by Pullias, humility is the opposite of an overwhelming pride. "It helps one to understand his proper place in the larger scheme of things. Such humility of mind is the foundation of respect for other people and their varying abilities. "

6. Peace.[5] This is "essentially a philosophy of life that gives unity and meaning to the search and struggle. " This philosophy is made up of the basic beliefs an individual holds to be true--those principles one decides to live by, and by which his life is governed. When peace is achieved, the individual finds stability and poise in the midst of turmoil.

These six principles speak directly to the problem of the librarian's personality. Not until we as a group and as individuals recognize that the problem is with us and that it is serious, will we be able to change. After recognition must come a desire to improve our personalities. Our image as a profession, although improving, is far from ideal. We must not discard our scraps of information; we must not be merely well-informed. Rather, we must be receptive to "humane feeling" by continuing to grow as persons. Thus, the isolated information we provide, coming from and through us to the seeker, is no longer "scraps of information" but, because of what we as librarians are or are becoming, begins to take on the life and meaning of genuine learning. The personality of the librarian can make the difference.

Notes

1. Alfred N. Whitehead, The Aims of Education. New York: Macmillan Company, 1929, p. 13.

2. The thought is expressed in reference to teaching by a careful student of the teacher and the teaching art in this way: "the most fundamental principle of all we have considered about excellence in teaching is that if the teacher would effectively fulfill his role as a

teacher, he must constantly grow in greatness as a
person.   In deepest essence, a teacher can be no
greater as a teacher than he is as a person. "   Earl
V. Pullias in Toward Excellence in College Teaching.   Dubuque, Iowa: William C. Brown Company,
1963, p. 44.

3.   For a fuller discussion of these points, as well as a
     discussion of growth in knowledge, see his book pub-
     lished by Indiana University Press, 1963, chapter 24.

4.   For a profound study of this problem by a distinguished
     psychiatrist, see Rollo May's Love and Will; for a
     different but very insightful approach, see C. S.
     Lewis' The Four Loves.

5.   The most profound discussion of this problem I know
     may be found in Alfred N. Whitehead's great book,
     Adventures in Ideas, chapter 20.

39. Do's and Don'ts for Librarians
and Administrators

by Mary Louise Mann

Reprinted from Today's Education, October 1970,
by permission of the author and the publisher.

Over the years, I have developed two lists of do's
and don'ts--one for librarians and one for administrators to
use when communicating with one another. If both groups
follow these tenets, their library programs should improve,
and teachers and students will reap the benefits.

To librarians, I offer this advice about dealing with
your administrator:

Don't attempt to discuss library needs with him in
the school cafeteria, at the ball game, or when you can
corner him in the hall.

Do make an appointment. Let him know what you
want to discuss with him.

Do plan ahead. Make notes of the points you want
to emphasize, the questions you want to ask.

Do prepare a long-range plan with quantitative and
qualitative goals to be accomplished each year.

Don't use library terminology, such as carding, ac-
cessioning, Dewey decimal system. In fact, don't talk about
technical processes; they bore administrators.

Do take along statistics and other materials you may
need.

Do prepare and submit a detailed budget for the library.

Don't ask for funds for library use in a timid or
apologetic manner.

Don't beat around the bush. State needs with the
assurance that they are essential.

Don't bow your head in acquiescence if he says our
budget has been cut.

Do emphasize needs of pupils and teachers for library services.

Don't base your need for clerical or paraprofessional assistance on the amount of desk work to be done.

Do emphasize the importance of freeing you from clerical work so you can spend more time helping pupils and teachers.

Don't tell him how much cataloging you have to do-- he just might think you are inefficient.

Don't complain about the teachers, even those who send all the study hall students to the library so they can go to the boiler room and smoke.

Don't complain about your lot even if you do have the worst possible schedule.

Don't be afraid to ask--those who ask get.

For administrators, I have these suggestions about dealing with the school librarian:

Do take notes rather than trust your memory when he comes to you with problems or new ideas.

Do give your librarian a definite answer to questions or requests. If you feel that the request or suggestion is unwise, impractical, or impossible, substantiate your refusal with adequate reasons.

Don't hedge, or the librarian will go away feeling completely frustrated.

Do have an open mind and show interest and enthusiasm for new ideas that your librarian may propose, and give him an opportunity to try them out.

Don't give the impression that these ideas are doomed to failure or "won't work."

Do consider library needs in relation to the total school program.

Do consider the media center as a vital link rather than as an isolated unit.

Do restrain any criticism or misgivings you may have about your library service until you have listened to the librarian's side of the story.

Do praise your librarian now and then for a job well done.

Don't ever let him feel that his efforts have been in vain.

The administrator and librarian need to get together to plan, to dream, to work for solutions to problems, and to establish goals for providing the very best possible library service for their school.

40.   Things to Do When School Opens
      in the Fall

      by Pearl L. Ward

      1.   Be in the media center a few days before school
opens in order to open the mail, freshen up the rooms, rearrange books or equipment to suit your taste.

      2.   Enter your first month's schedule on your calen-
dar.   Type the schedule.   Include book orders, pamphlet
orders, binding, supplies, etc.   Then dismiss details and
routines from your mind; complete items on your calendar
as they come due.

      3.   Make an extra effort to have attractive and out-
standing flower arrangements in the library.

      4.   Have display cases and bulletin board areas in
the media center feature the newest and most appealing materials; include book and album jackets, for example.   Display the materials that appeal the most to children and
young people, such as mystery, adventure, and animal stories, light romance, hobbies, music, current problems
such as drugs.   Good displays are a silent invitation to
all students, young and old.

      5.   Make a good display in a case, if one is availa-
ble, in the main hall or outside of the media center.

      6.   At the first faculty meeting, if introduced and
allowed to say a word, do so in the warmest and most sin-
cere manner.   Wear a genuine smile.   Keep your comments
short.

      7.   Make an attempt to meet as many faculty mem-
bers personally as possible, both old and new ones.   Talk
with them enough to learn their special hobbies or interests.
Then remember to watch for new and current material concerning their interest and show it or send it to them.

      8.   Invite the faculty members, the principal, vice-

249

principals, attendance officer, and any other administrator
to come to the media center. Show them materials they
can use.

9. Arrange to have a conference with the English or
Social Studies teachers and plan for the orientation of the
freshmen. Work closely with the teaching staff in this program.

10. Prepare an enticing folder for freshmen and new
students, giving them a warm welcome to the media center.
Let them feel that the center is for them as well as for the
old students. Cartoons to liven the folder are good.

11. Have your own name on your desk, large enough
to be seen easily, so that all students and faculty coming to
the media center will be able to address you by name.

12. Prepare a short but lively article for the first
issue of the school paper, or give a reporter information
about yourself and the media center--your own introduction
to the school.

13. Attend all social functions of the faculty, be
friendly and cooperative if asked to serve on committees or
plan programs.

14. Accept the opportunity to give book reviews,
both at faculty meetings and for individual classes. Make
them the best reviews possible, entertaining as well as informational. Make the faculty and students glad that they
have you for their librarian.

15. By your words, and especially by your deeds,
let the students and faculty know that your primary purpose
for existence is to serve their needs, to make their individual instructional programs more effective.

APPENDICES

A. Criteria of Excellence Checklist

    by Robert N. Case

      Reprinted by permission of the American Library
      Association, from School Libraries, Spring 1969.

    The "Criteria of Excellence" was first used by the
School Library Manpower Project, funded by the Knapp
Foundation of North Carolina Inc. , as a guide in identifying
outstanding school library centers offering unified service
programs at the building level. The school libraries identified participated in a national survey to determine the
tasks presently being performed by all types of school library personnel.

    The criteria, while giving emphasis to the perform-
ance of service activities related to total staff function, is
however, an effective instrument to assess the ever changing role of the school library. School administrators and
school library personnel in cooperative study will discover
the "Criteria of Excellence" statements to be useful in
evaluating individual school library programs. Such evaluation and self-study on an annual and continuing basis will
allow the school district to activate plans for meeting future needs for the total education of its community's youth.

    It is necessary in using this criteria to understand
the implications for interpreting school library manpower
requirements. The growing demand for a variety of services from a school library calls for an early recognition to
study new ways to utilize a variety of levels of library personnel to perform these important functions. Educators,
who are becoming increasingly concerned with the national
shortage of trained school library personnel, are seeking
new ways to more effectively utilize librarians by supporting their roles with a variety of specialists, technicians,
aides, and additional support personnel.

    The "Criteria of Excellence" checklist will provide
the foundation for an initial evaluation of individual school

library programs. First it becomes necessary to determine what services and activities are presently actual operational functions of the school library. Secondly, quality school library service requires continuous study and revision of activities to keep pace with increased educational demands. Third, as the checklist begins to group and identify areas that require attention, school library personnel working with administrators will need to plan time schedules to realistically meet the high goals for quality performance in education.

While school districts may have many of the activities in the "Criteria of Excellence" presently in operation, it is important to understand that even successful functions of a library need to be studied and reviewed from time to time. Priorities established to meet these goals must relate to the total educational plan of the community.

The value of the checklist is not in the total score achieved however, but in the manner school library personnel and administrators will approach and use the "Criteria of Excellence" to study the progress of a school library program. In an overall plan to achieve excellence in school library development, administrators and key school library personnel must design a plan that will achieve a proper balance of the operational and service activities to a realistic approach to staff assignment. The decisions to meet and maintain this balance of staff to program should evolve naturally from results of studies made on a continual basis which relate to individual school needs.

As the school library directly or indirectly effects or is influenced by the entire school program, representatives from other disciplines need to be encouraged to participate in the evaluation and study of the library's role in the total instructional plan. Implementing time schedules to activate new programs will need to be carefully outlined, for timing is vital to budget planning, space requirements, and the assignment of staff.

Once a program is staffed, introduced and has become a functional part of the school library, a periodic review should be carried out to assess its initial impact and total effect upon the instructional program. It is through this evaluation, interpretation and implementation, that school libraries have been able to achieve the excellence which has so vitally influenced education.

Criteria of Excellence
Program Analysis Checklist

Directions: Read the statements carefully. In the spaces provided under each of the three broad categories; Program, Research, Implementation, check (√) the columns which best identify the school library.

The school library program, as an integral part of any school's instructional program contributing to the development and implementation of the total curriculum and achievement of the educational objectives of the school, shows evidence of the following:

	PROGRAM			RESEARCH			IMPLEMENTATION		
	Fully Operational A	Partially Operational B	Non Operational C	Presently Under Study A	Planned for Study B	No Study Planned C	Expect Achievement 1 - 2 Years A	Expect Achievement 3 - 5 Years B	Do Not Expect to Achieve C
1. At the district level, a school supervisor who gives direction and leadership in the development of a total district-wide school library program.									
2. At the building level, at least two trained librarians (and/or audiovisual personnel), with additional paid supporting staff.									
3. A unified program which reflects a depth and variety in the selection of all types of media, with the necessary equipment available for use in the support of the instructional program.									
4. Effective design in physical arrangement of facilities to accommodate use by teachers and students, individually and in small or large groups.									
5. Efficient organization and easy accessibility to all services, materials, and equipment for teachers' and students' use before, during, and after the school day.									

6. Provision for, and assistance to, teachers and students in the production of new materials for instructional use.

7. Participation of library personnel with teachers in the planning and implementation of the curriculum as a means of integrating library services with the instructional program of the school.

8. Planned and coordinated inservice for teachers to provide training in the production and use of instructional media.

9. Purposeful instruction for students, as individuals or in small or large groups, in library and research skills evolving from the needs of the instructional program.

10. Consultative and special services to teachers to provide support in the performance of their educational roles.

11. Availability of a wide variety of learning opportunities for the individual which offer the challenge and motivation necessary to aid a student in his intellectual, social, and emotional development.

12. Continuous evaluation of the library program in support of the educational philosophy and purposes of the school and the needs and interests of the teachers and students served.

During the next five years the School Library Manpower Project will continue to study the changing roles of
school library personnel. Particular attention will be directed toward job analysis leading to new job definitions.
Once these new roles have been defined the Project will direct its attention and resources to advancing recruitment
activities which will lead toward new program designs for
training school library personnel. In the interim, local
school districts will want to begin a self-study of individual
school library performance to prepare for anticipated new
designs in school library services.

B. Instructional Programing:
    Structuring and Instructional Sequence*

    by Frederick G. Knirk

    Programed instruction is a process whereby a series
of instructional objectives are: 1) identified, 2) written into
an instructional program, 3) evaluated and revised, until
4) the resulting program is evaluated. If it works for a
specified population in an efficient way, it is adopted. If
the program is found not to work well, it is rejected.

    The process of programing begins with the identifica-
tion of a series of instructional goals, or objectives. These
relevant objectives should include both cognitive (content) objectives and the affective (attitudinal) goals. It is desirable
that these objectives be written in behavioral terms implies
identification of a goal which can be measured. Writing
these kinds of measurable objectives will permit the instructional programmer and other evaluators to know when the
student actually achieves the identified objectives.

    Further, the development of instructional objectives
can be the framework within which the required instructional
materials, are organized. The objectives can be related to
each other sequentially with illustrative and drill items built
into the program to encourage retention. These illustrations
and repetitive exercises would be similar to those conducted
by the teacher, but might not be included in the usual abbreviated lesson outline. In a very real sense, the development
of programed materials can be likened to the development of
a detailed lesson outline with all of the illustrative positive-
ly reinforcing and repetitive information built into it. Further, a program is written so that students can easily understand it.

    The program itself consists of a series of relatively
small steps or frames with questions on the content of that

_____

*Reprinted by permission of the author (Unpublished).

or previous frames. This questioning insures that students
will know by their correct or incorrect answers exactly
which materials need restudy. The questions are relevant,
straight-forward, and easy to answer; not so easy that the
student is bored, but easy enough that he can progress con-
fidently. He is constantly reinforced by this positive feedback as he works through the program.

The students, by continually answering the questions,
will be kept mentally active and "with the program!" This
involvement of students with the materials and the use of
positive reinforcement, or feedback, is found in almost all
programs.

There are basically two types of programs. Linear
programs, also called Skinner Programs, usually have short
frames and look like the illustration below.

EXAMPLE FRAMES FROM A LINEAR PROGRAM

Answers to   There are 10 decimeters in 1
Questions at   meter, just as there are 12
Right   inches in 1 foot. There are
          20   _____ decimeters in 2 meters.

         100   Just as there are 10 decimeters
                    in 1 meter, there are 10 centi-
                    meters in 1 decimeter. In 1
                    meter there are _____ centi-
                    meters.

       1,000   We know there are 100 centi-
                    meters in 1 meter. Appendix C
                    tells us that there are 10 mil-
                    limeters in 1 centimeter.
                    There are _____ millimeters
                    in 100 centimeters.

Excerpt from: The Metric System
               of Measurement.
               by F. G. Knirk.
               Detroit Public
               Schools, 1961.

Branch programs use a student's past knowledge and
abilities to procede through a programed text at his own

speed. Inaccurate perceptions can be diagnosed by the use
of these texts and then remedied by specific illustrations
and background information.

The branch program "frames" are usually larger than
those for linear program frames. Questions are of the multiple choice type, which facilitate branching. A frame to an
incorrect response in a branching program is included below.

EXAMPLE FRAME FROM A BRANCH PROGRAM

Your answer was: The atomic weight of the following atom is 7.

7e	M	shell
8e	L	shell
2e	K	shell

17 P
18 N

Your answer was incorrect. You may be confusing
the number of electrons in the outer shell for the
atom weight.

There are 7 valence electrons, in the above atom,
but this is not the answer to our question. The
question was:

What is the atomic weight of the above atom:
If your answer is: Turn to page:
17........................16
35........................21
I don't know.............. 17

Frame from: The Halogen Family.
by F. G. Knirk.
Detroit Public
Schools, 1962.

There is no one best way to develop programed materials. Program materials may be linked together by relating objectives, or they may be developed by a teacher
with a rational science-oriented teaching style without explicit objectives well identified in advance.

Almost <u>any medium</u> can be programed. Most program materials today are found in a printed or programed text. Sometimes the printed materials are put into devices called "teaching machines" which, in essence, merely turn the pages of a programed text for a student. Films can be programed in the sense that information can be presented and then be the subject of questions as the film pauses momentarily. Following a few moments during which the student is to respond either overtly on paper or mentally, the correct response is then given on the film.

Evaluation and revision procedures leading to the adoption or rejection of a film are also an important aspect of developing motion picture film programs. Television materials, language laboratories, taped materials, computers and other media can be similarly programed.

Most programed materials are designed for <u>individual student</u> use. This individualization of instruction <u>may be one of the</u> greatest characteristics of programed materials, and its most valuable contribution to modern instruction. This permits students with varying backgrounds and goals, and learning styles, etc., to be directed to the more appropriate programs. They can then work through these materials at their own rate. This means all students can successfully complete an instructional unit. It will, obviously, take some students longer to complete the materials than others. However, in the case of program materials on film, or audio tape, it is difficult to allow the student's reading or listening rate to modify his pace as he proceeds through the materials. A motion picture projector and tape recorder will go along and set speed's, unless the student stops it for time for introspection, or reshows segments for review.

The final step in developing program materials involves an <u>evaluation of the materials.</u> Materials should be continually evaluated both during development and after completion. This evaluation must involve the same types of students as those who are eventually to use the program. Wherever student difficulties with vocabulary, pacing, the illustrations, or other methodological and pedagogic concerns occur, they can be then corrected until the program works effectively for that student population. If the program cannot be made to work, then the program must be rejected.

This ability to evaluate and revise materials until they work effectively (relatively well, and thus) and make efficient use of the student's time is a strong reason programing is often liked by students and teachers.

Back to the lesson outline model of programing: if a teacher were able to evaluate each lesson outline used, and continually revise it until it worked as well as possible with a particular type of student, his presentations would continually improve as a result of the evaluation and revision process. It is for exactly this reason that the programed materials are so effective.

While much of the research in education today shows no significant difference between programed and traditional learning, it is expected that most programed instruction-related studies will result in either: 1) the same cognitive gain in one-half to one-third, or 2) that the student will learn more in the same amount of time required by students taught in the traditional manner. If the objective gain obtained by the traditionally taught students is acceptable to the programed student, then he would have additional time to take further courses, to socialize, or to utilize his extra time as he sees fit.

Many students find it difficult to learn in a programed situation. Generally, the younger students who have not yet learned "how to learn," are more positive about their programed materials. Older students frequently find it difficult to modify their learning styles, possibly because they have not learned to take the responsibility for their own learning and moniter the use of their own time. A continuous program of self-directed learning develops within the individual an ability to identify and resolve problems which may or may not originate within a school, producing a citizen who is able to make meaningful decisions that affect his well being.

C. Selecting Materials
    for School Media Centers:

    Guidelines and Selection Sources
    to Insure Quality Collections

    Prepared by the American Association
    of School Librarians

Foreword

This third edition of <u>Selecting Materials for School
Media Centers</u> was occasioned by the increasing demand for
copies of the 1967 revision, the significant number of new
selection tools made available since 1967 as well as the
many new publications worthy of identification, the updating
of certain 1967 listed sources, and the experiences of field
use with consequent re-evaluation of previously listed selection aids.

The extension of federal and state aid for the purchase
of multi-media instructional materials and the resultant establishment and development of school library media centers'
collections, continues the demand and the dilemma of identifying appropriate materials from the thousands of new titles
produced each year as well as identifying the availability of
blacklisted titles. In an effort to resolve these problems,
this bibliography has been compiled by the American Association of School Librarians. In its previous editions, it
has been accepted as the standard list of selection aids by
many state departments of education, state libraries, and by
local school districts. To these ends, this current edition
is offered.

The 1971 revision reflects the professional evaluation
and recommendations of many materials specialists and other
educators who have worked with the tools and found them to
be exemplary. A marked increase in specific subject area
aids is noted as is the increase of evaluative lists of audio-
visual materials. The wider range of educators concerned
with materials selection since 1965--teachers, administrators,
curriculum specialists in teams and individually--has enriched

the expertise of evaluation and raised the level of sophistication in identifying motivational content and design. Further,
several of the sources include student recommendations.
This welcome involvement is recognized in this list.

Judicious use of any selection aid is strongly recommended: prefatory remarks together with statements regarding intended audiences, scope, purpose, bias, and qualifications of editors, compilers and contributors should be noted
in order to appropriately characterize the citations within
the sources themselves. And, finally, physical examination
of both print and nonprint materials is encouraged prior to
purchase. The growing number of education media selection
centers throughout the country is extending the opportunity
for this desirable practice. Used in conjunction with the
sources listed here, the examination centers' collections can
greatly augment the efficiency, accuracy and quality control
of the selection process.

The AASL Committee consisted of: Frances Fleming,
Coordinator, Library Services, Baltimore County Board of
Education, Towson, Maryland; Elizabeth Hodges, formerly
Supervisor of Library Services, Baltimore County Board of
Education, Towson, Maryland; Virginia McJenkin, formerly
Supervisor of Library Services, Fulton County, Georgia; and
chairman, Dorothy McGinniss, Associate Professor, School
of Library Science, Syracuse University. The Committee
worked on the lists of print materials while the lists of nonprint materials were compiled by a representative of the Department of Audiovisual Instruction, Dr. Frederick Knirk,
Associate Director for Academic Affairs, Center for Instructional Communications, Syracuse University.

The following national organizations also contributed
suggestions: American Association for Advancement of Science; Music Educators National Conference; National Council
for the Social Studies; and National Council of Teachers of
Mathematics.
                     John Rowell, President, 1969-70
                     American Association of School Librarians

Guidelines for Selection of
Material for School Media Centers

The expansion of school library media programs to
include a diversity of materials is a natural outgrowth of

the acceptance of the concept of the library or school media center as an integral component of the instructional program of the school. It is the function of the school media center to provide materials which undergird the school curriculum, and it is no longer realistic to think of teaching and learning materials only in terms of the printed word. To support its educational program, a school needs material in many forms related to all curriculum areas.

Intelligent selection of these materials is a time-consuming task which requires professional competence as well as the ability to profit by the professional competence of others. The first requisite is depth of knowledge of the curriculum and the second is knowledge of the needs, interests and abilities of the school clientele. Related factors are the amount of money available, the materials already available in the school media center and materials available from other sources.

Selection of the type of material--printed, pictured or recorded--should be made on the basis of the medium available that most effectively conveys or interprets the content or the concept; in many instances, material in one format is useful in supplementing that in another. The same information may be needed in various forms to accommodate individuals and groups with varying abilities, interests and needs. Regardless of format, all materials selected for the school library media center should meet high standards of excellence. Materials which deal with current topics should be up to date; those which reflect a biased point of view should make the prejudice recognizable.

The individual school media collection should support all facets of the curriculum with materials which reflect different points of view on controversial subjects and which provide opportunities for students and teachers to explore widely in their search for information and inspiration. Since there is within a school little homogeneity of either ability or interest, the collection should contain both easy and difficult materials.

Media selection is a cooperative process which should involve teachers and students, with the final decisions being vested in the media staff. Teachers are subject specialists; therefore, it is the responsibility of the media staff to consult with teachers and to secure their assistance in evaluating instructional resources. Students should be involved in evaluating and selecting print and nonprint materials. Direct participation of faculty and students should be standard procedure in determining the curricular value and the student appeal of instructional materials.

The safest method for selection is, of course, a firsthand knowledge of the material itself; the next is the perceptive use of reliable lists and reviews. Factors to consider in evaluating lists include the reliability of the person or organization who prepared them and their recency. Many school districts and some county and state departments of education now provide examination centers where print and nonprint materials may be previewed or examined. Where such service is available, teachers and librarians should be given the opportunity to become familiar with the materials and should avail themselves of this opportunity before recommending their purchase.

Many school districts, too, have developed statements of policy which govern their selection of materials. Such statements include the philosophy for selection, the agency and staff responsible for implementing the policy, the types of materials included, criteria and procedures for their selection, and procedures for handling problems which arise when a particular piece of material is questioned. When such statements are cooperatively developed, accepted and adhered to, they provide both guidance and protection for all who are involved in the selection of materials.

Other publications which are useful in the preparation of a policy statement are: The School Library Bill of Rights for School Media Center Programs (endorsed by the American Association of School Librarians, 1969); Policies and Procedures for Selection of Instructional Materials (Revised and endorsed by American Association of School Librarians, 1970); The statement from the Committee on Treatment of Minority Groups in Library Books and Other Instructional Materials, "Resolution for Publishers, Editors and Reviewers" (adopted by American Association of School Librarians, 1971); and The Students' Right to Read, prepared by the National Council of Teachers of English, 1962.

Sources of Selection for Print Materials

General Book Lists

Adventuring with Books: A Reading List for Elementary Grades compiled by the Elementary Reading List Committee, National Council of Teachers of English. Over 1, 250 titles arranged in twelve categories. 1966. NCTE. 75 cents.

Best Books for Children compiled by Doris Solomon. A list of recommended books, grouped by age level and grade along with several subject groupings. Contains some suitable adult titles. Revised annually. Bowker. $3. 50.

A Bibliography of Books for Children by Association for Childhood Education International. Annotated list of about 1, 300 books for supplementary reading by children ages 2 thru 12. 1968. ACEI. $1. 50.

Book Bait: Detailed Notes on Adult Books Popular with Young People compiled by Eleanor Walker. Descriptive annotations more detailed than usually found in such a list. Titles arranged by age and type of reader; follow-up titles also included. 1969. ALA. $2. 00.

Books and the Teen-Age Reader by G. Robert Carlsen. Articles about work with young people. Bibliographies of more than 700 books for teen-agers. 1967. Harper. $4. 95. Bantam. 75 cents.

Books for Children 1960-65. 3, 068 titles listed and recommended for library purchase in the Children's Books Section of Booklist from September 1960-August 1965. 1966. ALA. $10. 00; 1965-66 supplement. $2. 25; 1967-68 supplement. $2. 50; 1968-69 supplement. $3. 00.

Books for College Libraries prepared by Melvin Voigt and Joseph Treyz. About 53, 000 titles chosen for an undergraduate library, many of which might be useful for mature readers in senior high. 1967. ALA. $45. 00.

Books for Elementary School Libraries: An Initial Collection compiled by Elizabeth D. Hodges. 3, 077 books annotated. 1969. ALA. $7. 50.

Books for Junior College Libraries compiled and

edited by James W. Pirie. 20, 000 books to meet needs of mature senior high school students. 1969. ALA. $35. 00.

Books for the Teen Age. Annual selection of about 1, 500 books including both recent and older books. One-line annotations for books of the current year. Gives publisher but not price. Published each January. New York Public Library. $2. 00.

Books for You compiled by Committee on the Senior High Book List, NCTE. Annotated list of leisure reading for high school students. 1964. NCTE. 90 cents.

Children And Books by May Hill Arbuthnot. Articles on all phases of children's literature plus excellent detailed bibliographies. 1964. Scott Foresman. $15. 00.

Children's Books compiled yearly by Virginia Haviland and Lois B. Watt. Over 200 titles evaluated yearly. Back numbers available. U. S. Government Printing Office. 15 cents.

Children's Books Too Good to Miss compiled by May Hill Arbuthnot and others. Helpful list for parents and teachers. 1966. Case Western Reserve University. $3. 25; paperback $1. 50.

Children's Catalog. A classified annotated guide to 4, 274 books for elementary school and children's libraries. Price includes four annual supplements. 1966. Wilson. $17. 00.

Children's Literature in the Elementary School by Charlotte Huck and Doris Kuhn. Articles on use of books in elementary school plus excellent bibliographies. 1968. Holt. $9. 95.

Doors to More Mature Reading: Detailed Notes on Adult Books for Use with Young People compiled by the Young Adult Services Division, ALA. Detailed annotations of nearly 150 adult books. 1964. ALA. $2. 50.

The Elementary School Library Collection compiled by a committee of specialists in children's materials, Mary Virginia Gaver, chairman. A list of "high quality materials on all topics included in the elementary curriculum and of wide interest to children. " Special features include: selection policy, audiovisual materials, periodicals, professional tools, lists of large print books. 1970. The Bro-Dart Foundation. $20.00 (includes supplement).

Fiction Catalog. Guide to 4,097 works of adult fiction. 1960. Wilson. $9.00. 1961-65 volume with four supplements, $11.00.

4,000 Books for Secondary School Libraries. A basic list compiled by the Library Committee of the National Association of Independent Schools. In addition to books, includes listings of magazines and audiovisual materials. 1968. Bowker. $5.25.

Good Books for Children edited by Mary K. Eakin. Books published during the years 1960-65. Chosen from titles reviewed in Bulletin of the Center for Children's Books. 1966. University of Chicago. $7.95.

Introducing Books: A Guide for Middle Grades by John Gillespie and Diana Lembo. Eighty-eight books grouped into eleven goal-theme areas described and analyzed for effective booktalks. 1970. Bowker. $9.25.

Junior High School Library Catalog. 3,278 books selected for use in junior high schools. 1965. Wilson. With four annual supplements. $20.00.

Juniorplots: A Book Talk Manual for Teachers and Librarians by John Gillespie and Diana Lembo. Eighty books evaluated for young people 9 to 16. 1967. Bowker. $7.95.

Let's Read Together: Books for Family Enjoyment selected and annotated by a special committee of the National Congress of Parents and Teachers and the Children's Services Division, ALA. Books for the very young child to 15-year-olds, grouped by reader interest and age level. 1969. ALA. $1.50.

The Paperback Goes to School. Annual list of paperback titles considered useful and available for classroom and supplementary use in elementary and secondary schools by a joint committee of NEA and the American Association of School Librarians. Bureau of Independent Publishers and Distributors. Free.

Parent's Guide to Children's Reading by Nancy Larrick.

Articles and bibliographies. 1969. Doubleday. $5. 95. Pocket
Books.   95 cents.

Public Library Catalog.   11, 001 nonfiction titles for
small and medium sized public libraries, of which many
might be useful with senior high students. 1968.   Wilson.
$50. 00 with four supplements.

Reference Materials for School Libraries prepared by
Cora Paul Bomar and others.   Designed as a guide in se-
lecting and using reference materials in North Carolina
Schools, grades 1-12.   Division of Public Information and
Publications, State Department of Public Instruction, Raleigh,
North Carolina. 1968. $2. 00.

Senior High School Library Catalog.   List of 4, 231
books. 1967. Wilson. $25. 00 with five annual supplements.

Subject Index to Books for Intermediate Grades compiled by Mary K. Eakin.   Analyzes the contents of 1, 800
books, primarily trade books, under 4, 000 subject headings
which meet today's curriculum and interest needs for grades
4-6. 1963. ALA. $7. 50.

Subject Index to Books for Primary Grades compiled
by Mary K. Eakin.   Indicates independent reading level and
interest level of over 900 trade books and readers. 1967.
ALA. $4. 00.

Subscription Books Bulletin Reviews.   Detailed evaluation of reference books reprinted from The Booklist and Subscription Books Bulletin.   ALA. 1956-60, $1. 25; 1960-62,
$1. 50; 1962-64, $2. 00; 1964-66, $2. 25; 1966-68, $2. 25.

Your Reading, a Book List for Junior High prepared
by the Committee on the Junior High School Book List,
NCTE.   Brief descriptive annotations, grouped under subjects. 1966. NCTE.   75 cents.

Lists of Specialized Materials

The AAAS Science Book List for Children compiled
by Hilary J. Deason.   Books in science and mathematics
for grades 1-8.   Arranged by Dewey classifications and
annotated to indicate content and grade level.   First purchase items starred.   Useful as suggested coverage of

subjects for school and public libraries.   American Association for the Advancement of Science.   Revised edition, 1971.
$10. 00.

The AAAS Science Book List for Young Adults prepared under the direction of Hilary J. Deason.   Lists 1, 500 selected, annotated science and mathematics books suitable for high school and junior college students.   1970. AAAS.
$3. 50.

American History Booklist for High Schools: A Selection for Supplementary Reading, edited by Ralph A. and Marian R. Brown.   Bulletin No. 42 of the National Council for the Social Studies.   A comprehensive bibliography of resource readings for American History, annotated and cross-indexed.   Books are graded for various learning levels, and categorized according to fiction, nonfiction and original source material. 1969. NEA. $2. 50.

American History in Juvenile Books: A Chronological Guide by Seymour Metzner.   Books available concerning American History for elementary and junior high school students arranged according to period with which they are concerned.   Not selective; not annotated.   Reading level indicated. 1966. Wilson. $7. 00.

A Bibliography of Children's Art Literature by Kenneth Marantz.   An annotated listing of books, particularly useful for stimulating and enriching the visual imagination of the child.   Books were chosen for the quality of the illustrations, appeal of the story, and accuracy and comprehensibility; lively comments make the booklet interesting reading in itself. 1965. NEA, National Art Education Association.   40 cents.

Bibliography of Negro History and Culture for Young Readers by Miles Jackson.   Annotations of 500 items including print and nonprint materials for elementary and secondary levels. 1968. University of Pittsburgh. $2. 50.

Bibliography of Selected Children's Books About American Indians.   Sixty-three books, each reviewed by an American Indian.   For ages six through young adult. 1969. Association of American Indian Affairs.   50 cents.

Books for Friendship: A List of Books Recommended for Children.   Graded, annotated list of about 300 children's books which foster understanding and appreciation of other human beings. Children's program publications, American Friends Service Committee. 1968. $1.25.

Books in American History: A Basic List for High Schools compiled by John E. Wiltz. Comprehensive annotations of more than 300 titles suitable for high schools arranged by historical period. Gives publisher and price; includes paperback editions where available. 1964. Indiana University Press. $1.00.

Building Bridges of Understanding compiled by Charlotte Keating. An annotated bibliography of books for recreational reading about minority groups for children of all ages. 1967. Palo Verde Publishing Co. $2.95.

Catalog of Language Packages. Children's books in foreign languages, principally French, German and Spanish, selected by a committee of the Children's Services Division, ALA. Books may be bought in packages or as separate volumes. Package Library of Foreign Children's Books. Catalog Free.

Children's Books to Enrich the Social Studies for the Elementary Grades by Helen Huus. Bulletin No. 32 of the National Council for the Social Studies, NEA. An annotated list of books grouped by categories and covering subjects usually included in the social studies curriculum of grades k-6. 1966. NEA. $2.50.

Free and Inexpensive Learning Materials by George Peabody College for Teachers. More than 3,000 items evaluated for accuracy and usefulness in schools. Revised yearly. George Peabody College. $2.00.

Free and Inexpensive Materials on World Affairs by Leonard Kenworthy. Practical list with brief annotations; includes all kinds of materials. 1969. Teachers College, Columbia University Press. $1.95.

Gateways to Readable Books edited by Ruth Strang and others. "An annotated graded list of books in many fields for adolescents who find reading difficult." 1966. Wilson. $5.00.

General Encyclopedias in Print compiled by S. Padraig Walsh. Practical guidelines for choosing a general knowledge encyclopedia. 1969. Bowker. $3. 00.

Good Reading for Poor Readers compiled by George
Spache.   Useful in elementary and junior high school. 1968.
Garrard. $3. 75.

A Guide to Science Reading compiled and edited by
Hilary J. Deason. Annotated bibliography of more than
1, 000 paperback science books, keyed to four reading and
comprehension levels. 1966. New American Library. 75 cents.

High Interest-Easy Reading for Junior and Senior High
School Reluctant Readers by Raymond Emory and Margaret
B. Houshower.   Contains reading activities, an interest in-
ventory and bibliography. 1965. NCTE. $1. 00.

High School Mathematics Library compiled by the
National Council of Teachers of Mathematics. 1967. NEA.
$1. 00.

History in Children's Books by Zena Sutherland.
Semiselective subject list for grades k-8.   Includes biogra-
phy and fiction. 1967. McKinley. $8. 50

Hooked on Books: Program and Proof by D. N.
Fader and E. B. McNeill.   Articles about using books with
juvenile delinquents and bibliographies of paperbacks popular
with poor and reluctant readers. 1968. Putnam. $5. 95.

"I Can Read It Myself" compiled by Frieda M. Hefler.
Titles selected for independent reading and grouped for the
beginning reader in grades 1-2 and for the primary reader
ready for longer books. 1965. Ohio State University. $1. 25.

Magazines for Libraries by Bill Katz. Useful for
selecting the more sophisticated magazines for high school.
1969. Bowker. $16. 95.

Mathematics Library--Elementary and Junior High
School compiled by the NCTM. 1968. NEA. 80 cents.

MLA Selective List of Materials: For Use by Teachers of Modern Foreign Languages in Elementary and Secondary Schools edited by Mary J. Ollmann.   A comprehensive
bibliography which includes titles in ten modern languages.
Also includes nonprint materials. 1962. Modern Language
Association of America. $1. 50; Supplement for French. 1964.

$1. 00; Supplement for Spanish and Portuguese. 1964. $1. 00; Supplement for Italian. 1964. $1. 00; Supplement for German, Norwegian, Polish, Russian and Swedish. 1964. $1. 00.

Music Education Materials; A Selected Annotated Bibliography includes teacher and student references in the field of music. All items arranged by topic for easy reference. 1968. NEA. $2. 50.

Negro in Schoolroom Literature: Resource Materials for the Teacher of Kindergarten through the Sixth Grade by Minnie Koblitz. Annotated listings of over 250 books for children and for teachers; includes some audiovisual materials. 1966. Center for Urban Education. 60 cents.

Negro Literature for High School Students by Barbara Dodds. Reviews 150 books. 1968. NCTE. $2. 00.

Periodicals for School Libraries edited by Marion Scott. Evaluates 429 periodicals for children and young adults from kindergarten through grade 12. 1969. ALA. $3. 50.

Reading Guide in Politics and Government by Robert H. Connery and others. A well-balanced annotated list of books in the field of political science for teachers and students of history and government. 1966. NEA. $1. 50.

Reading Ladders for Human Relations edited by Muriel Crosby. An annotated list of over 1, 000 books for children and young people, developed around six human relations themes. 1964. American Council on Education. $4. 00.

Teachers' Guide to American Negro History by William Katz. Annotated bibliographies as well as units of work in the field. 1968. Quadrangle. $5. 50.

The Teachers' Library: How to Organize It and What to Include. Suggested materials--books/magazines/AV materials--for professional libraries. List prepared by a committee representing ALA and NEA. 1968. NEA. $1. 50.

We Build Together--A Reader's Guide to Negro Life and Literature for Elementary and High School Use edited by Charlemae Rollins. Lists books for preschool child to the ninth grade. 1967. NCTE. $1. 50.

World Civilization Booklist: Supplementary Reading for Secondary Schools prepared by the World Civilization Booklist Committee of the NCSS. Bulletin No. 41 of the National Council for the Social Studies. Contains a listing of over 1,200 books annotated and cross-indexed, covering world history, world affairs, and area studies. 1968. NEA. $3.50.

Reviewing Tools for Current Books

Appraisal, Reviews of books on science topics done by librarians and scientists. Useful for elementary and junior high level. Children's Science Book Review Committee, Harvard Graduate School of Education. $3.00.

Booklist. A guide to current books and audiovisual material published twice a month, September through July, and once in August. Reviews recommended books and audiovisual material for children, young people and adults, giving full buying and cataloging information and analytical notes. Includes annual list of notable children's books. ALA. $10.00.

Bulletin of the Center for Children's Books. Published monthly except August. Reviews books for children and young people, including marginal and not recommended titles. University of Chicago. $4.50.

Choice. A monthly magazine which reviews carefully and in detail books for colleges. Especially valuable for selecting books for mature high school students. ALA. $20.00.

Elementary English. A magazine devoted to better teaching of elementary language arts. Contains articles and in each issue, reviews of new books for children. Included with membership in Elementary Section of NCTE. $10.00.

The Horn Book Magazine. Discriminating reviews of books for children and young people, along with articles on children's literature. Carries regular section on science books and on adult books for young people. Includes annual list of outstanding books. The Horn Book, Inc. $6.00.

Library Journal. Published twice monthly. Value for reviews of adult books and audiovisual materials for high schools on all subjects. In the 15th of the month issue, School Library Journal is included. Bowker. $10.00.

School Libraries. Quarterly. Reviews professional books and audiovisual materials including selection aids. American Association of School Librarians. Single copy $2.00.

School Library Journal. Monthly, September through May. Brief reviews of books and audiovisual materials recommended and not recommended for grades K-12. Articles of interest to teachers and school librarians; special lists (professional reading, free and inexpensive materials, paperbacks). Bowker. $7.00 (Part of Library Journal).

Science Books; A Quarterly Review. Careful, detailed reviews of science books for use with elementary, secondary and junior college students. American Association for the Advancement of Science. $6.50.

Directory of Publishers

American Association for the Advancement of Science, 1515 Massachusetts Avenue, N. W. , Washington, D. C. 20005.

American Council on Education, 1785 Massachusetts Avenue, N. W. , Washington, D. C. 20036.

American Friends Service Committee, 160 North 15th Street, Philadelphia, Pennsylvania 19102.

American Library Association, 50 East Huron Street, Chicago, Illinois 60611.

Association for Childhood Education International, 3615 Wisconsin Avenue, N. W. , Washington, D. C. 20016.

Association of American Indian Affairs, 432 Park Avenue South, New York, New York 10016.

Bantam Books, 271 Madison Avenue, New York, New York 10016.

R. R. Bowker Company, 1180 Avenue of the Americas, New York, New York 10036.

The Bro-Dart Foundation, 113 Frelinghuysen Avenue, Newark, New Jersey 07114.

Bureau of Independent Publishers and Distrubutors, 122 East 42nd Street, New York, New York 10017.

Case Western Reserve University, 2029 Adelbert Road, Cleveland, Ohio 44106.

Center for Urban Education, 105 Madison Avenue, New York, New York 10016.

Columbia University Press, 2960 Broadway, New York, New York 10027.

Doubleday and Company, 277 Park Avenue, New York, New York 10017.

Educational Materials Laboratory, U. S. Office of Education, Washington, D. C. 20402.

Garrard Publishing Company, 1607 North Market Street, Champaign, Illinois 61821.

George Peabody College for Teachers, Division of Surveys and Field Services, Nashville, Tennessee 37203.

Harper & Row, 2500 Crawford Avenue, Evanston, Illinois 60201.

Harvard Graduate School of Education, Longfellow Hall, Appian Way, Cambridge, Mass. 02138.

Holt, Rinehart and Winston, 383 Madison Avenue, New York, New York 10017.

The Horn Book, Inc. , 585 Boylston Street, Boston, Mass. 02116.

Indiana University Press, Bloomington, Indiana 47401.

McKinley Publishing Company, 112 South New Broadway, Brooklawn, New Jersey 08030.

Modern Language Association of America, 62 Fifth Avenue, New York, New York 10011.

National Council of Teachers of English, 508 South Sixth Street, Champaign, Illinois 61820.

National Education Association, 1201 16th Street, N. W.,
Washington, D. C. 20036.

New York Public Library, Fifth Avenue and 42nd Street,
New York, New York 10018.

Oceana Publications, Dobbs Ferry, New York 10522.

The Ohio State University, Publications Office, 2500 Kenny
Road, Columbus, Ohio 43210.

Package Library of Foreign Children's Books--Department T,
119 Fifth Avenue, New York, New York 10003.

Palo Verde Publishing Company, Tucson, Arizona 85702.

Quadrangle Books, 180 North Wacker Drive, Chicago, Illinois,
60606.

Scott Foresman and Company, 1900 East Lake Avenue, Glen-
view, Illinois 60025.

State Department of Public Instruction, Raleigh, North Carolina 27602.

U. S. Government Printing Office, Washington, D. C. 20402.

University of Chicago Press, 5750 Ellis Avenue, Chicago,
Illinois 60637.

University of Pittsburgh, Cathedral of Learning, Pittsburgh,
Pennsylvania 15213

The H. W. Wilson Company, 950 University Avenue, Bronx,
New York 10452.

Sources of Selection for Nonprint Materials

When selecting nonprint materials, it is desirable to
examine carefully before purchase to make sure they meet
the needs of the particular clientele with whom they will be
used.

General Lists

Audiovisual Instruction.   Periodic listing of sources

of evaluation. Association of Educational Communications
and Technology/NEA, 1201 16th Street, N. W. , Washington,
D. C.   20036.   Monthly, September-May. $12. 00 per year.

Guides to Newer Educational Media: Films, Filmstrips, Kinescopes, Phono-Discs, Phono-Tapes, Programmed
Instruction Materials, Slides, Transparencies and Videotapes
by Margaret Rufsvold and Carolyn Guss.   Handbook describing available catalogs, lists, services, professional organizations, journals, and periodicals which regularly provide information on newer educational media.   Third edition, 1971.
ALA.   In preparation.

Instructional Materials for Teaching Audiovisual
Courses.   Center for Instructional Communications (Film
Rental Library), Syracuse University, Syracuse, New York
13210.   1968. $2. 00.

Instructional Materials for Teaching the Use of the
Library: A Selected Annotated Bibliography of Film, Filmstrips, Books and Pamphlets, Tests and Other Aids.   Compiled by Shirley L. Hopkinson, Claremont House, San Jose,
California 95114.   1966. $1. 00.

Sources of Audiovisual Materials by Milbrey L. Jones.
U. S. Government Printing Office, Washington, D. C.   Order
No. FS 5. 235:35090.   1967.   15 cents.

A Working Bibliography of Commercially Available
Audiovisual Materials for the Teaching of Library Science
compiled by Irving Lieberman.   Occasional Papers # 94,
University of Illinois, Graduate School of Library Science,
Urbana, Illinois 61801.   1968. $1. 00.

Reviews of new audiovisual materials also appear in
Booklist, Library Journal, School Library Journal and other
education and library periodicals.

Lists of Films and Filmstrips

Bluebook of Audiovisual Materials.   Educational
Screen, Inc. , 434 S. Wabash, Chicago, Illinois 60605.   (In
August issue of Educational Screen and Audiovisual Guide.)
Annual. $2. 00.

Educator's Guide to Free Films.   Annual compilation

of films available from industry and nonprofit organizations without charge. Educators Progressive Service, Randolph, Wisconsin 53956. Annual. $10.75.

EFLA Evaluation. 1948 to date. Monthly listings on 3x5 cards. Educational Film Library Association, Inc., 250 West 57th Street, New York, New York 10019. Membership $15 per year plus service basis charge depending on size of film library. (See below compilation in book form entitled Film Evaluation Guide, 1946-1965.)

8MM Film Directory, edited by Gran Ann Kone for Educational Film Library Association. Distributed by Comprehensive Service Corporation, 250 West 64th Street, New York, New York 10023. 1969. $10.50.

Film Evaluation Guide, 1946-1964. Educational Film Library Association, Inc., 250 West 57th Street, New York, New York 10019. 1965. $30.00. Supplement 1965-67, $10.00.

Film Library Quarterly. Includes articles and film reviews for libraries and film collections. Film Library Information Council, 101 West Putnam Avenue, Greenwich, Conn. 06830. Quarterly. $8.00 per year.

Film News. Monthly reviews and suggested uses for films and filmstrips. Published six times a year. Film News Co., 250 West 57th Street, New York, New York 10019. $6.00 per year.

Film Review Digest. Published four times a year. Educational Film Library Association, 250 West 56th Street, New York, New York 10019. Rates on request.

Index to 8MM Motion Cartridges. National Information Center for Educational Media. R. R. Bowker Co., 1180 Avenue of the Americas, New York, New York 10036. 1969. $16.00.

Index to 16MM Educational Films. National Information Center for Educational Media. R. R. Bowker Co., 1180 Avenue of the Americas, New York, New York 10036. 1969. $39.50.

Index to 35MM Educational Films. National Information Center for Educational Media. R. R. Bowker Co.

1180 Avenue of the Americas, New York, New York 10036.
1969. $34. 00.

Landers Film Reviews.   June 1956 to date.   Monthly
except July and August.   (Annual volume available since
1965.)   Landers Associates, P. O. Box 69760, Los Angeles,
California 90069. $35. 00 per year, plus vinyl binder.

Silent Film Loop Source Directory.   Lists silent
8mm loop films by subject area, title and educational level.
Technicolor, Commercial and Educational Division, 1300
Frawley Drive, Costa Mesa, California 92626.   Free.

Sound Film Loop Source Directory.   Lists sound
8mm loops by subject, title and educational level.   Technicolor, Commercial and Educational Division, 1300 Frawley
Drive, Costa Mesa, California 92626.   Free.

Lists of Overhead Transparencies

Source Directory, Prepared Transparencies.   Lists
transparencies by source, subject matter and educational
level.   Grafle, Inc. , Rochester, New York 14601. 1966.
(Revised periodically.) $1. 00.

Index to Overhead Transparencies.   National Information Center for Educational Media.   R. R. Bowker Co. ,
1180 Avenue of the Americas, New York, New York 10036.
1969. $22. 50.

Lists of Tape and Disc Recordings

Audio Cardalog.   1958 to date.   Monthly except July
and August.   3x5 cards.   Edited by Max U. Bildersee, Box
1771, Albany, New York 12201. $25. 00 per year.

Educators Guide to Free Tapes, Scripts and Tran-
scriptions.   Lists free audio materials by service, subject
and educational level.   Educator's Progress Service, Randolph, Wisconsin 53956.   Annual. $6. 75.

National Audio Tape Catalog.   Lists available tape
recordings by title and subject.   Department of Audiovisual
Instruction/NEA, 1201 16th Street, N. W. , Washington, D. C.
20036. 1967. $3. 00.

Recordings for Children: A Selected List. Children and Young Adults Services Section, New York Library Association. Available from Mrs. Augusta Baker, New York Public Library, 20 West Fifty-third Street, New York, New York 10018. 1964. $1.00.

Lists of Programmed Instruction, Slides and Pictures

Learning from Pictures by Catharine M. Williams. A guide and source book on the use of pictures for all grade levels. Department of Audiovisual Instruction/NEA, 1201 16th Street, N. W. , Washington, D. C. 20036. 1968. $4.50.

Programmed Learning: A Bibliography of Programs and Presentation Devices edited by Carl H. Hendershot. Basic Bibliography and 1967 and 1968 supplements including vinyl binder and index. Order from Mr. Carl H. Hendershot, 4114 Ridgewood Drive, Bay City, Michigan 48707. $21.50.

Lists of Television Program Materials

Instructional Television Materials: A Guide to Films, Kinescopes Available for Televised Use. National Instructional Television Library Project, 10 Columbus Circle, New York, New York 10019. 1964. Free.

NCSCT Telecourse Catalog. The National Center for School and College Television, Box A. , Bloomington, Indiana 47401. 1966. (Spring). Free.

SELECT BIBLIOGRAPHY

With few exceptions, the items selected for inclusion in this book of readings were taken from periodicals. This select bibliography, which includes books only, will provide additional sources to broaden the scope and balance the reading of the librarian/media specialist.

American Library Association and National Education Association. Standards for School Media Programs. Chicago and Washington, D. C. , 1969.

Brown, James W. and others. Administering Educational Media: Instructional Technology and Library Services. 2nd ed. New York: McGraw-Hill Book Co. , 1972.

Davies, Ruth Ann. The School Library; a Force for Educational Excellence. New York: R. R. Bowker Co. , 1969.

Ellsworth, Ralph E. and Wagener, Hobart D. The School Library; Facilities for Independent Study in the Secondary School. New York: Educational Facilities Laboratories, 1963.

Erickson, Carlton W. H. Administering Educational Media Programs. New York: Macmillan, 1968.

Gaver, Mary. Services of Secondary Schools Media Centers; Evaluation and Development. Chicago: American Library Association, 1971.

Gerlock, Vernon S. and Ely, Donald P. Teaching and Media; a Systematic Approach. Englewood Cliffs, N. J. : Prentice Hall, 1971.

Hensel, Evelyn. Purchasing Library Materials in Public and School Libraries. Chicago: American Library Association, 1969.

Hicks, Warren B. and Tillin, Alma M. Developing Multi-
    Media Libraries. New York: R. R. Bowker Co., 1970.

Kemp, Jerrold E. Planning and Producing Audiovisual Ma-
    terials. San Francisco: Chandler Publishing Co., 1968.

Miller, Shirley. The Vertical File and Its Satellites; a Hand-
    book of Acquisitions, Processing, and Organization. Lit-
    tleton, Colorado: Libraries Unlimited, 1971.

Peterson, Carolyn Sue. Reference Books for Elementary
    and Junior High School Libraries. Metuchen, N.J.:
    The Scarecrow Press, 1970.

Rossoff, Martin. The School Library and Educational Change.
    Littleton, Colorado: Libraries Unlimited, 1971.

Rowell, John. Educational Media Selection Centers; Identifi-
    cation and Analysis of Current Practices. American Li-
    brary Association, 1971.

Scott, Marian H., ed. Periodicals for School Libraries; a
    Guide to Magazines, Newspapers, and Periodical Indexes.
    Chicago: American Library Association, 1969.

Wittich, Walter Arno. Audiovisual Materials; Their Nature
    and Use. 4th ed. New York: Harper and Row, 1967.

CONTRIBUTORS

Positions noted are either current or ones held at time materials were originally published.

BEACHNER, Anna M. Field Worker, Knapp School Libraries Project and Curriculum Consultant, Richland, Washington.

BEACON, Robert. Instructor, Department of Instructional Technology, University of Southern California, Los Angeles; Teacher, Los Angeles Unified School District.

BLAY, Andre A. President, Magnetic Video Corporation, Farmington, Michigan.

CASE, Robert N. Director, School Library Manpower Project, American Library Association.

CHALMERS, John J. Assistant Audiovisual Supervisor, Edmonton Public School Board, Edmonton, Alberta, Canada.

CROSSMAN, David M. Assistant Director of Libraries, Hillman Library, University of Pittsburgh.

DARLING, Richard L. Dean, Columbia University School of Library Service, New York; formerly Supervisor of Library Services, Montgomery County Public Schools, Rockville, Maryland.

EGAN, Mary Joan. Chairman, School Library Media Department, Burnt Hills-Ballston Lake Central Schools, Scotia, New York.

ELLSWORTH, Ralph E. Director of Libraries, University of Colorado, Boulder; now retired.

FORSDALE, Joan R. Consultant in educational media design specializing in 8mm films.

284

FRASE, Larry. Elementary Associate, College of Education, Arizona State University, to the Arizona-Mesa Differentiated Staffing Consortium.

GOLDSMITH, Stephanie. A librarian of the Laboratory High School, University of Chicago.

GORDON, Garford G. Research Executive, California Teachers Association.

HALL, Clem M. Formerly Assistant Director of the Washington office, American Library Association.

HENNE, Frances. Professor, Columbia University School of Library Service, New York.

HIGGINS, James J. Writer-researcher for Project Information Exchange, Philadelphia School District.

KAZLAUSKAS, Edward. Assistant Professor, School of Library Science, University of Southern California, Los Angeles.

KNIRK, Frederick G. Associate Professor, Department of Instructional Technology, University of Southern California, Los Angeles.

LEWIS, Philip. President, Instructional Dynamics, Inc., Chicago, Illinois.

LOWREY, Anna Mary. Associate Director, School Library Manpower Project; former director of libraries for the San Leandro, California Unified School District.

McBRIDE, Otis. Professor of Education and Head, Academic Department of Librarianship-Educational Media, University of Colorado, Boulder.

McCAULEY, Elfrieda B. Coordinator, Secondary School Libraries, Greenwich, Connecticut Public Schools.

MANN, Mary Louise. Formerly school library supervisor, Metropolitan School District of Washington Township, Indianapolis, Indiana.

MORRIS, Barry. Assistant Superintendent for Instruction, Fairfax County Public Schools, Fairfax, Virginia.

NICHOLSEN, Margaret E.   Head Librarian, Evanston,
Illinois Township High School.

NICKEL, Mildred L.   Director of School Libraries, Lansing
School District, Lansing, Michigan.

PEGAN, Thomas A.   Operations Manager of Magnetic Video
Corporation, Farmington, Michigan

RILEY, William C.   Principal, Lomond School, Shaker
Heights, Ohio.

ROWELL, John.   Director, Program for School Libraries,
Case Western Reserve University; Director, Educational
Media Selection Centers Project, the National Book Com-
mittee, Inc.

TABA, Hilda.   Professor of Education, San Francisco State
College.

TALBERT, E. Gene.   Professor of Elementary Education,
Arizona State University, Tempe.

VEIHMAN, Robert A.   Materials Preparation Consultant,
College of DuPage, Glen Ellyn, Illinois.

VOGELER, John G.   Free lance writer specializing in data
systems reporting.

WAGENER, Hobart D.   Architect, Boulder, Colorado.

WARD, Pearl L. Assistant Professor, School of Library
Science, University of Southern California, Los Angeles.

WEDGEWORTH, Robert.   Executive Director, American Library Association.

INDEX

("n" Following a Page Number Refers to Footnote)

287

Education of the Handicapped Act, 129-132. See also Handicapped
Education of Vision, 218
Education Professions Development Act, 26
Eine Kleine Nachtmusik mentioned, 199
Electronics Industries Association, 226
Elementary and Secondary Education Act
grant, 42
library implications, 25-26, 42, 65
purpose of, 65
support of, 108
Title I, 123-124
Title III, 65, 124-126
Title V, 126-127
Title VII. See Bilingual Education Act
when passed, 26
Engelmann, Seigfried, 214
England mentioned, 14
Environmental Learning Center
advantages of, 43, 58-59
evolution of, 35, 57
implications, 35-36
role of librarian, 43
staff requirements, 45
use of materials, 42, 43, 44-45
See also Audiovisual center; Instruction Media Center; Instructional Resources Center; School libraries
Equality of Educational Opportunity, 75n
Equipment
audiovisual, 4, 17, 26-27, 80
electronic, 16-17
Erasmus, Desiderius mentioned, 9
Erickson, Carlton W. H. 75n

ESEA See Elementary and Secondary Education Act
ETV See Television, educational
Exceptional children, 32
Exhibits, programmed, 17
Expenditure, 76 See also Budget
Exposure meter, 191-192

Faulkner, William, 24, 28n
Federal aid. See Funding
Federal Communications Commission, 227
Filmloop
cataloging, 160
intershelving, 157
processing, 43, 159
uses of, 157, 216-218
value of, 212-215, 218-219
Films
cataloging, 159
implications for library, 3, 18, 19, 21, 26, 42, 43, 46, 157, 260
importance of, 9, 188, 212
popular sizes, 189
problems of, 10, 159
8 mm, 17, 43
16 mm, 43
32 mm, 191-194
Filmstrips
cataloging, 159
preparation, 193-194
problems, 10
processing, 159
shelving, 43, 157
uses, 13, 17, 43, 57, 157
viewer, 36
Fleming, Frances, 263
Fogg, Museum, 174
Ford Foundation, 54, 57, 58
The Four Loves, 246n
France, Paris, 2, 176, 178
Francis I mentioned, 9
Freiser, Leonard, 31

materials in, 46-47, 196, 207

mechanics of, 50-51, 52, 57, 58

problems of, 8, 52, 64, 65-66, 86-89, 144-151 passim

programs, 32, 33, 37, 62, 63, 78-79, 107, 108

purpose of, 46, 51-52, 54, 90, 114-115

role of principals, 54-55, 57-58, 89

room requirements, 50-51

selection policies, 134-140

services provided, 47-48, 56

staff responsibilities, 36, 48-50, 52, 57, 59, 87, 95, 134, 249-250

use of photography, 188-190

See also Audiovisual Center; Environmental Learning Center; Instructional Resources Center; School libraries

Instructional programming
Explanation of, 100, 257-261

Instructional Resources Center
at College of DuPage, 157, 161
use of cassettes, 203-204
See also Audiovisual Center; Environmental Learning Center; Instructional Media Center; School libraries

Intercom, 238

Intershelving, 157

Italy, Rome
mentioned, 2

Ithaca College, New York, 230-231

Jobbers, 146, 147

Kennedy, John F.
mentioned, 142

Kepes, Gyorgy, 218

Keysort, 162-165 passim

Keyword In Context index, 167

Keyword Out of Context index, 167

Kits, 43, 157, 160

Knapp Foundation, 26, 92, 252

Knirk, Frederick, 258, 259, 263

Knowledge, carriers of See Carriers of knowledge

Knox, William T., 172, 173n

Krathwohl, David R., 117

Kruse, Edward K., 107

Kurland, Norman, 45

KWIC See Keyword In Context index

KWOC See Keyword Out of Context index

Language
development of, 9
importance to library, 9
laboratories, 17, 38, 47, 100, 226-227, 229

Lea County, New Mexico, 171

Learning
implications of, 4, 24, 30, 62, 142
importance of, 27, 29, 30
individualized, 25, 27, 113, 114, 227-228
new concepts, 54-60
problems, 15
programmed, 18 See also Teaching machines

Lefevre, Alice L., 64, 74n

Legislation, 25-29 passim, 65, 123

Lennon, John
mentioned, 184

Lewis, Clive Staples, 246n

Librarians
accountability, 91
communicating with ad-

Microreader, 36, 38
Minneapolis, Minnesota, 171
Morphet, Edgar L., 173n
Morris, Barry, 66, 75n
Morrison, Perry D., 64, 74n
Morton, F. Rand, 229
Moscow, Russia, 178
Mosher, Frederick C., 67,
71, 75n
Motion pictures See Films
Mt. San Antonio College, 175
Museums See Cleveland Mu-
seum of Art; Fogg Mu-
seum; Metropolitan Mu-
seum of Art; Pushkin
Museum
Music Educators National
Conference, 263

National Council For Geo-
graphic Education, 103
National Council For the
Social Studies, 263
National Council of Teachers
of English, 265
National Council of Teachers
of Mathematics, 263
National Defense Education
Act, 26, 65, 127-128, 153
National Education Associa-
tion, 28n, 92, 204
National Geographic, 149
National Geographic Society,
147
NEA See National Education
Association
New York Times Index, 237
The New Yorker, 11n
Nixon, Richard M., 65
Nonbook materials
advantages, 62, 184
cataloging, 153, 158-161
passim
evaluation of, 141-143
intershelving of, 157
processing, 158-161 passim
problems, 10, 141-142,
143, 182

uses, 9, 142-143, 184-187
North Carolina, 92
North, Stafford, 231
Notched-card system, 162-
165 passim
Novick, David, 75n

Occupational Definitions For
School Library Media Per-
sonnel, 92-96
Office of Education See U. S.
Office of Education
Ofiesh, Gabriel D., 229, 232
Ohio State University, 23,
231, 233
Oklahoma Christian College,
231, 233
Oral Roberts University, 231
Oxford University, 16

Pamphlets
acquisition, 149
cataloging, 239
processing, 43
sources, 238-239
use of, 19, 43, 46, 236-237
Paraprofessionals, 37, 59,
106
Parent Teacher Association,
58
Parallel access, 230
Parr, Jack
mentioned, 113
Patterns of Development In
Elementary School Libraries
Today: A Five Year Re-
port On Emerging Media
Centers, 75n
Periodicals, 43, 46, 149
Philadelphia, Pennsylvania,
185, 232
Philips Company, 200, 206
Philips, Murray, 45
Phonograph records
uses, 9, 12, 17, 18, 21,
26, 43, 46, 56, 57
Pittsburgh, Pennsylvania, 172

improvement of, 87, 152-156, 252, 253
influences on, 25
organization of, 13-16, 78
problems, 5, 6-11 passim, 15, 25, 28, 35, 36, 38-40, 41, 61, 64, 68-69, 87, 94, 108-109, 152
public library cooperation, 154
purpose of, 2-14 passim, 16-23 passim, 25, 29-31, 33, 35-36, 39, 41, 107, 113, 135
selection of materials, 262-265
trends, 5, 10, 12-23 passim, 24-27, 29, 38, 40, 46-52, 111, 252, 253
use of book catalogs, 155-156, 168
See also Audiovisual center; Environmental Learning Center; Instructional Media Center; Instructional Resources Center
School Library Bill of Rights For School Library Media Programs, 136, 265
School Library Development Project, 26
School Library Journal, 75n
School Library Manpower Project, 26, 92-94, 252, 256
School library media specialist
budget implications, 77
explanation of, 62
limitations, 86
responsibilities, 10, 27, 30, 49, 62, 63, 77, 78, 86, 91-92, 94, 97-101, 144-146
School Library Personnel: Task Analysis
School media center See School libraries
School media specialist See

School library media specialist
Scientific American, 23n, 237
Sears List of Subject Headings, 239
The Selected List of U. S. Government Publications, 238-239
Selecting Materials For School Media Centers, 262-265
Selection policies, 134-140
Serial access, 230
Serials, 149
Shaker Heights, Ohio, 54
Shippensburg State College, 232
Simons, Wendell W., 179n
Single lens reflex See Cameras
Sixth Report and Order, 227
Skinner, Burrhus Frederic, 19, 23n
Skinner Programs, 258
A Slide Classification System, 174, 178, 179n
Slides
classification, 159-160, 174-176
processing, 43, 159-160
use of, 17, 19, 26, 42, 46, 157
Smith, Susan, 45
Sohn, David A., 183
Sputnik
mentioned, 3
Standard Book Number, 169
Standards For School Library Programs, 109
Standards For School Media Programs
formulation, 25, 66, 137
implications, 25, 66, 69, 76-81 passim, 85, 86-87, 91, 167-169
interpretation of, 26, 33, 39, 42, 66, 69, 76, 85-89, 107, 116, 137

Vaux Junior High School,
184-187
Vertical File Index, 238
Vertical files, 56-57
Viewfinder, 192
Vinson, Lu Ouida, 115
Vocational Education Act, 26

Wallace, George
mentioned, 184
Wayne, Pennsylvania, 162
West Hartford, Conneticut,
231
Whitehead, Alfred N., 242,
245n, 246n
Wildavsky, Aaron, 67, 75n
Wilson Library Bulletin, 74n
World Book Encyclopedia,
238

Young, Roberta E., 107-108

Ziskind, Sylvia, 64, 74n